THE
ATTENTION
COMPASS

Suncoast Digital Press, Inc.
Sarasota, Florida
www.suncoastdigitalpress.com

Paperback ISBN 978-1-964143-16-3
eBook ISBN 978-1-964143-18-7

Cover design and interior by Elijah Toten

Suncoast Digital Press

THE ATTENTION COMPASS

A Come-Back Story of Collapse,
Renewal, and the Simple Tool
That Changed Everything

ERIC EDWARD WILSON

To my wife, Michelle,

This journey was only possible because you walked beside me,

believing in wholeness when I could only see broken pieces.

Everything that follows is built on the foundation of your love.

CONTENTS

"The cave you fear to enter holds the treasure you seek."—Joseph Campbell

The Dream

It was 2003, and by all apparent measures, I had *made it*. I was a successful television meteorologist with a beautiful home, a loving family, and the respect of my community. I operated at what I would later understand as a level of consciousness that was driven by the fear of losing what I had, while craving more validation, more success, more external proof of my worth. And beneath this carefully constructed identity, a growing emptiness was beginning to make itself known.

What I didn't realize then was that this emptiness was actually my first hint of something profound—the absence of flow in my life. Despite external achievements, I hadn't yet discovered the alignment of gut, heart, and mind that creates access to that centered awareness where the Universal Mind speaks through us, and where our deepest creativity and wisdom emerge. I call this the Flow State, and if you stick with me through my story, you'll not only understand this magical space, you will be able to access it, to tune into it and all its profound gifts.

The Dream

As if I had a "dream catcher" over my bed, I woke up one morning with the most vivid, fully formed dream playing like a movie in my head. I was, of course, in the starring role—but nothing else was familiar, at least not the first time the dream came to me. As I recall, the dream started with a sensation of anxiousness in my body…

———◆———

Here I am, realizing that everything hinges on my next move. If I don't qualify, if I don't make the group, it would mean years and years of work wasted…for naught. For some, just to get invited to join was enough to be proud of; yet not for me. The pride of my ancestors and the fate of my descendants depend on this. This is about honor. It's my moment, and I'm very nervous.

In the near distance, an unsettling commotion grows louder. The noise is affecting my concentration. *What is that?* I strain to see through the trees—it looks like a person. How could this be? No one uninvited is allowed on site for any reason. Those in charge are watching me, waiting to see what I will do in the face of unforeseen circumstances. I am in a panic. *Why aren't they doing something about that guy, and all that noise he is making?* I struggled to put the distraction out of my head and concentrate.

Then everything goes black.

"Welcome back!" exclaims a large man I assume is the leader of this event that I can sense but not explain.

"Thanks," is all I could come up with. I am baffled. I don't remember a thing. I have no idea why a crowd is gathering in this Great Hall (somehow I know that is what it's called). I understand that everyone is here to acknowledge and congratulate me on my success, which I cannot name. *Can they tell I have forgotten my feat?*

Displayed on all four walls of the Great Hall are all the Enlightened Ones. I am being summoned to the head table in front of this large room, now full of too many people to count. I see arms waving to catch my attention from those who didn't know I existed before. Some people come up to give me pats on the back, which at times takes my breath straight from me. *Man, if I could only remember what I did!*

In the distance, a lone man smiles…*is that my father?*

The dinner chatter is full of compliments, congratulations, and expectations. As the lights dim, the leader moves to the center of the room. The nobility at my table immediately rise and stand at attention, and I clumsily follow.

Suddenly, it seems as if the only light in the room is on me...and him. He gestures to me, and I hurry toward him, nearly trembling with trepidation. *What if he asks me about the feat of which I have no recollection?* He lowers his eyes into mine; the moment is upon us.

My fear subsides and there's only a feeling of acceptance, finally. For generations have dreamt of this moment...and it is happening now...to ME, of all people. Then, the moment releases. The doors to the Great Hall burst open. Three men move from the entrance towards the outside of the circle where the leader and I stand alone.

We turn and face the three. I am really curious. As the men on each end of the trio bow their heads, the middle one looks directly forward. *Why does he not bow his head? What a jerk,* I think. The light is behind them, giving them only silhouettes.

"Who dares disturb this ceremony?" demands the leader.

"Forgive us," the center man says. "We are humble servants delivering a message to the group.".

The leader will have none of this. "A message? What is so important?" He indicates that the man should continue.

What comes forward, now more in focus, is a shameful, disgusting, and obviously angry shell of a man. Closer now, the smell of his stench is so awful, it's embarrassing. I can tell, whoever it is, he's a pitiful soul— and now I realize he's the man I'd seen in the distance.

When asked his name, he turns and stares straight at me. I sense his glare is screaming,

"Why do you reject me!?!"

"I...am...sorry, but I don't know who you are."

He takes a step forward and comes into the light. The crowd gasps. I, too, am shocked. I have no words.

"Exactly..." he says, leaning his face to mine.

It is me.

Introduction to the Code Connection: Consciousness is Not What it Appears to Be

I awoke from this dream in a cold sweat, heart pounding. I didn't need to replay the dream to understand it—the message couldn't have been clearer if it had been written in neon lights: I had been rejecting the most essential part of myself.

Before I share what this dream ultimately led me to discover, I need to warn you—we're about to venture into territory that might challenge everything you think you know about yourself and reality. But stay with me, because this understanding changed my life in ways I could never have imagined. All good.

Years after this dream, as I walked miles each day trying to make sense of my collapsing life, I began to realize something profound: Consciousness isn't what we've been taught it is. We're raised believing we're separate individuals, that our thoughts and feelings are confined to our minds, and that the world "out there" exists independently from us. But what if this separation is just an illusion?

I'd never been particularly interested in quantum physics, but I couldn't ignore how scientific discoveries were pointing to the same truths that ancient wisdom traditions had taught for millennia. Scientists found that particles remain mysteriously connected regardless of distance— what happens to one instantly affects the other. I began to wonder: *If the building blocks of reality behave this way, could our minds work similarly?*

This dream was my first glimpse behind the veil—a momentary recognition that what I called "me" was actually an entity divided against itself. The successful weatherman standing in the spotlight was only one fragment of who I was. The rejected, disheveled man at the door represented everything I had denied in order to maintain my illusion of success.

This division in consciousness is something we all experience. We operate at different levels of awareness—what I later came to understand as the **nine levels of The Code.** That night, in my dream, I experienced a profound collision between my Level 5 consciousness (the celebrated weatherman craving external validation) and the parts of myself I had pushed into the lower levels of Shame, Guilt, and Apathy (the rejected figure at the door).

In our society, we're taught to identify exclusively with our "presentable" selves—our achievements, social roles, and acceptable emotions. We push away our fears, doubts, and authentic needs, banishing them to the shadows. But what I discovered is that consciousness cannot be divided, and the enormous (failing) efforts we make at that attempt do have consequences. What we reject doesn't disappear—it returns, often in ways we don't recognize until it's too late.

My dream showed me something essential: Without the integration of all aspects of self, the Flow State remains inaccessible. The weatherman receiving accolades *and* the rejected figure at the door were both me— and until I could embrace and include these, I would remain cut off from the deeper wisdom trying to emerge through me.

But in that moment in my dream, all I felt was the painful shock of seeing myself as both the celebrated success and the rejected failure. Little did I know this confrontation would be the catalyst for everything that followed.

This pattern of rejection and eventual confrontation isn't unique to me—it's a human theme as common as "hero's journey." In *Star Wars*, Luke Skywalker had to face that with Darth Vader as his father—a part of himself he'd rejected. In *The Hobbit*, Frodo Baggins confronted his shadow through the Ring's corrupting influence. Harry Potter discovered that his connection to Voldemort represented aspects of himself he feared. These aren't just entertaining stories—they're archetypal patterns of consciousness that resonate because they reflect a universal truth about our own challenging journey to wholeness.

My understanding of Consciousness levels and The Code would eventually lead me to discover the Flow State—that centered awareness where the gut, heart, and mind align perfectly. This disappearance of separate compartments creates access to a universal wisdom beyond the individual mind. The Flow State isn't just a concept; it's the natural condition of consciousness when we're no longer fragmented and divided against ourselves.

Exercise: "Dream Reflection"—Your Inner Messengers

Dreams often serve as messengers from parts of ourselves we've disconnected from in waking life. If you don't go to sleep feeling full, satisfied, and complete (and who does, actually) then your dreams are a way to better understand how to become more whole, full, and satisfied. Often, we call them *weird* or *strange*, but if you concentrate on *how you felt* during the dream, you will get a glimpse of what is missing in your life. What is keeping you from being *whole* again?

The dream I shared represented my first real introduction to and confrontation with my rejected self. Your own dreams, recurring thoughts, or unexpected emotions might contain similar messages waiting to be recognized.

Take a few moments to reflect on the following questions. Write your answers in a journal or speak them aloud—something powerful happens when we externalize these reflections:

1. Recall a dream, intuition, or persistent thought that felt significant but that you may have dismissed. What was the main feeling or core message it conveyed?

2. If this dream/thought could speak to you directly, what would it say? Don't analyze—simply allow words to flow as if this part of you finally has a voice.

3. Who or what in your life might represent your "rejected self"? These could be qualities you admire in others but deny in yourself, or aspects of yourself you try to hide or overcome. (Hint: Look into any pockets of shame.)

4. What would happen if, instead of pushing away that rejected part, you simply asked: "Who are you and what do you need?"

Remember, this exercise isn't about finding the "right" interpretation, but about opening a dialogue with aspects of yourself that may have been trying to get your attention. Just as my dream was the catalyst for my journey, your own inner messages might contain the seeds of your transformation.

As you explore these questions, notice moments when you feel a sense of flow or alignment—times when thinking subsides and a deeper knowing emerges. These glimpses, however brief, are tastes of the Flow State we'll be exploring throughout this book—your birthright as a conscious being.

Allow these questions to sit with you in the coming days. You might be surprised at what emerges when you create space for all parts of yourself to be heard.

"Night, the beloved. Night, when words fade and things come alive. When the destructive analysis of day is done, and all that is truly important becomes whole and sound again. When man reassembles his fragmentary self and grows with the calm of a tree." —Antoine de Saint-Exupery

"As above, so below; as within, so without; as the universe, so the soul."—Hermes Trismegistus

The Consciousness Code

Have you ever had one of those perfect moments when everything just clicked? Maybe you were playing an instrument and time seemed to melt away. Perhaps you were engaged in a conversation that flowed so naturally you lost track of where your thoughts ended and the other person's began. Or maybe you were simply walking in nature when suddenly the boundary between you and the world around you softened, and you felt a profound sense of connectedness to everything.

These aren't just pleasant experiences. They're glimpses of what I call the Flow State—moments when the fragmentation we normally experience gives way to wholeness. And they hold the key to understanding the hidden code that governs our lives.

I don't remember walking down here from the house, but here I am at the lake. I'm always drawn to the lake when the noise of worries and woes gets so loud I feel my head will explode if I don't change the channel. As I look down, slowly putting one foot in front of the other, I notice the soft lapping sound of the water on the shore. A much bigger wave has come over me, one of peace, a quiet clarity. I gaze out over the water, so still, reflecting the sky so completely that I can't tell where the water ends and the air begins. My mind feels clean, a freedom that seems to come from everywhere and nowhere at once.

My analytical mind kicked back in. *That's interesting, but what good is a moment of peace when my real problems are still waiting for me?* Little did I know that this brief experience was offering me my first clue to a completely different way of being—one that would ultimately transform not just my inner experience but my external reality as well.

The Mystery of Different Realities

Here's something I've always found fascinating: two people can experience the same external circumstances in completely different ways. Have you noticed this?

Take a simple rainy day. One person curses the weather, feeling that the universe has personally conspired to ruin their plans. Another sees an opportunity to enjoy the cozy feeling of being inside with a good book. A third feels a child-like excitement at the chance to splash in puddles. Same rain, drastically different experiences.

Or consider something more significant—like losing a job. One person sinks into despair, seeing it as proof of their inadequacy and believing they'll never recover. Another experiences anxiety but manages to see it as a temporary setback. A third, rare individual might even recognize it as an opening for something better, feeling a sense of anticipation despite the uncertainty.

What explains these different reactions? We might attribute them to personality, past experiences, or coping skills. All of those play a role, but there's something even more fundamental at work—something that determines those very personalities, interpretations of experiences, and coping mechanisms in the first place.

That something is consciousness itself, or more specifically, the level of consciousness from which a person is operating.

The Nine Levels of Consciousness

Through my personal journey of transformation, I discovered that consciousness operates along a spectrum of frequencies or levels—what I came to understand as "The Code." These nine distinct levels aren't just theoretical constructs; they're experiential states that determine how we perceive and interact with reality.

I like to think of these levels as different radio stations, each broadcasting a completely different version of reality. When you're tuned to one station, you literally can't hear what's playing on the others. Similarly, when operating from one level of consciousness, you cannot perceive the reality available at other levels—until you change the frequency.

Let me take you through these levels, not as abstract concepts, but as lived experiences that you might recognize from your own life:

Level 1: Shame (Energy of Hopelessness)

Imagine feeling like you don't even have the right to exist. Not just unworthiness, but a profound sense that your very presence is somehow wrong. I remember days when I could barely look at myself in the mirror, when the weight of shame felt so physical I could hardly lift my body out of bed. At this level, the world appears actively hostile, and opportunities don't even register because you feel fundamentally undeserving of them.

A friend once described this state perfectly: "It's like being invisible but also feeling that everyone can see right through you to all your flaws." People operating at this level often self-sabotage because success feels more threatening than failure.

Level 2: Guilt (Energy of Regret)

Have you ever been caught in that mental loop of "If only I had..." or "I should have..."? That's the energy of guilt—slightly lighter than shame but still incredibly heavy. At this level, you're constantly punishing yourself for past mistakes, real or imagined.

I recall a period when every decision I made was filtered through a lens of anticipated regret. "If I try this and fail, I'll never forgive myself." This paralysis by guilt prevents forward movement because the past seems to have more gravity than the future. Dwelling in guilt closes any window of optimism.

Level 3: Apathy (Energy of Resignation)

"What's the point?" This is the mantra of Level 3 Consciousness. It's not active despair but a numbed resignation—the emotional equivalent of a shrug. What makes apathy particularly insidious is that it masquerades as rationality. "I'm just being realistic," says the apathetic mind, mistaking cynicism for wisdom.

I've watched people in this state systematically dismantle every suggestion for improvement with seemingly logical arguments. "That won't work because..." becomes the reflexive response to any possibility of change. There's almost a comfort in the certainty of hopelessness. This level of apathy helps one to avoid risk, at the cost of actually living life.

Level 4: Fear (Energy of Survival)

This is where most of society operates—not in terror, but in a constant state of low-grade anxiety about the future. At Level 4, we make decisions based on avoiding what we don't want rather than moving toward what we do want. We don't even allow ourselves to identify what we really want.

Think about the choices you've made to be safe rather than fulfilled; the stable job you don't even like instead of following your passion; the relationship that's comfortable but not inspiring; the opinions and unmet needs you keep to yourself to avoid potential conflict.

I lived at this level for years, building a career that looked successful from the outside but was fundamentally driven by a fear of insecurity. Every accomplishment was less a celebration than a temporary relief from anxiety—a brief respite before the next worry appeared.

Caution and risk analysis has its place in good decision-making. Level 4 of consciousness is not that—it's where fear is your lens for life, and it's become chronic.

Level 5: Desire (Energy of Craving)

If you've ever convinced yourself, "I'll be happy when..." you've experienced Level 5 Consciousness. This is where we attach our fulfillment to external conditions—the promotion, the relationship, the house, the recognition. It's seductive because it contains more energy than the lower levels, but it's still fundamentally a state of lack.

I remember achieving a career goal I had been working toward for years. The rush of satisfaction lasted less than three days before my mind locked onto the next milestone that would "really" make me happy. This is the hamster wheel of desire—always chasing, never arriving.

Level 6: Anger (Energy of Breakthrough)

Surprisingly, anger represents a significant step up in consciousness. Why? Because it contains movement. After the heaviness of shame, the self-punishment of guilt, the resignation of apathy, the caution of fear, and the endless chase of desire, anger says, "Enough! This needs to change!"

The key is not staying in anger but using its energy for transformation. Its power can change feeling like a victim to feeling a sense of determination. Think of it as the force needed to break out of old patterns. A friend who had been in an unhealthy relationship for years finally found the courage to leave when she accessed her anger. Not hatred for her partner, but a healthy anger at the situation and the patterns she had accepted.

Level 7: Acceptance (Energy of Flow)

This is where resistance begins to dissolve. Not with a sigh of resignation (that's Level 3 apathy), but in a clear-eyed recognition of reality as it is, without the need to fight against it. At Level 7, you stop arguing with what's happening and instead ask, "Given that this is the situation, what's my best next step?"

I experienced this shift after being let go from a substandard job, just out of the blue. Me!? The educated professional just 'let go and sent home'!? I remember sitting in the parking lot just thinking to myself, *I can't fight this anymore. I know I'm worth more than this job and I know I have to just let this job go. I have to let everything go.* It was a peaceful drive. After months of resisting circumstances I couldn't change, I finally surrendered—not giving up, but giving in to the flow of life. Shortly afterwards, solutions appeared that I couldn't see when I was caught in resistance—in this case fighting the substandard job. It wasn't about fixing everything immediately but about finding the path of least resistance through the situation. Sometimes you just drive home and watch the sunset knowing the sun will rise again.

Level 8: Peace (Energy of Stillness)

At Level 8, the compulsive need to control outcomes falls away. You begin to feel a profound trust in the unfolding of life, not because everything will go as you want, but because you recognize a deeper order beyond your personal preferences.

This doesn't mean passivity. In fact, action at this level is often more effective because it's not distorted by fear, desperation, or attachment to results. I've observed how people operating from peace seem to experience an unusual number of "coincidences" or synchronicities—as if the universe itself is collaborating with them.

Level 9: Enlightenment (Energy of Wholeness)

Few people stabilize at this level permanently, but most of us have had at least glimpses of it—moments when the boundary between "self" and "other" temporarily dissolves. In these states, what we normally perceive as separate objects and beings are experienced as expressions of a unified field of consciousness.

A musician friend described entering this state during a performance: "I wasn't playing the music; the music was playing me. There was no separation between me, the instrument, the audience, or the sound. It was all one movement." Artists, athletes, dancers and meditators often report similar experiences of boundaries dissolving in moments of peak performance or deep presence.

In the following diagram I have drawn an example of where the transition point is when you move out of the lower levels of survival and into the higher levels of thriving. There is a clear distinction in the wavelength of vibrational consciousness, and the higher you vibrate the tighter the peaks and valleys are. Subsequently the lower vibrations have very few peaks and valleys. Much like the experience you have when vibrating at the level. Use this chart to identify where you might be operating from right now, and the possibilities that await your ascension.

The Nine Levels of Vibrational Consciousness

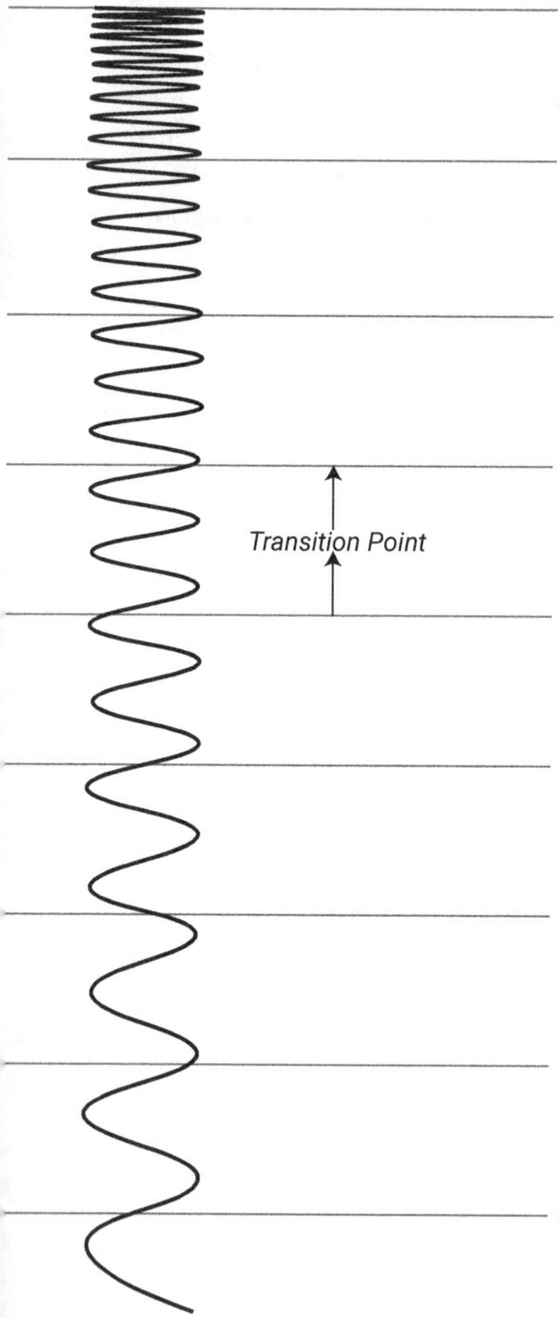

Level 9: **Enlightenment** (Energy of Non-Duality)
Experience: 'Self' and 'Other' Dissolves
Manifests as: Spontaneous Wisdom
Physical: Extraordinary Coherence
Key Phrase: "I am That"

Level 8: **Peace** (Energy of Stillness)
Experience: Inner Stability
Manifests as: Synchronistic Timing
Physical: Radiating Calm
Key Phrase: "All is well"

Level 7: **Acceptance** (Energy of Flow)
Experience: Working With Reality
Manifests as: Creative Solutions
Physical: Relaxed Alertness
Key Phrase: "I can work with this"

Level 6: **Anger** (Energy of Breakthrough)
Experience: Energy For Change
Manifests as: Setting Boundaries
Physical: Increased Vitality
Key Phrase: "This Must Change"

Level 5: **Desrie** (Energy of Craving)
Experience: Constant Wanting
Manifests as: Never Feeling Enough
Physical: Scattered Attention
Key Phrase: "I'll be happy when..."

Level 4: **Fear** (Energy of Survival)
Experience: Worst-Case Scenarios
Manifests as: Defensive Living
Physical: Tense Muscles, Shallow Breath
Key Phrase: "I need to be safe"

Level 3: **Apathy** (Energy of Resignation)
Experience: Lack of Care, Numbness
Manifests as: Giving Up Before Trying
Physical: Sluggish Movement
Key Phrase: "What's The Point?"

Level 2: **Guilt** (Energy of Regret)
Experience: Self Punishment about Past
Manifests as: Aplogetic Existence
Physical: Slumped Posture, Downcast
Key Phrase: "I made a mistake"

Level 1: **Shame** (Energy of Hopelessness)
Experience: Feeling Flawed, Unworthy
Manifests as: Self-Sabotage, Isolation
Physical: Barely Moving, Heavy
Key Phrase: "I am a mistake"

What makes these levels significant isn't just their description but how they function. Each level operates at a specific frequency or vibration. The lower levels (1-5) vibrate slowly and densely, creating experiences of separation, struggle, and limitation. The higher levels (6-9) vibrate more rapidly, creating experiences of connection, ease, and expansion.

The level you operate from isn't just a psychological state—it's an energetic frequency that literally attracts corresponding experiences into your life. Two people in the same situation but operating from different levels will perceive and experience that situation in completely different ways. One will see problems everywhere; the other will find opportunities.

These distinctions of consciousness levels align remarkably well with established scientific understanding.

Levels 1-3 (Shame, Guilt, Apathy) correlate with what neuroscience identifies as parasympathetic freeze responses—characterized by reduced prefrontal cortex activity, heightened amygdala activation, and biochemical patterns associated with withdrawal and depression.

Levels 4-5 (Fear, Desire) correspond to sympathetic nervous system dominance—fight-or-flight physiology characterized by heightened cortisol, narrowed perceptual focus, and reward-seeking behavior that neuroscience links to anxiety disorders and addiction patterns.

Level 6 (Anger) represents a transitional state where the defensive posture begins shifting toward engagement—neurologically marked by increased blood flow to the prefrontal cortex while still maintaining heightened arousal.

Levels 7-9 (Acceptance, Peace, Enlightenment) correlate with what researchers call coherent or integrated brain states—characterized by synchronized alpha wave patterns, balanced sympathetic/parasympathetic activation, and neurochemical profiles associated with both alertness and calm (heightened GABA, serotonin, and oxytocin with moderated cortisol and adrenaline).

The progression from fragmented consciousness (Levels 1-5) to integrated consciousness (Levels 7-9) isn't only subjectively meaningful but objectively measurable through technologies such as EEG, heart rate variability analysis, and functional MRI.

These nine levels of consciousness aren't merely conceptual frameworks, but correspond to measurable physiological states. Research from the HeartMath Institute has documented distinct patterns in heart rate variability (HRV) that align remarkably with these consciousness levels. When operating at lower levels (1-5), researchers observe chaotic, disordered heart rhythm patterns characteristic of stress and anxiety. As consciousness rises to Levels 7-9, HeartMath's measurements show a shift toward what they term *psychophysiological coherence*—a state where heart rhythms display a smooth, ordered sine-wave-like pattern indicating optimal communication between heart and brain.

This coherence state, measured through HRV analysis, corresponds precisely to the higher consciousness levels where the three brains—gut, heart, and mind—operate in harmony rather than conflict. HeartMath scientists have demonstrated that this coherence state enhances cognitive function, emotional stability, and intuitive capacity—the very qualities that naturally emerge at higher consciousness levels. Their research provides compelling physiological evidence for what ancient wisdom traditions have recognized for millennia: consciousness exists along a spectrum from fragmented to integrated, and this spectrum has measurable correlates in our biological functioning.

Throughout this book, I'll share how I moved through these different levels of consciousness—experiencing their limitations and gifts firsthand. My journey through these levels revealed something extraordinary: we are not permanently fixed at any level but can learn to shift our frequency intentionally through what I call the Flow State.

The Flow State: Defined

The Flow State is the natural condition of consciousness when your three neural networks—gut, heart, and mind—align in coherent harmony. This isn't just a pleasant experience but a distinct neurophysiological state where scattered attention unifies, allowing access to higher consciousness levels (7-9) and connection to the universal field of intelligence. In this state, you experience reality not as separate problems to be solved, but as a unified field to be navigated with wisdom that transcends individual limitation. We will dive further into the Flow State in later chapters and incorporate its harmonial brilliance for your life.

When Three Brains Harmonize

Did you know you have not one brain but three? This isn't metaphorical— it's a biological fact.

The brain in your skull is the one you're most familiar with— the magnificent organ that handles analytical thinking, language, and conscious decision-making. But you also have complex neural networks in your heart and gut that function as specialized "brains" in their own right.

The heart contains approximately 40,000 neurons that can sense, learn, remember, and even feel. The gut contains roughly 500 million neurons—more than in your spinal cord! Both send more signals to your cranial brain than they receive from it, suggesting they're not just passive receivers of instructions but active participants in your cognitive and emotional processing.

I discovered the importance of this three-brain system during a pivotal conversation with a friend who was studying neuro-cardiology. She explained how heart rhythm patterns change dramatically depending on our emotional states. "In states of frustration or stress," she said, "heart rhythms become chaotic and disordered. But in states of appreciation and love, they become incredibly coherent and ordered."

This hit me like a lightning bolt. I realized that in my most flow-like states—those moments of clarity by the lake—my three brains weren't fighting each other. My gut wasn't sending anxiety signals that my heart was trying to soothe while my head was attempting to rationalize everything. Instead, all three centers were aligned, creating a coherent field that allowed a different quality of awareness to emerge.

Think about times when you've felt conflicted: Your head says one thing ("This job pays well, I should be grateful"), your heart feels another ("But I'm miserable here"), and your gut sends yet another signal ("Something about my boss feels off"). This internal conflict creates what scientists call "psychophysiological incoherence"—a measurable state of disordered energy that blocks access to higher consciousness levels.

Conversely, when all three brains align—when your thoughts, emotions, and instincts point in the same direction—you enter a state of coherence that serves as a gateway to higher levels of consciousness. This is the Flow State—not just a psychological experience but a measurable state of physiological harmony.

The beauty of this understanding is its practicality. **We don't need to achieve some exotic spiritual state to access higher consciousness**. We simply need to create alignment among our already-existing neural networks. The tool I discovered for creating this alignment—the Attention Compass—will be explained in detail in Chapter 4. I call it a *tool* because you will be able to grasp it and use it in a powerful and practical way, starting immediately.

Consciousness as Frequency: Your Vibrational Broadcast

Have you ever walked into a room and immediately sensed the energy there? Or met someone and felt either drawn to or repelled by them before they even spoke? These experiences hint at something science is beginning to confirm: Consciousness operates as a vibrational frequency that extends beyond our physical bodies.

Every thought, emotion, and belief generates an electromagnetic field that can actually be measured with highly sensitive enough instruments. HeartMath Institute research has shown that the heart's electromagnetic field extends several feet beyond our bodies and changes measurably based on our emotional states.

This isn't just interesting biology—it's the key to understanding how consciousness shapes reality. You're constantly broadcasting a vibrational signature based on your predominant emotional and mental states. This broadcast doesn't just affect your internal experience; it literally interacts with the quantum field around you, attracting resonant experiences and repelling discordant ones.

I first noticed this in my own life through what seemed like strange coincidences. During periods when I operated primarily from fear and scarcity (Levels 3-4), I would repeatedly encounter situations that reinforced those exact emotions—unexpected bills, difficult people, opportunities that fell through at the last minute. It was as if the universe was conspiring to confirm my worldview.

But during periods when I managed to maintain states of acceptance and peace (Levels 7-8), a different pattern emerged. Helpful people would appear at just the right moment. Resources I needed would become available in unexpected ways. Solutions to problems would present themselves with minimal effort on my part. Some of my experiences seemed like miracles.

Was the universe treating me differently? Not exactly. My frequency was attracting different experiences—like a radio tuning into different stations. Life "happened" one way when tuned into one level, differently when there was only static, and then clearly more positive when tuned into higher levels.

This understanding transforms how we approach manifestation. It's not about using visualization techniques or positive affirmations to "trick" the universe into giving you what you want. It's about shifting your actual vibrational frequency through the alignment of your three brains, which naturally attracts corresponding experiences.

Ever wonder how a tuning fork works? In the world of music, when you strike a tuning fork and hold it near another tuning fork of the same frequency, the second fork will begin to vibrate in resonance with the first—without any physical contact between them. Similarly, when you maintain a consistent vibrational state, you cause resonant experiences to "vibrate" into your reality.

The Quantum Connection: You Are Not Separate

Modern physics has revealed something that ancient spiritual traditions have taught for millennia. At the most fundamental level, separation is an illusion. The apparently solid, separate objects that make up our world—including our bodies—are actually dynamic patterns of energy and information in a unified field.

The famous double-slit experiment demonstrates that particles behave differently when observed versus when not observed (Wheeler, John Archibald, and Wojciech Hubert Zurek, eds. *Quantum Theory and Measurement*. Princeton University Press, 1983). This isn't a minor curiosity; it suggests that consciousness itself plays some role in the formation of physical reality.

A physicist I know gave me more clarity. "It's not that your thoughts are directly creating reality in a simplistic way," he explained. "It's more that consciousness and matter are different expressions of the same underlying field. They're intimately connected because they were never truly separate to begin with."

This understanding doesn't mean you can simply think a mansion into existence. The quantum effects we're discussing operate within probability fields governed by natural laws. But it does mean that consciousness is not just passively perceiving a fixed external world; it's actively participating in shaping that world through its focus, intention, and vibrational state.

When you enter the Flow State—when gut, heart, and mind align—you're operating from a more coherent quantum field. Your thoughts, emotions, and intentions are no longer working against each other but unifying into a single clear signal that interacts with the universal field more powerfully.

This is why the practice of "feeling it in" (which we'll explore in Chapter 7) is so powerful. When you can fully embody the emotional state of already having what you desire—not just thinking about it but feeling it in every cell of your body—you're actually shifting your vibrational frequency to match that reality. From that shifted state, what once seemed impossible becomes the natural unfolding of events.

What This Journey Offers You

These chapters will detail for you many practical tools for transformation—tools I've tested through my own journey from lower to higher levels of consciousness. This book isn't about escaping your current reality but transforming it from within by shifting the frequency from which you're operating.

Imagine moving through life from Level 8 (Peace) instead of Level 4 (Fear). Same circumstances, entirely different experience. Imagine you are driving along in your neighborhood, not too fast, and up ahead you see something in the middle of your lane on the road. It's black and white and red but you cannot yet see exactly what it is. Your brain identifies it as probably a neighbor's cat that has been run over. You know "Oreo" and start to feel upset. Your breath and heart rate quicken, you clinch your jaw in dread as you get closer. You're almost starting to cry. The small heap OCCURS for you as a tragically dead pet and your body responds accordingly. Then you pull up close enough to identify it—it's only rags in the road. Your body and mind are relieved and begin to calm down as you drive on.

Challenges don't disappear, but your relationship to them fundamentally changes. Solutions appear more readily. Synchronicities increase. Life begins to feel more like a collaborative dance and less like a struggle against resistance.

Throughout the chapters that follow, you'll learn:

- How to identify which consciousness level you're currently operating from

- Practical techniques for shifting to higher levels, even in challenging circumstances

- The Attention Compass method for bringing your three brains into alignment

- How to access the Flow State reliably rather than waiting for random moments of inspiration

- The art of "feeling it in"—living FROM your desired reality rather than FOR it

- How to maintain higher consciousness levels amid daily life

Each chapter includes exercises designed to help you experience these concepts directly rather than just understanding them intellectually. Because ultimately, this knowledge is valuable only to the extent that it transforms your lived experience.

I remember a woman I worked with who had been struggling with chronic health issues and financial problems for years. Through our coaching sessions, she learned to identify her consciousness level in real-time and practiced the Attention Compass technique (which we'll explore in Chapter 4) to bring her three brains into alignment. After several weeks of consistent practice learning to access the Flow State and live from Level 7 (Acceptance) rather than Level 4 (Fear), she reported that her physical symptoms began to improve, and unexpected financial opportunities appeared. "The circumstances of my life haven't completely changed yet," she told me, "but I'm experiencing them in a completely different way. And that difference is everything."

This transformation is available to anyone willing to learn the code of consciousness. It doesn't require special talents, spiritual gifts, or years of meditation practice. It simply requires understanding how your consciousness operates and learning to align your three brains into coherence.

My Promise to You

My promise is this: if you approach this journey with an open mind and heart, if you practice the tools with an intention to have a life-changing experience, and if you trust the wisdom emerging from your centered awareness, you will experience shifts in consciousness that will transform not just how you feel but the reality you perceive and create.

The Flow State isn't some exotic achievement reserved for monks, mystics, or specially gifted individuals. It's your natural condition when the fragments of your being realign into wholeness. And in that alignment, you'll discover that what you've been seeking—peace, fulfillment, purpose, joy—was never outside you. It was always within, waiting for you to come home to yourself.

Let's begin the journey.

Forecasting Everything But Myself

"40 below keeps out the riff raff" was a popular saying in the only town within miles of my duty station at Minot Air Force Base in North Dakota. I joined right after high school and quickly realized my peer group had changed drastically from what I was used to. I peered out the frosty window of the truck, on my way to fix a 40-year-old toilet in a rural missile silo out in the barren, white, frozen fields. I was aware of the pain in my fingers and toes, their unfortunate state due to heaters that never quite overcame the temperatures below zero that were the norm. I longed for the sunny days of California, where I had lived with my parents, who met there in college. I had never experienced the cold like this. It was otherworldly, and I was sure didn't belong there. This was not what I signed up for. Instead of seeing the world, I was in a frozen hell. I fantasized about escape.

Before the service, I went to three different high schools when my parents divorced and I bounced around between them. I could have qualified to go to college, but didn't know what I wanted to pursue. But I didn't want to live in a fractured family anymore, so I left to see the world through the military. Little did I know about any climate east of the Rocky Mountains, especially the brutal winters in North Dakota. Moving around as the son of a military family, and as a child of a divorced family, I developed strong social skills. I had to. I desperately needed to be wanted, validated, sought-after, and popular at an early age. So, even though I didn't know anyone for more than 2-3 years during my school years, I searched for quick approval from new friends. This became my personality. It was how I survived. I counted on the instant camaraderie I imagined would be part of the military experience.

Yet here I was, in the middle of nowhere, while everyone I knew was having the college experience, and for the first time, I found myself aching to escape my life. It was right after the Gulf War, and I had about a year left in my commitment when I decided I had two choices: 1. Rejoin for another four years or, 2. Try and get a job in the small town of Minot, 30 miles south of the base. I chose the latter.

During my last year in the service, I attended night school to learn broadcasting, hoping to one day be a radio broadcaster or "DJ." In 1992, I got a job doing overnights. Just getting the job was quite a feat of trust and faith, as everyone told me there were no openings. But I made it. In December of that same year, I was working full-time as an afternoon drive-time jock for the AM radio station in Minot. I was elated! My drive was to prove to everyone I was worthwhile; to all of my family…to the girl who broke my heart in High School…anyone who used to know me. I was going to be popular once again, and radio was just the start. I was seeking outside validation with a passion. (It was also the first time I used visualization to create my eventual reality, although I didn't know it at the time.)

In Minot in 1992, there were many roles in the company filled by the same person. The market was very small, with little money, but I KNEW this was my calling. Then one day, the weather person, a very popular lady, had to choose to be with her kids or continue doing the 6 p.m. and 10 p m. weather. She chose to keep the 6 o'clock position, which left the 10 pm position open. Not many people wanted to move to Minot in 1992 (before the Oil Boom years later), so there weren't many options for the station. Some reference is needed here; the radio station I worked at also had an FM station and a TV station, all in the same building. Maybe that makes more sense now as to why I was asked to do the 10 pm weather cast. I was not a meteorologist; I didn't even have a suit to wear on TV. But I knew that if I could just make this work, it would be my ticket to making it to larger markets. I was sure I could handle the hard work and brutal daily rituals.

What no one saw was me, minutes before that first broadcast, locked in a bathroom stall, my stomach in knots, fighting waves of nausea. The fluorescent lights buzzed overhead as I gripped the cold metal partition, trying to steady my breathing. I'd never felt such opposing forces at war within me—terror at the possibility of humiliating myself on live television versus the absolute certainty that if I didn't walk out of that bathroom and onto that set, I'd be trapped in Minot forever. The thought of permanent (and brutally cold) stagnation terrified me more than temporary failure. With shaking hands, I straightened my borrowed tie, splashed cold water on my face, and walked toward the studio lights.

I became the 10 p.m. weathercaster. I was awful. I "performed" the weather rather than being myself. I was like Jim Carrey in a bad Saturday Night Live skit. But I knew I could get better, and I pleaded with the News Director to let me stay on until they found a better weathercaster.

When nobody applied, I poured myself into the position. I took "correspondence courses" through the mail (pre-internet) to get my diploma for Atmospheric Science (3 ½ year journey) and became the first ever meteorologist on TV in North Dakota. I created a segment called *Weather Scouts* where people could send in questions about the weather, and I would answer them. The "weather lady" eventually left, and I was the only meteorologist for both radio stations and also the TV station. I got much better thanks to excellent mentors and really great people who saw my dedication to becoming the best I could be. One of those mentors told me something that changed everything: "When you are on the air, never address the camera with 'Hello, everyone.' Remember that there is only one person watching, no matter how many 'ones' there are."

That simple insight calmed me immensely. It transformed my approach from performing weather to sharing it with a single person in their living room. It humanized what had been a terrifying technical exercise. That shift in perspective allowed me to take my career to the next level—to connect rather than just broadcast. There is always just one person listening, one person my words need to connect with, even when the room is crowded or the audience is large. This truth would later take on profound meaning beyond my career, though I couldn't see it then.

So I talked a lot about snow for three more years in the frigid conditions of that very small town, but deep inside, I knew there was more I could become. I was doing well, and I began to feel like they needed me more than I needed them. It was my first glimpse of popularity as a young adult. I had made it! Yet, I felt the first of many pangs of the heart—I was empty inside and confused. I tried harder, got an agent, and moved to a big city.

Being on television and radio in the 90s was a big deal since no other live media existed—no internet, no YouTube, no social media. My high-profile role was, to me, very important, and I treated the position as such. Honor, commitment, and being correct had been my upbringing, so I fit right in. There was more, however—the feeling you get in a town or city where everyone knows who you are, even when you don't know them back. I had become a part of their morning, afternoon, and evening routines. I was on both the radio (2-5:30 p.m.) and TV (6, 10 p.m.). People "invited" me into their homes each day. I unknowingly became part of their family. There were few options (nothing like today), and once a family decided I was "their weatherman," it was like going steady. I came to understand this because whenever I was out in public, I was recognized and greeted as if I were a favorite family member. My deep longing for connection and a sense of family, which I'd wanted my whole life, was being filled in the most amazing way.

For me, since I had desired such a feeling with such intensity as a child, then later in the service, it was like a drug. I loved it. My false ego was in full swing. I loved giving information to those who depended on me. I loved the responsibility that came with being a Broadcast Meteorologist. Unlike the other "on the desk" TV positions, I was an expert—the only expert. I was asked each day/night for my opinion. I felt smart, needed, wanted, and important. It fed my ego and created a false yet concrete description of who I thought I was.

External validation is very much like a drug; it wears off. When that started to happen, I sought out larger markets, more responsibility, and more money. Finding that also meant stability. I got married, bought a beautiful house, picked out a boat, had a great truck, and bought my wife a Cadillac. Life on the outside was amazing. We became pregnant with our son soon thereafter, and I was on cloud 9. I would look around at all that I had achieved, imagine the father I would soon become, and admire the wonderful wife I found to share my life with. Everything was great on the outside—but when I really reflected inside, I was still empty…so I pushed away those pangs of inner strife,

My achievements were accompanied by a constant need for validation and recognition for my efforts, which my TV position satisfied—but the fulfillment was fleeting. Who was "I" outside of my role as a meteorologist? A husband? Father? Many other people my age had these roles, some even had TV roles. A burning question started to haunt me: *What am I missing?* In 2003. I began a search for the truth to life overall, to find the purpose beyond my roles. It unraveled right in front of me, taking me on the scariest journey, like I have only seen in movies. My curiosity about the nature of life, the reality behind the screen of what appeared to be real, would start a thirst for *more information*. Knowledge is good for the brain, but I wanted to fill my heart and spirit, as well. I wanted to *experience* the things I was discovering.

The Code Connection: Levels 4–5 (Fear and Desire)

My weather maps themselves were perfect metaphors for the illusion in which I lived. Each day, I'd stand before these colorful images that showed pressure systems, fronts, and storm cells—all appearing as separate objects moving independently across the screen. I'd point to these systems as if they were distinct entities: "This cold front will move through overnight, followed by this high-pressure system tomorrow."

But the atmosphere doesn't actually work that way. There are no lines in the sky separating one air mass from another. Weather is a single, continuous flow of energy and matter—we draw boundaries to make sense of it, to predict it, to feel some control over it.

This is exactly how we experience reality itself. We perceive separate objects—my body, your body, this job, that house, my successes, my failures—when in truth, everything is connected in ways our ordinary awareness can't perceive.

The emptiness I felt despite all my achievements was my first clue that something was fundamentally wrong with how I was seeing reality. I was treating my identity as a meteorologist as separate from my true self. I was seeing my accomplishments as objects to acquire rather than expressions of who I really was.

Looking back on my life as a weatherman, I operated primarily between Level 4 (Fear) and Level 5 (Desire) consciousness. My entire career path was motivated by the Level 4 fear of rejection, of being unloved, of not mattering. I joined the military to escape my fractured family (avoidance), and I pursued broadcasting because it promised the validation I craved.

As I achieved success, I shifted more into Level 5 (Desire) consciousness. I believed happiness lay in the next market, the next promotion, the next possession. The boat, the Cadillac, the beautiful house—these weren't just things; they were conditions I had set for my fulfillment. Yet when I acquired them, the happiness they brought was gone in a flash.

What makes these lower levels so deceptive is that society fosters and celebrates them. My fear-based drive for security and desire-based achievement were rewarded with praise, money, and status.

Everyone thought I was thriving, including me—at least consciously. But my emptiness was my heart's way of signaling that I was operating at a level of consciousness too confined for my true nature.

The greatest illusion—the one that caused my suffering—was the belief that I was separate from everything else. That I, Eric the Weatherman, was a distinct entity whose worth depended on the validation of *other* separate entities. This illusion of separation is the foundation of the lowest levels of consciousness, where fear, desire, and the endless chase for external approval dominate our experience.

My viewers saw me as the authority who could tell them about tomorrow's reality, never realizing I couldn't even see the storms brewing within my own.

Exercise: "Reality Check" – Identifying Your Own External/Internal Disconnects

External Success vs. Internal Truth

Before we go further on this journey together, I invite you to try a simple but profound reality check—one I wish I'd done long before my life had to collapse to get my attention.

1. **Achievement Inventory**: Take a moment to list your three to five most significant external achievements or roles. These might be career accomplishments, relationships, possessions, or social

positions—the things that define "successful you" to the outside world.

2. **Fulfillment Assessment**: For each achievement or role, ask yourself: "If this were suddenly taken away from me, how would I feel?" and "Does this truly fulfill me at my deepest level?" Rate each from 1-10, with 10 being completely fulfilling.

3. **The Quiet Moment Test**: Find a quiet space where you won't be disturbed. Sit comfortably and close your eyes. For just two minutes, set aside all thoughts of your roles, responsibilities, and achievements. Ask yourself: "Who am I when all of that is stripped away?" Don't analyze—just notice what arises.

4. **Whispers of Emptiness**: Recall moments when, despite outward success, you've felt an inexplicable emptiness or longing. What were you doing? Who were you with? What might that emptiness have been trying to tell you?

5. **Your Alternative Timeline**: If external validation and security weren't concerns, what would you be doing differently in your life right now? Allow yourself to imagine without judgment.

This isn't about judging your life choices or achievements as "wrong." The external world and personal accomplishments have their place and purpose. This exercise is simply about noticing the gap—if there is one—between your external success and your internal truth. Awareness of this gap is the first step toward bridging it.

Unlike my journey, which required the complete collapse of my external identity, yours might unfold more gently through consciousness and choice—but only if you're willing to look honestly at where you stand right now.

For me, there came a point when the gap between my external success and internal emptiness had grown to a chasm I could no longer ignore. It was 2003, and I had achieved everything I'd dreamed of—the career, the recognition, the beautiful family—yet when I'd lie awake at night, staring at the ceiling of my beautiful home, I felt like a stranger to myself. A hollowness had taken residence in my chest, an unnamed yearning that neither professional accolades nor material possessions could touch.

The weather maps were just like my life—systems moving across surfaces while deeper currents remained invisible. I'd become an expert at predicting atmospheric changes but remained deaf to the rumbling thunder within.

I remember one evening, after finishing the 10 p.m. broadcast, I stood alone in the parking lot under a vast North Dakota sky. Stars stretched endlessly above me, and for a brief moment, I felt my smallness in the face of such immensity. Who was I, really, beneath all these layers of carefully constructed identity? What was I missing that left me feeling so incomplete, even though I possessed everything I thought I wanted?

That question—*What am I missing?*—became the first illuminating flash of lightning in a storm that would eventually wash away everything I thought I knew about myself and reality.

I didn't realize it then, but I was standing at the edge of what The Code would reveal as the great division between lower and higher consciousness. I was about to embark on a search for meaning that would challenge everything I believed.

The weatherman could predict tomorrow's conditions, but he had no idea of the spiritual tempest that was about to engulf his life—or the profound clarity that would eventually emerge from its center.

CHAPTER 1
The Divided Self

Each chapter of this journey includes three elements: the external story of transformation, practical tools you can apply in your own life, and glimpses into the continuing dream that served as my inner guide through two decades of awakening. These dream sequences aren't just metaphorical flourishes—they represent the actual inner dialogue that paralleled my outer journey, showing how the psyche works to heal its own divisions when we're finally ready to listen.

———◆———

Have you ever noticed how easy it is to smile for a photo while feeling completely broken inside? To say "I'm fine" when you're anything but? To build a life that looks perfect from the outside while feeling a profound emptiness within?

That was my daily reality for years, and chances are, you've experienced some version of this division yourself. This gap between our outer presentation and inner experience isn't just occasional discomfort—it's the fundamental split that prevents us from accessing the Flow State and higher levels of consciousness.

I remember the exact moment I first recognized this division in myself. I was standing in front of the weather map during the 6 o'clock news, pointing confidently at cold fronts and pressure systems, my voice steady and authoritative. "We can expect clearing skies by morning as this high-pressure system moves through," I assured the viewers. Everything about me projected confidence and certainty. All I did was look at the camera during a commercial break and thought, *who is it that is talking?* It was like I was hovering above myself watching me do the broadcast. And it lasted only a second or two, but it was enough to set everything apart.

Inside, just beneath that polished exterior, a very different weather system was brewing—one filled with doubt, confusion, and a growing sense that something essential was missing from my life. What made this split so insidious wasn't just its existence but how normal it had become.

This division had been my constant companion for so long that I no longer questioned it.

The Successful Weatherman's Secret Storm

Back when I was living "the American Dream," my day would typically begin at 3:00 AM when my alarm jolted me awake. By 4:00 AM, I'd be in the studio, reviewing data, preparing graphics, and getting ready for the morning broadcast. Hair and makeup would transform me from sleepy human to camera-ready professional, and by 5:00 AM, I'd be on air, delivering the forecast with energy and enthusiasm that my body definitely wasn't feeling naturally at that hour.

"Good morning! I'm Eric Wilson and there are changes coming. We're tracking a system moving in from the northwest that could bring significant rainfall by this afternoon..."

The red light on the camera would blink off, and I'd immediately drop the animated expression, taking a quick sip of coffee before the next segment. On and off, all morning long—the weather personality and then the real me, weatherman and then just Eric, back and forth like flipping a switch.

By noon, the morning show would wrap, and I'd head to my office to analyze data for the evening broadcasts, record radio spots, update the station's website, and handle various other responsibilities. Between segments, colleagues would stop by to chat, viewers would send appreciative emails about how they planned their day around my forecast, and the news director would occasionally pop in to congratulate me on the ratings…when they were good, that is.

From the outside, it all looked so seamless and successful. And in many ways, it was. I had worked hard to get there—starting at small stations in places like Minot, North Dakota, gradually moving to larger markets, investing years in education and training. I took genuine pride in providing accurate forecasts that helped people plan their lives. There were aspects of the job I truly loved, particularly the blend of science and communication.

But beneath the surface, a quiet desperation was growing. While delivering the forecast about external weather patterns, I was increasingly aware of an internal storm that no meteorological training had prepared me for.

It would hit me at odd moments—sitting in my car after a broadcast, driving home as the rest of the world was just beginning its day. I'd feel a wave of emptiness wash over me, a sense that despite all the apparent success, something fundamental was missing. Was it "depression"? I did not think it was dramatic enough to call depression, but rather a persistent, low-grade sense of disconnection—from myself, from others, from any sense of meaning or purpose. *Is this really all there is?* I'd wonder, staring at the morning traffic. *Is this what I'm going to do for the next twenty years until retirement?* The thought filled me with a vague dread that I couldn't quite name but also couldn't shake.

What made it all so confusing was that I couldn't point to anything specifically wrong with my life. I had achieved the goals I had set for myself. I was respected in my field. I had a loving family. By any reasonable standard, I should have been content, even happy.

Yet the gap between my outer success and inner emptiness continued to widen. At social gatherings, I'd find myself playing the role of "Eric the Weatherman"—telling the same anecdotes, answering the same questions about extreme weather events, smiling and nodding while a part of me watched from a distance, wondering who this person was and why he felt so unfamiliar.

I developed countless strategies to cope with this growing division. I threw myself even more intensely into my work, taking on additional projects and responsibilities. I focused on material acquisitions—a nicer car, a boat, home renovations—hoping each new purchase would somehow fill the void. I consumed endless self-help books and motivational content, thinking perhaps I just needed to adjust my attitude or develop better habits.

Nothing worked. In fact, these coping mechanisms only widened the gap by reinforcing the external identity while neglecting the internal reality. I was becoming more and more divided against myself, living simultaneously as two people—the successful professional everyone knew and the increasingly hollow person I was becoming. *Is this schizophrenia?* I wondered. I thought not, but certainly did not feel *well*.

The Weather Map Illusion

The irony of my situation wasn't lost on me, even then. As a meteorologist, my entire career centered around creating artificial separations that don't actually exist in nature.

Think about it: have you ever seen a cold front in the sky? Have you ever looked up and noticed the boundary between a high-pressure and low-pressure system? Of course not. These lines don't exist in the actual atmosphere. They're conceptual tools meteorologists use to make sense of what is, in reality, a single, continuous fluid system in constant motion.

This is exactly what we do with ourselves and our experience of reality. We draw artificial boundaries where none actually exist. We separate our "professional self" from our "personal self," our "public face" from our "private feelings," our "mind" from our "body" from our "spirit." We slice and dice our unitary experience into manageable pieces because it feels safer, more controllable that way. Some call this "compartmentalizing."

One morning, I was standing in front of the green screen, illustrating the boundaries of an approaching storm system with sweeping gestures. "Here's where the cold front will move through, creating a sharp division between the warm, humid air to the south and the cooler, drier air pushing down from Canada."

Suddenly, I was hit with the realization that I had been doing exactly the same thing with my life—drawing sharp divisions between aspects of myself that were never meant to be separated. The weatherman versus the husband and father. The public personality versus the private individual. The outer success versus the inner emptiness.

Just as there are no actual lines in the sky, there are no real divisions within us. The boundaries we create—between thoughts and emotions, between mind and body, between work and life—are conceptual tools, not realities. Useful in certain contexts, perhaps, but ultimately artificial.

And here's where the weather map analogy gets even more interesting. When meteorologists create these artificial divisions, they do it with a purpose—to understand and predict the behavior of a complex system. The problem comes when we forget that the human-constructed map is not the actual natural territory. We confuse our models with reality itself.

This is exactly what happens in our lives. We confuse the roles we play, the identities we construct, and the boundaries we establish with who we actually are. We begin to believe in the divisions we've created. We become fragmented, living in a state of low-grade internal conflict where different aspects of ourselves are working at cross purposes.

For years, I maintained these artificial separations with meticulous care.

Living at Levels 4–5: The Fear and Desire Treadmill

Looking back, I can now see that my divided existence kept me firmly anchored in Levels 4 and 5 of consciousness—Fear and Desire. These levels aren't just psychological states; they're distinct energy frequencies that shape how we perceive and interact with reality.

Level 4 (Fear) manifested in my constant anxiety about maintaining the success I had achieved. I wasn't just afraid of failing; I was afraid of being exposed as somehow fraudulent or inadequate despite my achievements. This fear created a perpetual background tension that colored everything I did. It expressed itself in seemingly responsible behaviors—triple-checking forecasts, obsessively monitoring ratings, staying late to prepare for broadcasts—that were actually driven by a deep insecurity.

Sometimes I couldn't hold the fear at bay. I remember one evening when a competing station's meteorologist predicted a major snowstorm while my models suggested it would mostly miss our viewing area. The pressure I felt was enormous. If I stuck with my forecast and was wrong, viewers might switch to the competition. If I adjusted my prediction to match theirs without believing it was accurate, I'd be compromising my professional integrity. I stayed with my own forecast, which meant hours of being on the edge of terror.

The physical symptoms of fear were unmistakable—a tightness in my chest, shallow breathing, racing thoughts, disturbed sleep. Sadly, I had become so accustomed to this state that it felt normal. I didn't recognize it as fear; I called it "taking my job seriously." Alongside this fear ran the equally powerful current of Level 5 (Desire)—the constant craving for more. More recognition, more success, more security, more possessions. In this state, happiness always exists in the future, contingent upon achieving the next goal or acquiring the next thing.

"I'll feel fulfilled when I reach the top market." Then, "I'll feel fulfilled when I get the prime time slot." Then, "I'll feel fulfilled when I win the regional Emmy." The target kept moving, but the promised full and lasting satisfaction never arrived.

The insidious thing about Levels 4 and 5 is that society celebrates and rewards them. My fear-based hypervigilance was praised as "attention to detail" and "dedication." My desire-driven ambition was applauded as "motivation" and "drive." Far from being recognized as limitations, these consciousness levels were reinforced at every turn.

What I couldn't see then was how these levels were keeping me locked in a divided state, always fragmented, never whole. Fear causes us to contract, to separate ourselves from potential threats, to draw boundaries between "safe" and "unsafe." Desire causes us to project fulfillment onto future conditions, creating a division between "now" and "then," between "what is" and "what should be."

Together, fear and desire create a treadmill of endless striving without arrival, of constant motion without rest. They maintain the illusion of separation between self and other, between present and future, between who we are and who we think we should be.

I was caught in this treadmill for years, moving faster and faster while essentially staying in the same place. My external circumstances changed—better job, bigger house, more recognition—but my internal state remained constant: divided, conflicted, and secretly hollow.

The Symptoms of a Fragmented Consciousness

The division in our consciousness manifests in very real, often painful ways. Having lived with this fragmentation for years, I became intimately familiar with its symptoms. Perhaps you'll recognize some of these in your own experience:

Chronic Exhaustion: Not just physical tiredness, but a bone-deep weariness that sleep doesn't seem to touch. It takes enormous energy to maintain artificial divisions within yourself. I would get eight hours of sleep and still wake up feeling depleted, not understanding that the true exhaustion was coming from the constant internal conflict rather than external demands.

The Mask Phenomenon: That uncanny sense of "putting on a face" for different situations and the relief of "taking off the mask" when alone. I had different masks for different contexts—the authoritative weatherman, the engaged colleague, the caring father and husband. Each required a slightly different version of myself, and switching between them required a subtle but constant vigilance.

Emotional Disconnection: A growing difficulty in accessing or expressing authentic emotions. I found myself intellectualizing feelings rather than experiencing them directly. When asked how I felt about something, I would respond with what I thought about it instead. The connection to my emotional life had become so tenuous that I hardly noticed its absence. Truly, I was numb.

Decision Paralysis: Increasing difficulty making decisions, especially about important life matters. When different parts of ourselves want different things, even simple choices can become battlegrounds for internal conflict. I would analyze decisions endlessly, making pros and cons lists that never led to clarity because the divided parts of myself couldn't reach a consensus. Anything that called for thinking was met with overthinking.

The Impostor Syndrome: A persistent feeling that your achievements are somehow fraudulent and that you'll eventually be "found out." Despite objective evidence of competence and success, I constantly fought the sense that I was fooling everyone, including myself. This wasn't just occasional self-doubt but a fundamental uncertainty about my own authenticity. This contributes to feeling stuck in a cycle of shame (Level 1).

Meaning Deficit: A growing sense that life lacks deeper meaning or purpose, despite external achievements. I remember standing in my driveway one evening, looking at my home, my car, all the tangible symbols of success, and feeling absolutely nothing. It was as if I was looking at someone else's life, one that had no real connection to anything I actually connected with or valued.

Relationship Distance: A subtle but growing disconnection from those closest to you. When we're divided within ourselves, authentic connection with others becomes increasingly difficult. I was physically present with my family, but emotionally elsewhere, unable to bridge the gap between my outer performance and inner emptiness enough to create true intimacy. I wanted to care, be present, and be a good family man—so that's how I acted. This only made me feel more alone.

Synchronization Problems: Alignment is crucial. When our thoughts, emotions, and actions are misaligned, life itself seems to become less fluid. I noticed that during my most fragmented periods, nothing seemed to flow smoothly. Simple tasks took more effort, opportunities fell through, interactions became strained. It was as if the division within was creating friction in my external experience as well.

These symptoms aren't signs of personal failure or weakness—they're the natural consequence of living in a divided state. Our consciousness isn't designed to function in fragments. Just as a car engine can't run smoothly when its parts are misaligned, we can't operate at our full potential when we're divided against ourselves.

I lived with these symptoms for years, not recognizing them as connected or understanding their common source. I tried to address each one separately—time management for the exhaustion, communication techniques for the relationship distance, motivational content for the meaning deficit. But these approaches never created lasting change because they didn't address the fundamental issue: the division itself.

It wasn't until my complete collapse (which I'll share in Chapter 3) that I was forced to confront the unsustainability of this divided existence. But you don't need to wait for a crisis to begin recognizing and healing the divisions in your own consciousness. Awareness itself is the first step toward integration.

Though I couldn't see it then, this division I experienced wasn't a permanent condition but a necessary recognition. What felt like an insurmountable split between my public and private selves would eventually become the doorway to a more integrated way of being. The fragmentation I struggled with—between the weatherman persona and my authentic self—contained within it the seeds of wholeness I would later discover. Like a map that first shows us how lost we are before guiding us home, recognizing this division was the essential first step toward the coherence I would find through the Attention Compass and Flow State. The journey to wholeness begins not with denial of our fragments but with honest acknowledgment of them.

The dream that opened this book became a recurring visitor throughout my journey—sometimes arriving during the darkest periods of collapse, other times emerging as I began to rebuild. These weren't random nighttime images but profound dialogues with the divided aspects of myself, each dream deepening my understanding of what integration truly means. Throughout this book, I'll share how these dreams evolved alongside my external transformation, serving as an inner compass guiding me toward wholeness. What began as a terrifying confrontation with my rejected self gradually became a reunion—a coming home to parts of myself I'd spent a lifetime avoiding. This part of the book's chapters will be called "The Dream Deepens."

The Dream Deepens: The First Glance

I couldn't outrun the dream. Just weeks after that first haunting encounter, sleep pulled me back to the Great Hall.

Golden light spills across marble floors. Faces are turned expectantly toward me. The disheveled man appears at the door asking, "Why do you reject me?" Something inside me—some thin thread of recognition—keeps me from recoiling. Instead, I take one small, trembling step toward him. My heart hammers in my chest so violently, I am sure everyone can hear it.

"I don't know who you are," I say, my voice steadier than the earthquake in my bones.

His eyes—my eyes—hold mine with an intensity that makes my skin prickle. Eyes like deep wells. Wells of sorrow so deep I could drown in them, yet somehow also filled with a patience older than time. "Look harder," he says. It sounds more like an invitation than a command. But I feel like he's asking me to do something I have spent a lifetime avoiding.

I woke with his words echoing in my consciousness, tears cooling on my cheeks though I hadn't been aware of crying. Something fundamental had shifted. The man I had previously seen as disgusting and shameful— someone to be banished from the celebration of my accomplishments— now appeared simply... wounded. Human. The boundary between us had thinned, just slightly, but enough to create a hairline fracture in the fortress I'd built against myself.

As I mapped my inner divisions through the exercise at the end of this chapter, tracing the geography of my fragmented self, I kept returning to one unsettling question: What if those very divisions were keeping me from seeing who that man really was—and by extension, who I really was beneath the weatherman's carefully constructed persona? What if the parts of myself I'd worked so hard to hide away contained not shame but salvation?

Exercise: Mapping Your Inner Divisions

This exercise is designed to help you identify the divisions that might exist in your own consciousness. Unlike some practices that focus immediately on healing or integration, this one is about awareness—simply recognizing the splits that might be operating in your life.

Remember, these divisions aren't character flaws or problems to be fixed. They're natural adaptations to a culture that encourages fragmentation. The goal isn't to judge them but to bring them into awareness, which is the necessary first step toward wholeness.

Find a quiet space where you won't be interrupted for about 30 minutes. Have a journal or several sheets of paper handy, along with something to write with. Then follow these steps:

1. Identity Inventory

Make a list of the different "selves" or roles you present in various contexts of your life. Be as specific and honest as possible. For example:

- Professional self (How you behave and what you value at work)
- Social self (How you present yourself with friends or in social settings)
- Family self (Who you are with family members)
- Private self (Who you are when completely alone)
- Online self (How you present yourself on social media)
- Any other distinct "versions" of yourself you're aware of

For each identity, write down:

- Three words that describe this version of you
- What this version values most
- What this version hides or suppresses
- When this version typically appears

2. Contradiction Mapping

Now look for contradictions between these different selves. For example:

- Your professional self might value efficiency and productivity, while your private self craves rest, less structure, and more spaciousness.
- Your social self might be outgoing and agreeable, while your private self is introspective and has strong opinions.
- Your family self might emphasize stability and tradition, while another part of you yearns for adventure and novelty.

Write down any contradictions you notice without trying to resolve them. Just bring awareness to these internal tensions. No need to edit, this is just for you.

3. The Unconscious Interview

This part of the exercise accesses aspects of yourself that might not be immediately obvious. Write down these questions, then write your answers without censoring or editing:

- What parts of myself do I hide from others?
- What aspects of myself am I ashamed of or uncomfortable with?
- If I could live without concern for others' approval, what would I do differently?
- What unacknowledged desires do I have that conflict with my external life?
- What truths am I afraid to admit to myself?

Write quickly and don't overthink. The goal is to bypass your usual filters and access deeper layers of awareness.

4. Body Awareness Check

Our bodies often hold the truth of our divisions, even when our minds are expert at maintaining them. Sit quietly, gently close your eyes, inhale deeply and exhale, and scan your body from head to toe. Notice any areas of tension, discomfort, pain, or numbness. For each area you identify, ask:

- What might this physical sensation be telling me?
- Is there a division or conflict that this part of my body is expressing?
- If this tension/discomfort could speak, what would it say?

Record any insights that arise, even if they seem irrational or don't make immediate logical sense.

5. Reflection and Integration

After completing the previous steps, take some time to reflect on what you've discovered. Consider these questions:

- What patterns do I notice across these exercises?
- Which divisions feel most significant or painful?
- Are there any divisions that surprise me?
- How might my life be different if these aspects were more integrated?

This isn't about solving or fixing anything yet. It's simply about bringing awareness to the divisions that might be operating in your life. This awareness itself is transformative, as what we can see clearly begins to shift naturally.

Share your insights in your journal, and consider revisiting this exercise periodically. As your awareness grows, you'll likely discover deeper layers of division as well as natural movements toward integration.

Remember, the goal isn't to eliminate all the different aspects of yourself—diversity within unity is healthy and natural. The goal is to transform fragmentation into differentiation, division into multiplicity. In an integrated state, different aspects of yourself can still exist, but they work together harmoniously rather than at cross-purposes.

In the chapters ahead, we'll explore how the Attention Compass can help you move from awareness of these divisions to actual integration and alignment, opening the door to the Flow State and higher levels of consciousness. But recognition is always the essential first step. What we can see clearly, we can transform.

"When you are inspired by some great purpose, some extraordinary project, all your thoughts break their bonds."—Patanjali

CHAPTER 2

Ignoring The Call

Do you remember the last time something whispered to you? Not a person—something deeper. That subtle nudge when you're about to make a decision. An internal inkling. The persistent thought that keeps returning despite your attempts to dismiss it. The strange coincidence that seems too meaningful to be random. These aren't just psychological quirks or statistical flukes. They're the language of your deeper self trying to communicate with your conscious mind.

I missed this language for years. Or more accurately, I heard it but refused to listen. Ignoring whispers became habitual and automatic.

I can see now that long before my life collapsed, long before I experienced the dream that opened this book, my deeper self was sending signals—persistent, increasingly urgent messages that something needed to change. These weren't dramatic interventions. They were soft but nagging disruptions in the narrative I had constructed about my life and who I was.

But the noise of my divided self—caught in Levels 4 and 5 of consciousness, between fear and desire—drowned out these subtle communications. The weather sirens of external demands were always louder than the distant rumble of inner knowing.

The Whispers Before the Storm

It started with little things—moments of disconnection that I quickly dismissed and moved past.

I remember standing in front of the green screen one morning, delivering the forecast with my usual polished, bright and sunny voice. The words flowed automatically, my gestures precise and practiced. "We're looking at a beautiful weekend ahead, folks, with temperatures in the mid-70s and plenty of sunshine—perfect for outdoor activities."

And then, mid-sentence, the strangest sensation washed over me. It was as if I stepped outside myself and was watching this performance from a rafter above the set, gazing down. *Who is this person? What is he doing? Why does any of this matter?* The questions arose unbidden, cutting through the familiar rhythm of the broadcast.

In that moment, the whole scenario—me gesturing at digital weather patterns that weren't actually there, smiling into a camera, telling strangers what to wear tomorrow—seemed utterly absurd. Not wrong, exactly, just deeply strange and somehow disconnected from anything real or meaningful.

The moment passed. I completed the forecast without missing a beat...no viewer would have noticed anything amiss. But something had shifted internally, a brief tear in the fabric of my constructed reality, allowing a glimpse of something beyond it.

That was the first instance of what I came to call a "step out," but not the last. Suddenly finding myself in the role of observer of my own persona became more frequent over time. It could happen during meetings when colleagues were earnestly debating the placement of a graphics package or the phrasing of a weather warning. It could happen at industry events when meteorologists (myself included) were comparing market sizes and career trajectories as measures of success. At home, this sometimes occurred when I was going through the motions of domestic life while my mind was still caught in work concerns.

Each time, there was that same quality of suddenly seeing the situation from outside, with a stark clarity that revealed its artificiality. And each time, I would quickly step back in, dismissing the insight as meaningless distraction. I became proficient at moving past the unsettled feeling in a nanosecond.

But these weren't the only signals. There were dreams—not as dramatic as the confrontation in the Great Hall that would come later, but persistent and thematically consistent. I often dreamed of being unable to speak on air, opening my mouth but producing no sound while the red light of the camera stared impassively. I dreamed of being lost in labyrinthine television studios, trying to find my way to the set but encountering only empty corridors and locked doors. I dreamed of standing in front of weather maps that kept changing unpredictably, making any forecast impossible.

I didn't need a psychology degree to recognize the anxiety in these dreams, but I interpreted them purely in terms of professional pressure—fear of failure, impostor syndrome, performance anxiety. I never considered that they might be pointing to something deeper, a fundamental misalignment between my authentic self and the life I was living.

Then there were the physical symptoms—subtle at first but increasingly difficult to ignore. Tension headaches that no amount of ibuprofen could touch. A persistent tightness in my chest that wasn't quite pain but never fully relaxed. Sleep disturbances that left me exhausted despite spending adequate time in bed. Digestive issues for which doctors could find no specific cause.

My body was trying to communicate what my conscious mind refused to acknowledge—that maintaining the division between my external persona and internal reality was creating unsustainable stress. But rather than listening to these signals, I treated the symptoms. More coffee to combat the fatigue. Sleeping pills to force rest. Antacids for the stomach issues.

Pushing through, maintaining the performance, keeping the show running at all costs.

Perhaps most telling were the unexpected emotional responses that seemed completely out of proportion to their triggers. I would feel a sudden, overwhelming surge of sadness while driving home after a perfectly successful broadcast. Or inexplicable anger would flare when colleagues complimented my work. Or most disturbing, a complete emotional flatness would descend during moments that should have brought joy—awards, recognition, even time with my family.

Eventually, I couldn't help but notice these emotional non-sequiturs. They were like static on a radio frequency—interference patterns created by the dissonance between the life I was living and the one my deeper self was calling me toward. But instead of tuning the dial to find clarity, I simply turned up the volume of my external activities, drowning out the static with more noise.

All of these signals—the step-out moments, the dreams, the physical symptoms, the emotional disconnects—were like weather patterns forming on the horizon of my consciousness. Had I been reading them with the same attention I gave to atmospheric conditions, I might have forecasted the storm that was coming. But I was too busy talking about the weather to notice I was standing in it.

The Synchronicities I Couldn't See

Beyond these internal signals were external patterns that, in retrospect, seem almost comically obvious—synchronicities and coincidences that kept pointing toward the same message through different channels. Many had given up whispering and began hollering.

Have you ever noticed how when something is trying to get your attention, it seems to appear everywhere? A word you've never heard before suddenly shows up in three different conversations. A book title keeps catching your eye in different contexts. A theme repeats itself across seemingly unrelated situations. These aren't random coincidences but patterns emerging from what Carl Jung called the "collective unconscious"—a field of shared meaning that communicates through synchronicity rather than linear causality.

Each and every one of us dwells in this unseen world of synchronicity—well, not always *unseen*, once you bring awareness to it. My life was filled with these patterns, but I was too caught in the identity-level consciousness to recognize them as meaningful.

One persistent synchronicity involved encounters with people who had radically changed their life paths. There was the former executive I interviewed for a human-interest weather story who had left his corporate career to become an organic farmer. "Best decision I ever made," he told me off-camera. "I was dying in that office, literally feeling my life force drain away. Now I feel alive again."

There was the station photographer who quit suddenly to pursue documentary filmmaking in developing countries. Her farewell email included a quote from Howard Thurman: "Don't ask what the world needs. Ask what makes you come alive, and go do it. Because what the world needs is people who have come alive."

There was the "chance" meeting with a college classmate who had abandoned a promising engineering career to become a meditation teacher. When I asked if he regretted leaving the security of his former field, he looked at me with genuine confusion. "Security? I was having panic attacks every Sunday night, thinking about Monday morning. How is that security?"

Each of these encounters left a mark on me—a momentary disturbance in the field of my certainty about my own path. But I quickly rationalized them away. These people weren't like me. They didn't have my responsibilities, my obligations, my particular circumstances. Their choices were available to them but not to me. Their freedom was the exception, not a possibility I could seriously consider.

Let me say that again: I had a rock-solid belief that they had a choice—and that I had no choice.

Another pattern involved books and articles that found their way to me through various channels. A colleague would mention a book that "reminded me of you for some reason." A magazine left in the break room would fall open to an article about finding purpose beyond success. A segment we covered on the morning show about career transitions would linger in my thoughts for days afterward.

These weren't random topics, but variations on a single theme: authentic living versus external achievement, meaning versus success, being versus performing. Yet I managed to engage with this content intellectually while keeping it safely separate from my actual life choices. I could discuss these ideas, even find them interesting and compelling, without ever applying them to myself.

I was operating from *fragmented consciousness* (a state we'll explore more fully in Chapter 4), where my mind could understand concepts while my emotions and instincts remained disconnected from this understanding.

This prevented the three-brain alignment (of heart, mind, and gut) that enables true change.

Perhaps the most powerful synchronicity involved repeated encounters with a particular phrase: "the divided self." It appeared in a psychology article I read while researching a human-interest story. It was the title of a book I noticed on a colleague's desk. It came up in a radio interview I overheard while driving to work. And most strikingly, it was the exact phrase my son used when asked about his career day presentation: "I told them my dad has a divided self—he's one person on TV and another person at home." *Wow.*

From the mouths of babes, as they say. My son's innocent observation hit me like a physical blow. For a moment, the pattern was undeniable—this concept of division kept appearing because it was the core issue I needed to address. But within hours, I had rationalized even this away. *Of course, there's a difference between professional and personal personas—that's just being an adult, having appropriate boundaries between different life domains. Nothing problematic there at all,* I deftly convinced myself.

This is how synchronicities or "signs" work—they're not usually dramatic burning bushes or voices from the heavens. They're subtle patterns that require a certain quality of attention to recognize. And when we're caught in lower levels of consciousness, dominated by fear and desire, that quality of attention isn't available to us. We miss the message not because it isn't being delivered but because we aren't tuned to the frequency where it's being broadcast.

The Code Connection: Emotional Gravity Pulls You Back

When I first discovered the consciousness levels of The Code, one concept in particular helped me understand why I had ignored so many clear signals: emotional gravity. This isn't just a metaphor but a genuine energetic phenomenon that keeps us anchored to familiar states of being, even when those states cause suffering.

Just as physical gravity holds objects in place on Earth, emotional gravity maintains our consciousness at particular levels by making any movement away from them feel threatening, difficult, or simply wrong.

This force becomes stronger the longer we've inhabited a certain level, creating the emotional equivalent of a deep groove that naturally pulls us back whenever we start to climb out. Part of the human experience is to sometimes be "stuck in a rut," yes?

For years, I had been operating primarily between Levels 4 (Fear) and 5 (Desire)—living from a place of anxiety about maintaining security and constantly chasing external validation. These states weren't fulfilling, but they were familiar. My neurological pathways were well-established in these patterns. My identity was constructed around them. My relationships and professional role reinforced them.

When signals arose suggesting a different way of being—whether internal voice prompts or external synchronicities—they represented a threat to this established order where I'd become comfortable. Moving toward a higher level of consciousness would require dismantling aspects of my identity that, while perhaps not serving my deeper well-being, were nevertheless central to my sense of self.

This explains why even positive growth can feel threatening. It's not just that we fear the unknown; it's that we intuitively sense that authentic transformation requires a kind of death—the dissolution of the self we've known, in service of a self we can't yet imagine. No matter how limiting our current state might be, at least it's familiar. We know how to be this person, how to navigate from this level of consciousness. Anything else is uncharted territory.

I experienced this emotional gravity most powerfully when moments of clarity temporarily lifted me to Level 7 (Acceptance) of consciousness. These brief elevations—usually occurring when out in nature, during creative activities, or in genuine connection with others—would bring a spacious awareness and sense of rightness that made my usual anxious striving seem unnecessary and even absurd.

But these states never lasted long. Within hours or sometimes minutes, the gravitational pull of my habitual consciousness would reassert itself. The spaciousness would contract. The clarity would cloud over. The old patterns of thought and emotion would return, often with redoubled force, as if to compensate for the temporary escape.

Vibrational Inertia

This isn't just psychological resistance—it's an energetic and neurobiological reality. When consciousness shifts to a higher level, it literally vibrates at a different frequency. This new vibration disrupts established neural patterns and energy fields. The body-mind system, designed for homeostasis (maintaining stable conditions), naturally resists this disruption by pulling consciousness back to its habitual "normal" frequency. It is vibrational inertia, resistance to change.

How does this work in practice? When signals of a higher calling would appear in my life, my system would respond with what felt like reasonable objections but were actually manifestations of emotional gravity. My "rational" voice said things like "This isn't the right time for big changes. Wait until Aidan is older/the mortgage is paid off/you have more savings." The voice was relentless:

"You've invested too much in this career path to consider alternatives now. Think of all you'd be throwing away."

"Who are you to want more meaning? Be grateful for what you have—many would love to be in your position."

"These feelings are just temporary dissatisfaction. Everyone goes through phases like this in their career."

"You have responsibilities to others. Pursuing your own fulfillment would be selfish."

These thoughts weren't lies, exactly. Each contained elements of truth. But their primary function wasn't truth-seeking; it was homeostasis—maintaining the familiar, even at great cost.

They were the voice of emotional gravity, pulling me back to the known whenever I began ascending toward the possible.

What makes emotional gravity so powerful is that it operates largely beyond conscious awareness. We don't experience it as an external force acting upon us but as our own thoughts, feelings, and intuitions. It masquerades as wisdom, as prudence, as responsibility—making the choice to remain in lower consciousness seem like the mature, sensible option.

We imagine that breaking free from the pull of emotional gravity must take a Herculean effort, and sometimes it does. Just as a rocket needs tremendous initial thrust to escape Earth's gravity, moving to higher levels of consciousness can require significant energy—often in the form of a crisis or breakthrough that temporarily disrupts the established patterns enough for a new possibility to emerge.

For me, that disruptive force would eventually come through complete collapse (which I'll describe in the next chapter). But it doesn't have to be that dramatic. The Attention Compass practice offers a different strategy to gradually weaken emotional gravity's hold—not by fighting against it but by consistently returning attention to center, where a different quality of awareness can begin to take root.

The key insight here is recognizing that resistance to your deeper calling isn't a personal failing but a natural function of consciousness seeking to maintain its familiar patterns. Understanding this can help transform self-judgment into compassion, which itself is a movement toward higher consciousness. The question shifts from "What's wrong with me that I keep ignoring what matters?" to "How can I work with these natural forces rather than against them?"

The Addiction to Familiar Identity

Closely related to emotional gravity is what I've come to understand as identity addiction—our profound attachment to who we think we are. This isn't just about roles or labels; it's about the entire constellation of thoughts, behaviors, preferences, and narratives that constitute our sense of self.

Think about how you would complete the sentence "I am the kind of person who..." The answers that automatically arise—whether they're "works hard," "never gives up," "puts family first," "succeeds at whatever I try," or any other self-definition—form the boundaries of your identity.

And like any boundaries, they both define what's inside and exclude what's outside.

My identity as "Eric the Weatherman" wasn't just a job title; it was a comprehensive self-concept that determined how I saw myself, how others saw me, and how I navigated the world. This identity included being knowledgeable, authoritative, helpful, professional, personable, successful, and respected. It excluded being uncertain, vulnerable, unattractive, confused, ordinary, or failed.

The power of identity lies in its capacity to create a sense of coherence and continuity in our experience. It tells us who we are and, just as importantly, who we are not. It gives us a framework for making decisions, a lens for interpreting events, and a basis for connecting with others who share aspects of our self-definition.

But this power comes at a cost. The more rigid and exclusive our identity becomes, the more it limits our capacity to grow, change, and respond authentically to new situations. It becomes a prison constructed of our own beliefs about ourselves, one that can be harder to escape than any external confinement. The identity rejects any intention to develop and maintain a "growth mindset."

I experienced this addiction most acutely whenever something threatened my established identity. When a forecast went wrong, when ratings dipped, when a colleague received recognition I felt I deserved—these situations triggered not just disappointment but existential panic. They threatened not just what I did but who I was.

This identity addiction explains why even unhappy situations can be so difficult to leave. The devil we know isn't just familiar; it's integrated into our sense of self. Leaving an unfulfilling career, ending a dysfunctional relationship, or abandoning a limiting belief system isn't simply about changing external circumstances; it's about abandoning oneself and becoming someone else. However promising in theory, that prospect, in practice, activates our deepest fears.

If you have witnessed a friend or family member in a toxic relationship, you likely were concerned for their safety and maybe even their life. It's very hard to watch someone you care about continue to tolerate abuse. You may feel compelled to say something, yet no matter what you say or do, they remain in an abusive relationship.

Over time, the person develops low self-esteem and begins to believe the lie that they are the problem in the relationship. All of these things work together to create dependency on the abuser, and their "new identity" is reduced to surviving through desperate attempts to please. Sporadic rewards of apologies, gifts, and false promises give them just enough hope that they opt not to abandon their victim identity.

For years, I maintained a death-grip on my weatherman identity despite the growing emptiness it contained. I invested enormous energy in protecting and reinforcing it—seeking validation, avoiding situations that might expose its limitations, curating a public image that matched the ideal. This wasn't just vanity; it was existential self-preservation. Without this identity, who would I be?

The most insidious aspect of identity addiction is how it distorts our perception. We don't see reality as it is; we see it as our identity needs it to be. Events, interactions, and information that confirm our self-concept are highlighted and remembered; those that contradict it are filtered out or reinterpreted.

This selective perception creates a closed feedback loop. My weatherman identity determined what I noticed, valued, and remembered, which in turn reinforced that very identity. Breaking this loop required not just new information but a fundamentally different way of seeing—a perspective that could encompass both the weatherman and something beyond it.

The deeper calling that I'd been ignoring wasn't just inviting me to do something different; it was inviting me to *be someone different*—or more accurately, to recognize that I already was more than the limited identity I'd constructed. This is why it felt so threatening and why I resisted it for so long. It wasn't just a career change or life adjustment at stake; it was my fundamental sense of who I was.

Understanding identity addiction has profound implications for transformation. When we recognize that our resistance to change is often about preserving identity rather than practical concerns, we can approach it with greater compassion and clarity. We can begin to loosen our grip on who we think we are to make space for who we might become.

This doesn't mean abandoning identity entirely—that's neither possible nor desirable. It means holding it more lightly, seeing it as a useful but limited tool rather than an absolute truth. It means expanding the boundaries to include more of our authentic experience, especially the parts that don't fit neatly into our preferred self-image.

My journey eventually taught me that true identity isn't something we construct and maintain; it's something we discover when we stop trying to be anyone in particular. It emerges naturally from the still center of the Attention Compass, where we're neither defending who we think we are nor striving to become who we think we should be. We're simply present, aware, and open to the fullness of our being—including the aspects we've previously rejected or ignored.

As I look back on these missed signals and synchronicities, I realize they weren't just random occurrences, but a coherent pattern trying to guide me toward greater wholeness. The whispers I ignored were actually invitations to a higher frequency of consciousness—one where gut, heart, and mind could align rather than conflict. What seemed like annoying interruptions to my carefully constructed life were actually doorways to the Flow State I would later discover.

◆

The Dream Deepens: The Voice in the Static

The night after I first recognized the patterns of my ignored calling, my dream carried me back to that otherworldly realm, but something had changed. This time, I found myself not in the Great Hall but in a dimly lit corridor outside it.

◆

Even through the heavy wooden doors, I can hear the muffled sounds of the ceremony continuing—glasses clinking, polite laughter, the symphony of social validation I have chased my entire life.

I know I should return to my place of honor inside the Great Hall. The weatherman is expected, after all. His absence would be noticed, remarked upon. But I feel much more strongly drawn away from the doors to the Great Hall. Something pulls me down that shadowed hallway, a magnetic force more compelling than applause.

At the corridor's end stands the disheveled man, his back to me. His shoulders are hunched beneath a threadbare jacket, his hair wild as a winter storm. He is focused intently on what looks like an old radio, the kind my grandfather kept in his workshop. His fingers move delicately across the dials, turning through wavelengths of static with the reverence of someone searching for a precious but lost frequency.

Heart in my throat, I approach. "What are you looking for?" My voice sounds different here, stripped of the polished broadcaster's tone.

Without turning, he continues adjusting the dial with meticulous patience. "I've been trying to tell you something for years," he says, his voice carrying the weariness of a thousand unanswered calls. "You hear the static, but not the message."

He turns the dial once more, and through the white noise, I hear a voice that makes me gasp. It's my voice, but deeper, more resonant, unburdened by performance. I cannot quite grasp the words, but feel my eyes filling with tears, anyway.

The sound of the voice vibrates not in my ears but somewhere behind my sternum; a truth my body recognizes before my mind can name it.

"That's the calling you keep ignoring," the unkempt man says, finally turning to face me. I see that he still bears the weight of rejection in the lines around his eyes, but now I notice something else—a clarity in his gaze that no mirror had ever shown me. The realization comes that what I'm witnessing is a depth of seeing untainted by the need for others' approval.

I reach for the radio dial, my fingers trembling with the intuition that touching it would change everything. I awaken. My hand is outstretched to empty air. Tears are streaming down my face.

◆

During my walks in the days that followed, I found myself listening differently—not just to the world around me, but to the spaces between thoughts, to the silences between heartbeats. I began to wonder what signals I had been filtering out all these years, what wisdom had been broadcasting on frequencies my blind and deaf ambition had drowned out. What might I hear if I finally stopped running from the voice beneath the static?

Exercise: It's Time to Tune In!

The deeper self speaks in whispers, not shouts. Messages come through subtle channels that are easy to miss amid the noise of daily life. This exercise is designed to help you tune into those channels and recognize the callings you might be ignoring.

Find a quiet space where you won't be interrupted for about 30 minutes. Have a journal or several sheets of paper handy, along with something to write with. Then follow these steps:

1. Persistent Thoughts Inventory

What thoughts, questions, or ideas keep returning to you despite your attempts to dismiss them? These might be:

- Activities you've always wanted to try but have rationalized away

- Questions about your life path that arise in quiet moments

- Interests that don't fit your current identity but consistently appeal to you

- Changes you've considered but keep putting off "until the time is right"

Write down everything that comes to mind without judging or analyzing it yet. Pay special attention to thoughts that have persisted over months or years rather than short-lived ideas or passing interests.

2. The Jealousy Compass

Our jealousy often points toward desires we're not acknowledging. Think about people whose lives, careers, or choices spark a sense of envy in you. Read between the lines—this isn't about coveting material possessions but about life design or ways of being.

- Who do you feel a twinge of jealousy toward when you hear about their work, relationships, or lifestyle?

- What specific aspects of their experience trigger this response?

- What might this jealousy be telling you about your own unacknowledged desires?

Be completely honest with yourself—this is private exploration, not public confession.

3. Body Wisdom Check

Our bodies often know our truth before our minds do. Pay attention to your physical responses when considering different aspects of your life:

- When you think about your current career path, what sensations arise in your body? Tension, expansion, contraction, lightness, heaviness?

- Are there activities or environments that consistently make you feel more energized and alive?

- Are there situations that regularly create physical symptoms like headaches, digestive issues, or fatigue?

Record these physical responses and what they might be communicating about alignment or misalignment with your deeper calling.

4. Joy Tracking

What brings you into a state of flow or timelessness? These experiences often indicate alignment with your authentic nature.

- When do you lose track of time because you're so absorbed in what you're doing?

- What activities make you feel most like yourself, without effort or performance?

- What did you love doing as a child that you've set aside as "impractical" or "childish"?

- When was the last time you recognized you had a sense of joy?

These flow states are often signposts pointing toward your deeper calling.

5. Synchronicity Awareness

Reflect on patterns, coincidences, or recurring themes that have appeared in your life:

- Are there books, ideas, or opportunities that have repeatedly crossed your path?

- Have strangers or acquaintances made similar observations about you that you've dismissed?

- Do certain symbols, images, or themes recur in your dreams or catch your attention in waking life?

These patterns often contain messages about your path that your conscious mind might be overlooking.

6. The Deathbed Perspective

Imagine yourself at the end of your life, looking back. From that perspective:

- What would you regret not having pursued or expressed?

- What would seem like a meaningful use of your remaining time and energy?

- What parts of your current identity and concerns would seem important, and which would seem insignificant?

This perspective often clarifies values and priorities that are obscured in day-to-day thinking.

7. Integration and Reflection

Review your responses to the above:

- What patterns or themes do you notice emerging?

- Where do you sense the strongest call or pull?

- What did you write that holds the most emotional charge?

- What aspects of your current identity feel most threatened by these callings?

- What small, low-risk step could you take to explore one of these callings more deeply?

Remember, recognizing a calling doesn't mean you must immediately upend your entire life to follow it. Often, the journey begins with simple acknowledgment, followed by small explorations that gradually create space for larger changes when the time is right.

The goal of this exercise isn't to create more pressure or expectations for yourself but to bring awareness to the wisdom that's already trying to reach you. Sometimes simply acknowledging a calling changes your relationship to it—from something threatening that must be suppressed to something valuable that can be gradually integrated.

Learning to listen to your deeper self is one of the most important skills you can develop for accessing higher levels of consciousness and the Flow State they make possible.

In the next chapter, I'll share what happened when I continued to ignore these signals—how my life collapsed completely before I finally began to listen. Essentially, when you become able to quickly tune into a message, you won't need to experience it getting louder and louder—that can be painful. Then, it will go Glenn Close on you and proclaim, "I will NOT be ignored!" This leads to having to "learn a lesson," and if you don't, you'll have a real problem on your hands.

Do you really want your life to be consumed with constant problem-solving?

My hope in sharing here the tools that I eventually developed is that your journey might be more graceful than mine was. My promise to you is that adopting my method for tuning into messages will give you more power, joy, and a sense of gratitude for all that life brings your way.

CHAPTER 3

The Necessary Collapse

Have you ever watched a building being demolished? There's something both terrifying and fascinating about that moment, when the carefully placed charges detonate and a structure that took years to build collapses in seconds. What stood firmly suddenly surrenders to gravity. The recognizable becomes imploded chaos.

But demolition experts know something the casual observer doesn't: collapse is not random. It's precisely engineered. And it's not the end, but a necessary beginning. Before something new can be built, what no longer serves must be dismantled—completely, structurally, from the foundation throughout.

My life collapsed with a similar brutal efficiency. One day I was Eric the Weatherman—a well-respected guy with financial security, professional identity, and a clear place in the world. The next, I was... No One. Nothing. A man without definition or form, stumbling in the rubble of what had been a carefully constructed life.

This wasn't just losing a job. It was an identity apocalypse. And while I couldn't see it at the time, this total dismantling was the most necessary thing that ever happened to me. A gift, actually.

The Collapse of Everything I Thought I Was

Orlando, Florida, July 2010. After years of climbing the broadcast ladder, I'd reached what appeared to be the summit. I was in charge of three weather stations and my salary had reached impressive levels. We owned a lovely home in Orlando, "The City Beautiful." Professional respect, financial security, social status—I had all the external markers of success.

But as we explored in the previous chapters, beneath this carefully constructed facade, emptiness was growing. The calls and pleas from my deeper self were getting louder, even as I tried desperately to ignore them.

Then came the moment that would change everything.

I was on the desk one Monday after being with this new TV Station for two and a half years. With no reason given, I was told to "Go see the GM before you leave." My co-anchor gave me a strange look that I brushed off. I felt secure in my position—I was handling the weather broadcasts, creating maps, blogging, and leading our social media efforts. I'd made myself important, safe in my role.

Until I opened the door and saw the faces of both the News Director and the new General Manager. There was a piece of paper in front of them with a pen to the side.

This can't be good, I thought.

"We have no idea why this is happening, Eric," they said. "We really like what you bring to our station and all the other things you are the lead on. This really makes no sense other than a money thing. That's all we can say."

I remember the look on their faces—they truly didn't know what was going to happen next. I looked around. No security escort, no banker's box for my belongings. What was on that paper? It read, "Effective Immediately."

The News Director couldn't handle it and stood up to get some water as the GM explained, "TV is not what it used to be, Eric." He mentioned others who had been let go in recent months—the old GM, the old News Director, main anchors who had been in the market for years. All too expensive. I was next.

The GM continued, "If you could just sign this and start training your replacement..." "WHAT?!" I exclaimed.

"We also need you to train three others on how to navigate this new social media. We will do everything we can to help you find another job."

"Three people?!" I asked in disbelief. "Why not just keep me?"

They didn't answer. I looked beyond them at the palm tree blowing in the window behind them and quietly said to myself, *So... this is where it ends, with a palm tree in paradise.*

Numb, I had no brain cells firing to put up a fight. I took the paper with me and told them I would talk to my agent first before signing anything. As I crossed the threshold of the GM's office, I said goodbye to his secretary. She sniffed and couldn't look up, just raised her hand. I sensed this had become a sad routine for her, seeing so many of us leave this way.

The timing couldn't have been worse. My wife Michelle and I had just come back from a meeting with our son's preschool teacher, who suggested he be held back another year before kindergarten. Aidan was five now and still not speaking clearly. We didn't know what was wrong and both felt that nightmarish mix of anxiety and helplessness. It had also been just over a year since my father's funeral. He died after a long struggle with pancreatic cancer.

From the parking lot, I called Michelle. "Honey, they are letting me go."

Silence on the other end. Finally, "What do you mean, letting you go? They are the ones who wooed us to come down here in the first place!" She was confused and in disbelief. So was I.

We couldn't afford our three homes (we still owned properties in other cities), while trying to find another home in yet another state. We made good money—or I did—but not that much. In fact, we had incurred crushing debt over the years that was catching up with us. There was just enough each month, but it wasn't enough for us to live on without my regular paycheck.

I zombie-drove my way home and sat in the driveway with nobody to talk to. My father was dead. I didn't want to share this news with my mother just yet. We had no support group, no close friends nearby. We were trapped in quicksand, and I froze. My mind stopped working. The positive outlook on life I had shared with so many viewers was gone. I'd seen some coal-black clouds in my life as a weatherman, but never expected to be inside and completely surrounded by one.

And it would get worse.

The lease on my car was ending in a month, and we had no income. We found out that our son had autism and required highly specialized treatments and therapy. Michelle stopped sleeping through the night. So did I.

We paid what we could with money borrowed from friends back in Detroit for the first couple of months, but there was no way we would make it long-term. Even though I had done nothing wrong, I felt like I had. I felt invisible. Hopeless. We became a one-car family. Even if I got a job, how would Michelle and Aidan get to school? Go to the store? I was trapped, and the walls kept closing in.

I had six months left on my contract, and my agent told me, "You have a contract to be the morning meteorologist. If they won't put you on the air, they are contractually bound to pay you until the end of the year. Good luck, buddy."

Good luck? I needed a miracle!

My sense of self was reduced to the lowest levels, and I lived in constant panic. I had six months—six months to save the day. Yet all I did during the day was worry and walk. Walk and worry.

I walked so much I lost 35 pounds, and it showed in my face. My neighbor asked why I wasn't on TV anymore. I told her everything. Her name was Rhoda, and she worked in radio sales but had no leads for me. One day I was mowing the lawn as she returned from shopping. She got out of her car and asked me to pull up my shirt. My shorts were baggy, and my belt was wrapped around my back. I was even surprised to see my ribs.

Rhoda came over that night and said she would "adopt" us. I was so embarrassed. But my family needed help, so I accepted her offer with immense shame and guilt. We waited each Sunday for her to stop by with money for the week and food she bought on sale or as buy-one-get-one-free. It was food. This was my new life.

The next year, we were in the courts trying to keep our home, paying a lawyer to "find the deed." Finding the deed to the house bought us some time as our mortgage had been bought, sold and traded many times in the three years we had it. Finding the deed became a way to buy time; for me to find my way out while staying in our house. All I thought about was, "How are we going to keep this up?"

During one meeting with the lawyer, riding in our only car with our son, I wondered what living in a car would be like. It was an awful yet real possibility, and I felt invisible. So I walked in nature to clear my mind and started my own weather business online. It didn't catch on. The "Midas touch" that seemed to follow me throughout my career had abandoned me. I felt invisible and ineffective. I constantly worried that Michelle would take Aidan and go live with her parents, but she didn't.

We needed more than physical help; we needed spiritual and mental relief.

Peace—of a sort—came that December in 2010 when we filed for bankruptcy to keep our home, a mark that would follow us for the next seven years. Walking out of the courtroom, I remember being asked by one of the creditors, "Do you think you will ever make this amount of money again?"

I was told to answer, "No." It felt like I was forecasting doom with my own words. While we were now free of the crushing debt, I still needed a job.

My false identity—being important to others, smart, needed, wanted, sought after—had vanished into the atmosphere. Now I felt so incredibly weighted down each morning, I was unable to find the strength to even get out of bed. *Why bother?* If it wasn't for our angel neighbor Rhoda, my family would be at the bottom of a well I couldn't imagine climbing out from.

Then my son broke his arm.

Michelle was volunteering at his school to ensure Aidan got the best teacher. She distracted herself from our new reality by staying busy there, later becoming the PTA President so she could be on campus all day. I was home alone. Michelle finally told one of the PTA parents about our situation, and her husband heard about Aidan's broken arm and our circumstances. He hired me—another angel, to say the least—to work at his carpet cleaning company. He gave me medical benefits on day one and my son got the treatment for his arm.

My soul was shrinking each day, but I was grateful for the job. I was not a good manager for a carpet cleaning company—or any company, for that matter—and felt guilty for the pity the owner took on me. After eight months of trying to make the best of it, I thanked him for his generous gift of employment but told him the job belonged to somebody who would make a difference rather than just take a paycheck.

Coming home again with news that I no longer had a job, Michelle was surprisingly supportive. We would find something…something would work out. We just needed to have faith.

Then, Rhoda died.

I was asked to do a reading at her funeral, and everyone in attendance was murmuring, "Who is that?" At the reception afterward, my family was introduced to Rhoda's family as, "This is the family Rhoda adopted." I felt four inches tall at best.

Desperate, I took a job at a university working all hours of the day and night watching students take tests. My job was to open the doors to the rooms, watch them, then close up and go home. The job paid below poverty level, and we were barely making it each month. We stopped buying anything for ourselves and focused on ensuring Aidan's childhood wasn't affected too negatively by our situation. He had us, he had his room, he had his favorite foods, so he was unscathed.

His autism is a blessing in many ways—this was one of them.

The university offered free schooling to faculty, and I took advantage of it. I poured myself into my studies, and in 2018, I earned another degree in computer science with a focus on app design and experience. Little did I know how crowded that marketplace was, and I was competing for jobs against people overseas who would take projects for a fraction of what it takes to make a living in America.

Descending Through the Levels: The Gravity of Consciousness

Remember the Consciousness Levels we explored in the Introduction? During my years as a successful weatherman, I operated primarily at Levels 4 and 5—Fear and Desire. Not the lowest states of consciousness, but certainly not the highest. There was enough energy there to function, achieve, and maintain the appearance of success.

But when everything collapsed, I didn't just lose my external achievements. I plummeted through the Consciousness Levels like a rock dropped into a deep well. This descent wasn't metaphorical—it was experiential, a tangible shift in the frequency of my awareness that affected everything from my thoughts to my physical body.

Level 3: Apathy (Energy of Resignation)

The first drop came in the form of apathy. After months of fruitless job searching, countless rejections, and the growing awareness that my career might truly be over, a deadening resignation set in. "What's the point?" became the background hum of my consciousness. I would sit for hours staring at the wall of our den, unable to motivate myself to even check email. The future—once so full of plans and ambitions—evaporated into a void I could neither imagine nor care about. The present became a waiting room with no exit. Even basic self-care fell away—why shower, why exercise, why engage with anything when nothing seemed to matter?

This wasn't laziness or even depression in the clinical sense. It was a complete energetic collapse—a state where the vibration of consciousness is so low that generating any movement, internal or external, feels impossible. Like trying to run through chest-deep mud. Have you ever felt *that* stuck?

Michelle would find me sitting in the same spot hours after she left for her volunteer work at the school.

"Did you apply for any jobs today?" my wife would ask.

"No," I would reply, my voice flat. "There's no point." The frightening thing wasn't that I was discouraged—it was that I truly, deeply meant it. I couldn't access any energy of hope or possibility.

This is the very definition of Apathy, or Level 3 Consciousness.

Level 2: Guilt (Energy of Regret)

Below apathy lurked something even heavier: crushing guilt. As our financial situation deteriorated and the impact on my family became impossible to ignore, guilt became my constant companion. Every look at Michelle's exhausted face after her long days of volunteer work felt like an indictment. Every compromise we made for Aidan—the therapies we could no longer afford, the homes we had lost, the stability that had vanished—twisted the knife deeper.

I should have seen this coming, I'd tell myself in endless loops of self-recrimination. *I should have saved more, spent less, been more careful, taken a different career path, made different choices at every turn.* The past became a minefield of regretful possibilities and missed opportunities. The present became nothing but painful *should-haves*.

The provider role had been central to how I understood myself in relation to my family. Without it, who was I to them? What value did I bring? These questions had no satisfying answers, only the heavy energy of having failed at what I believed was my most fundamental responsibility.

The guilt was physically palpable—a constant pressure in my chest, a perpetual knot in my stomach. I would wake at 3 AM, heart racing, mind spinning with scenarios of further deterioration. "If I had just..." became the beginning of endless mental sentences that led nowhere but deeper into regret.

The lowest point was accepting help from others—from Rhoda, from friends, from the carpet cleaning company owner. Each act of kindness, necessary as it was, reinforced my sense of failure. When I stood at Rhoda's funeral and heard myself described as part of "the family she adopted," the guilt was overwhelming. Not only had I failed, but my failure had created a burden for others.

Level 1: Shame (Energy of Hopelessness)

And then came the bottom: shame. Not guilt over what I had done wrong, but a more existential sense that I myself was wrong. Somehow defective at my core. Unworthy of success, happiness, even existence itself.

Shame is the lowest vibration a human can experience, and it feels like psychological death. Not just "I made mistakes" but "I am a mistake." Not just "I failed" but "I am a failure."

I avoided mirrors because I couldn't bear to see my own reflection. When I accidentally caught sight of myself—stepping out of the shower, passing a storefront window, glancing up while brushing my teeth—what looked back wasn't just a face but a living accusation. The eyes that once held confidence and purpose now seemed hollow, almost vacant. The mouth that had delivered weather forecasts with authority appeared smaller somehow, as if it had forgotten how to speak with conviction.

But it was more than just physical changes. Looking at my reflection felt like staring at evidence of my complete failure as a man, a provider, a human being. The person in the mirror wore the face of someone who had lost everything that mattered—not just the career and financial security, but the very identity that had held life together. I would see my father's disappointed expression superimposed over my own features, hear my mother's worried voice asking, "What happened to you?"

The shame was so visceral it felt like being punched in the stomach. My reflection seemed to be asking the question I couldn't answer: "How did you let this happen? How did you become this?" So I stopped looking. I brushed my teeth with my eyes closed, shaved by feel, and turned away from any surface that might show me the man I had become—because that man was someone I no longer recognized and couldn't bear to acknowledge as myself.

I avoided old friends and colleagues because their very existence reminded me of who I used to be. I avoided new social connections because—what would I say about myself? How could I explain this person I had become? Why would anyone care to know me, anyway?

There were moments when the shame was so intense I contemplated whether my family would be better off without me. Not active suicidal ideation, but a quiet, persistent question: "Does my existence add anything of value to the world?" The answer, from the bottom of Level 1 Consciousness, seemed overwhelmingly negative.

The brutal irony was that I had spent my entire adult life trying to avoid precisely this state. Every achievement, every career move, every financial decision had been, at some level, an attempt to outrun the shame I'd carried since childhood—the shame of the abandoned boy, the insecure teenager, the young man desperately seeking validation. Now, with all external buffers stripped away, I was drowning in exactly what I had feared most.

The Hero's Darkest Hour

If this were a movie script, this would be what storytellers call "the darkest hour"—that point in the hero's journey when all seems lost, when the forces of opposition appear to have won, when the protagonist faces not just external defeat but internal collapse.

Think of Luke Skywalker after losing his hand and learning Vader is his father, hanging in space with nowhere to go. Think of Frodo in Mordor, the Ring growing impossibly heavy, his strength failing, believing he will never complete his mission. Think of Harry Potter walking alone into the forest, believing his death is the only way forward.

These moments in storytelling reflect a profound truth about transformation: the darkest hour isn't just a dramatic device; it's often the necessary precursor to breakthrough. The hero must face a complete loss of their former self before they can be reborn into something greater.

In the terms of The Code, I had descended to the lowest 3 Consciousness Levels—shame, guilt, apathy—not as punishment but as preparation. Something was being dismantled that needed dismantling. Something was dying that needed to die.

The weatherman identity that had defined me for decades had crumbled. The provider role I had built my self-worth around had dissolved. The financial rock-solid stability I had used to measure my success had turned to dust. All the external scaffolding that had held up my sense of self had fallen away.

Painful as it was, something essential was being revealed—a self that existed before all those identities, a consciousness that didn't depend on external validation, a worth that couldn't be measured in salary or status.

I couldn't see this at the time, of course. From inside Level 1 Consciousness, the shame feels like truth rather than perspective, the hopelessness feels like reality rather than vibration. The discovery of the Attention Compass is what ultimately allowed me to begin the climb back up the Consciousness Levels.

But even in those darkest moments, seeds were being planted. My endless walks in nature, seemingly aimless at the time, were creating space for something new to emerge. My love for Aidan, which persisted even when love for myself had vanished, kept alive a flame of meaningful connection. Michelle's unwavering belief that "something will work out" maintained a tether to possibility I couldn't access myself.

The Code Connection: The Necessary Dismantling

Here's where the story takes an unexpected turn. This complete collapse—financial, professional, psychological, existential—wasn't actually the tragedy it appeared to be.

In the consciousness framework of The Code, what appears to be descent can actually be the beginning of ascent. But this process doesn't work the way our linear, progress-oriented minds expect it to.

Imagine your consciousness as a house. For years, I had been adding rooms, floors, elaborate facades—creating what looked from the outside like an impressive structure. But the foundation was cracked. The supporting beams were rotting. The whole thing was fundamentally unsound. Unstable consciousness—fear, desire, external validation, and the desperate avoidance of my deeper truths were all sinkholes under the foundation I pretended to have for the illusion of success. No amount of renovation could fix these problems. The entire building needed to come down so something authentic could be built in its place, only not on shaky ground but on a solid foundation of higher consciousness.

This is why spiritual traditions throughout history have recognized the transformative potential of complete collapse. The Christian concept of "dying to self" before rebirth. The Hindu understanding of Shiva as both destroyer and transformer. The Buddhist teaching that liberation comes when we let go of all attachments, including our identity. These aren't just poetic metaphors—they're describing the actual mechanics of consciousness transformation.

In fact, some view the butterfly metamorphosis as a metaphor for personal transformation. Did you know that the caterpillar, at one point on its journey, dissolves into a soup? That's right, there's no longer a caterpillar identity, yet it's exactly in the necessary and perfect state to then transform into a beautiful butterfly.

These traditions intuitively recognized what I would later discover through the Attention Compass (a practice for centering scattered awareness that I'll explain in Chapter 4)—that transformation requires letting go of our attachment to who we think we are before we can access who we truly are.

When everything you thought you were is stripped away, several crucial things happen:

First, the energy that was maintaining your false structures is released. Think of how much energy I had been investing in being "Eric the Weatherman"—the constant performance, the maintaining of appearances, the splitting of myself into public and private selves. When that identity collapsed, all that energy suddenly became available for something else. While I felt sad and dejected, I also had a sense of relief—at the time, I didn't understand that feeling at all.

Second, your authentic essence has space to emerge. Beneath all our constructed identities lies what some traditions call our "original face"— the pure awareness that is our birthright but becomes covered by layers of conditioning, trauma, and false self-images. These constructions can be so convincing that we mistake them for who we really are. Only when they fall away can we begin to glimpse our true nature.

Third, you develop immunity to your greatest fears. What was I most afraid of throughout my successful career? Failure. Loss of status. Financial insecurity. Being found out as somehow inadequate. When all of these fears materialized—and I survived—they lost their power over me. I had faced the worst and was still breathing. This is incredibly liberating.

Finally, you gain authentic compassion. Not the intellectual understanding of others' suffering, but the bone-deep recognition born of having been thoroughly humbled yourself. My collapse gave me access to a quality of compassion I could never have developed from the safety of success.

From the perspective of higher consciousness, what I experienced wasn't a fall but a clearing—painful but purposeful. Like a forest fire that, while devastating in the moment, creates the conditions for new growth that couldn't otherwise emerge.

Why Transformation May Require a Complete Breakdown

There's a question that often arises when I share this part of my journey: "Was the complete collapse really necessary? Couldn't there have been an easier way?"

I've reflected on this deeply, and the honest answer is: probably not. Not because suffering itself is inherently valuable, but because genuine transformation rarely happens without profound disruption to our existing patterns.

The reason is simple but challenging to accept: we don't change unless we have to. Humans are remarkably adaptive creatures, but this adaptability has a shadow side—we can adjust to incredibly dysfunctional situations rather than undertake the risk and discomfort of transformation.

Think about it: despite the growing emptiness I felt as a weatherman, despite the whispers from my deeper self, despite the synchronicities and messages appearing in my life—did I make any meaningful changes? No. I continued in the same patterns, making minor adjustments at best, until external circumstances forced a complete reckoning.

This isn't unusual. Throughout history, the most profound personal transformations often follow complete unraveling. Saint Paul on the road to Damascus. The Buddha abandoning his princely life. Countless spiritual biographies and timeless stories involve some version of hitting bottom before a breakthrough.

This pattern is easy to identify. Alcoholics Anonymous recognizes that people don't genuinely commit to recovery until they hit their personal "rock bottom." Career changes often follow layoffs or burnout rather than thoughtful planning or feeling free to make a choice. Relationship transformations frequently come after painful breakups rather than mutual growth.

Why is this? Several factors seem to be at work:

The Power of Identity Addiction: As we explored in the previous chapter, our attachment to who we think we are is incredibly strong. Even when that identity causes suffering, we cling to it because it provides a sense of continuity and familiarity. Only when that identity becomes absolutely unsustainable—when the pain of maintaining it exceeds the pain of letting it go—do most people surrender it.

"And the day came when the risk to remain tight in a bud was more painful than the risk it took to blossom."

Breaking free from identity addiction is about creating space for what I would later discover as the Flow State (which I'll explain fully in Chapters 6-8)—a quality of consciousness where gut, heart, and mind align to access wisdom beyond our limited identity.

The Comfort of the Known: Even uncomfortable patterns have the virtue of predictability. We know how to operate within them, how to protect ourselves, what to expect. The unknown, however potentially liberating, is terrifying to the ego-mind that craves certainty and control.

Loss of our put-together self forces us into the unknown when we would never voluntarily go there.

The Nature of Consciousness Evolution: Consciousness doesn't typically evolve gradually, like physical fitness which improves with regular exercise. It often shifts in quantum leaps, like water suddenly transforming into steam when it reaches a certain temperature. These phase transitions require specific conditions—including, sometimes, the complete disruption of existing patterns.

The Necessity of Surrender: Perhaps most importantly, genuine transformation involves a quality of surrender that our ego-driven culture neither values nor understands. Not giving up in defeat, but surrendering our illusion of control, our attachment to outcomes, our very definition of who we are. This surrender rarely happens without the humbling experience of a total cave-in of the persona we've constructed.

This doesn't mean we should seek suffering or create unnecessary trauma in our lives. But when collapse occurs—as it eventually does for most of us in some form—we can approach it not just as an ending, but as a potential beginning. Not as something that happened to us, but as something that happened for us. Not just as falling down, but as falling open to a larger possibility.

The complete dismantling of my identity, painful as it was, created the opening through which I would discover the Attention Compass and the Flow State. In the chapters ahead, I'll share how this tool emerged from the rubble of my former life. It was a lifesaver, helping me to find my center amid chaos and begin the journey toward higher levels of consciousness. I am deeply grateful for the opportunity to share this tool here with you, with every intention that you will find it accessible, practical, and life-changing.

***

The Dream Deepens: Shared Ruins

The day we received the final foreclosure notice, the dream returned with blazing clarity. This time, the Great Hall lay in ruins.

***

The ornate ceiling where crystal chandeliers once hung has crumbled away, leaving the space open to a sky the color of bruised skin. Marble floors where distinguished guests had gathered are now cracked and buckled, as if some great force had pushed up from beneath, shattering the foundation.

I stand in the middle of devastation, dust motes swirling in shafts of gray light. All is quiet. No ceremony, no crowd. The silence is broken only by the sound of my own ragged breathing. I turn slowly around and, among the debris, I spot him—the disheveled man—sitting calmly on a fallen column, watching me. Unlike everything around us, he appears unchanged by the destruction, as if chaos itself couldn't touch him.

"You look surprised," he says as I pick my way through rubble toward him, my shoes crunching on shattered crystal. His voice contains neither mockery nor pity, just a quiet observation.

"What happened here?" I ask, gesturing at the devastation around us, my voice breaking on the question.

His laugh is neither bitter nor joyful, but knowing—the sound of someone who had seen this coming long before I could admit its possibility. "The same thing that happened to your career, your finances, your identity." He pats the stone beside him. "Come, sit here amid our ruins."

"*Our* ruins?" I wonder to myself, noting that he has assumed our joint ownership in this disaster aftermath.

I feel confused and unprepared, but, hesitantly, I join him. I sit, feeling the cool stone beneath me, rough against my palms. For the first time, I notice we are breathing in the same rhythm—in and out, in perfect synchronization. I wonder if our lungs remember what minds forget— that we were never truly separate.

"Is anything salvageable?" I ask him.

He points to the center of the destruction, where something impossible is happening. Through the rubble of fallen stone and splintered wood, a small green shoot pushes upward toward the light— tender, vulnerable, yet possessed of a determination that defies the weight pressing down upon it.

"Only everything that matters," he says. And in his words, I hear not just consolation but revelation.

◆

I opened my eyes, aware of the taste of dust on my tongue and tears on my face. I felt grief, yet beneath that, a curious lightness had taken root in my chest—the weightlessness that comes when there is nothing left to lose, when the worst has already happened, and you find yourself, impossibly, still breathing.

As I navigated the very real rubble of my sans-identity life that day, I found myself looking for glimpses of hope, for green shoots, with a glimmer of optimism I hadn't felt in months. The transformation, if I had to pinpoint the moment, occurred with the revelation that what remains after everything falls apart might be the only thing that ever truly mattered.

Exercise: Finding Meaning in Your Own Collapses

While your experience may not mirror the totality of my collapse, most of us have encountered periods of significant breakdown—relationships ending, careers derailing, health crises, financial hardships, or other losses that shook our sense of identity and security.

This exercise invites you to revisit those experiences with fresh eyes, not to retraumatize yourself but to recognize their potential transformative value. Approach it with gentle curiosity rather than judgment. Approach it as a wise observer with a different perspective than when you were in the midst of it.

Find a quiet space where you won't be interrupted. Have a journal or paper ready to record your reflections.

1. Inventory of Collapses

Think back over your life and identify 2-3 significant "collapses"—periods when something important to your identity or security fell apart. These might include:

- Loss of a relationship
- Career setback or job loss
- Financial hardship
- Health crisis
- Discovery of serious betrayal
- Death of someone close
- Loss of faith or meaning system
- Major failure or disappointment
- For each experience, write down:
- What specifically collapsed or was lost
- When this happened
- How it affected your identity and sense of self at the time

2. Consciousness Level Tracking

For each collapse, reflect on what happened to your consciousness during this period:

- What emotions dominated your experience? (Refer to the nine Consciousness Levels if helpful)
- Did you notice yourself dropping to lower levels of consciousness during this time?
- Were there moments, even brief ones, when you accessed higher levels despite the difficulty?

3. The Space That Opened

Looking back with the perspective of time:

- What eventually filled the space created by this collapse?
- What aspects of yourself emerged that might not have otherwise?
- What became possible that wasn't before?
- What life lessons did you carry forward?
- What did you discover about yourself through this experience?

4. The Gifts (With Gentle Honesty)

Without minimizing the genuine pain of your experience:

- What strengths or capacities developed through this collapse?
- What illusions or attachments were you freed from?
- How did this experience change your understanding of yourself?
- How has it influenced your compassion for others?

5. Integration

Complete these sentences:

- "The collapse of _____________ initially seemed like the end of _____________, but eventually created space for _____________."
- "Through this experience, I discovered I am not just _________, but also _____________."

- "If this collapse hadn't happened, I might never have ________."

Remember, the purpose of this exercise isn't to sugar-coat genuine suffering or to suggest that all pain is somehow "for the best." Rather, it's to recognize how even our most difficult experiences can create openings for transformation that might not have happened otherwise.

Share these reflections with a trusted friend if helpful, but be gentle with yourself throughout the process. Revisiting collapse can stir strong emotions—approach them with the same compassion you would offer someone else describing such experiences.

In the next chapter, we'll explore the tool that emerged from my collapse—the Attention Compass that helped me find my center amid the chaos and begin the journey toward higher levels of consciousness. You'll learn how to pick up this tool and use it in ways you'll discover are accelerators for personal growth—mental, emotional, and spiritual.

"Where attention goes, energy flows; where intention goes, energy knows."—Ancient Yogic Proverb

CHAPTER 4
The Attention Compass

We're all guilty—nodding along to what's being said in a meeting, on the phone, or even during a face-to-face conversation while your mind is actually miles away. *When am I going to work on my presentation? What's for dinner? Why do I always have to be the first one to apologize...she was totally off base. Wait...I'm lost, let me go back and re-read that page...*This experience is common, often nearly a constant "attention drift." The mind tends to wander away from the present moment, pulled in various directions by habitual patterns of thought and emotion. This drift isn't random, it's directed by conditioning. It follows specific pathways that, once recognized, become predictable and ultimately manageable. Rather than aimless drifting with familiar currents, you can grip your oars and steer, stop, or change direction as you choose.

During my long walks through the darkest period of my collapse, when I had nothing but time and my own thoughts for company, I began to notice patterns in how my attention moved. Some days my mind would be consumed with regret about the past—choices I wished I could change, opportunities I'd missed, mistakes I'd made. Other days it would race anxiously toward the future—worst-case scenarios, unlikely catastrophes, desperate plans to avoid further pain.

Gradually, a metaphor emerged that helped me make sense of these patterns: the image of a compass with a plumb bob hanging from its center. This simple visual tool would eventually become my lifeline out of the lowest levels of consciousness—and the gateway to discovering the Flow State. I'm excited to share it with you.

The Plumb Bob Metaphor: Understanding the Mechanics of Attention

Imagine a compass lying flat, but instead of its face showing North, South, East, and West as geographical directions, it indicates **attention pulls**. Here is how the four opposing points represent the forces at work that take us out of and away from now: North represents identity concerns—thoughts about who you are or should be. South represents comparative thinking—measuring yourself against others or against your own expectations. West pulls attention into the past—regrets, nostalgia, or repetitive review of what's already happened. East draws attention into the future—planning, worrying, or fantasizing about what might happen.

Above this compass hangs a plumb bob—a weighted object suspended on a string, traditionally used in construction to find (with gravity's help) an accurate vertical alignment. This plumb bob represents your current focus of attention. When it's centered, your awareness rests in present reality, neither rejecting nor clinging to any aspect of experience. When the plumb bob swings toward any of the four directions, your attention has been captured by a particular pattern of thought or emotion.

Rarely, if ever, is the plumb bob completely still. It swings, sometimes subtly, sometimes wildly, pulled in different directions by thoughts, emotions, physical sensations, and external stimuli. This movement isn't just random noise—it follows specific patterns that correspond to different states of consciousness.

The Plumb Bob Metaphor

The plumb bob represents your current focus of attention - a weighted object suspended above the compass that naturally seeks center but is easily pulled in various directions. Unlike a compass needle that points in one direction, the plumb bob can indicate, through its movement, the current "pull" on your attention.

When the Plumb Bob is moving; one has attention "Pulled Away"

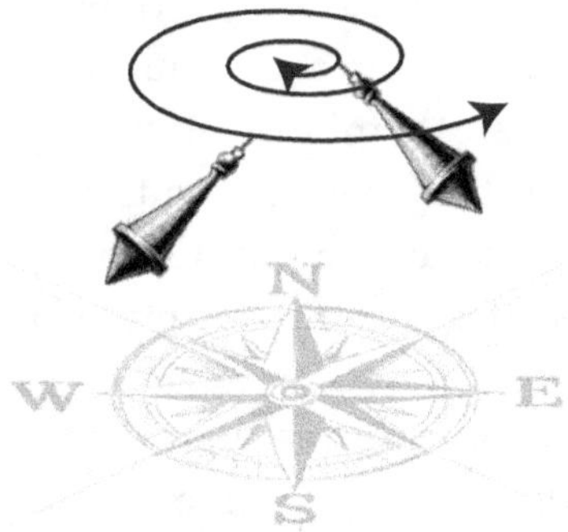

When the Plumb Bob is still; one enters "The Flow State"

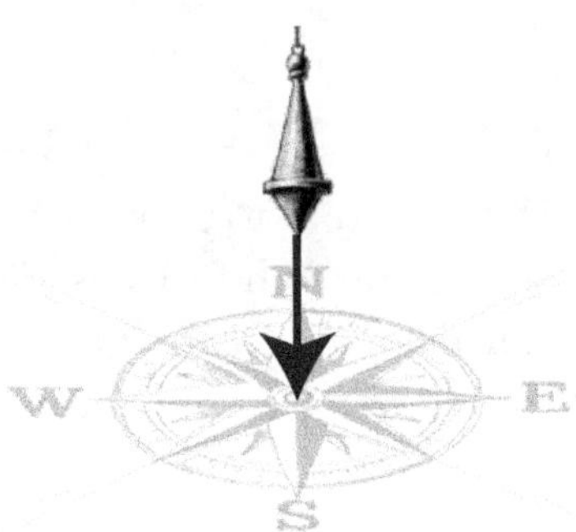

Let's take a deeper look into the meaning of the four metaphorical points of the Attention Compass:

North: When the plumb bob pulls northward, your attention is focused on **identity**—who you think you are. This might be expressed as either pride in your achievements and attributes ("I'm so successful/intelligent/attractive") or defense against perceived threats to your self-image ("How dare they question my expertise/integrity/worth?"). Either way, attention is consumed by maintaining and protecting the story of who you are.

South: A southward swing of the plumb bob indicates that your attention is caught in **comparison**—measuring yourself against other people, places, situations, or things. This can manifest as either superiority ("At least I'm doing better than them") or inferiority ("Everyone else has it figured out except me"). Either way, attention is trapped in a perpetual measuring contest that has no winner. Often the comparison is with a fantasy, some unrealistic ideal, destined to trap your attention in negativity.

West: When the plumb bob moves westward, your attention is pulled into the **past**. This might show up as repeated thoughts of regret or nostalgia, but both represent an inability to be fully present. The mind becomes caught in endless loops of "what if" and "if only," replaying scenes that cannot be changed and missing the only moment where life is actually happening—now.

East: When the plumb bob drifts eastward, your attention is projected into the **future**, typically through worry or fantasy. Both states remove you from present reality—one through fear-based speculation about what might go wrong, the other through escape into what might someday be better. Neither allows you to engage with life as it is unfolding in this moment.

"If you are depressed, you are living in the past. If you are anxious, you are living in the future. If you are at peace, you are living in the present,"—Lao Tzu.

The crucial insight of the Attention Compass is this: Only when the plumb bob rests at the center—when your attention is neither clinging to identity, nor trapped in comparison, nor lost in past or future—can you access the Flow State. Your heart, gut, and mind are only aligned when in the Flow State, allowing you to connect with and operate from a higher consciousness.

The Attention Compass isn't just a mental model but a felt experience. You can actually notice physical sensations in your body. When attention moves North into identity concerns, you might have a tightness in your jaw or forehead, for example. When pulled South into comparison, perhaps a hollowness in your stomach emerges. Westward pulls into the past often create a heaviness in the shoulders, while Eastward projection into the future commonly generates a fluttery sensation in the chest. Your body always knows where attention has gone before your thinking mind recognizes it.

And so, I discovered that my attention was almost never at *center*. It swung wildly between all four cardinal points—consumed with my lost identity as a successful weatherman, comparing my new circumstances to both my former lifestyle and others who seemed untouched by hardship, endlessly replaying decisions that led to my downfall, and alternating between catastrophic predictions and desperate fantasies about the future.

No wonder I felt so exhausted! The energy required to maintain this constant movement of attention was enormous. And each direction pulled me deeper into lower Consciousness Levels—Shame, Guilt, Apathy, Fear, and Desire.

A revelation came during what should have been an ordinary Tuesday morning walk. I had been practicing the compass metaphor for weeks, dutifully noting when my attention swung North into identity concerns or East into anxious future-planning. But on this particular morning, something felt different.

I was walking past the lake where I'd experienced those first glimpses of stillness, my mind caught in its familiar pattern—ricocheting between shame about our financial situation (South), anxiety about an upcoming bill (East), and desperate thoughts about rebuilding my professional identity (North). The plumb bob of my attention was swinging wildly, and I felt that exhausting sensation of being pulled in multiple directions simultaneously.

Then, mid-stride, it happened.

I suddenly *saw* myself from outside the pattern. Not just intellectually understanding that my attention was scattered, but actually witnessing the entire mechanism in action—like stepping back from a painting to see the whole canvas instead of being lost in individual brushstrokes. I could see the pull toward the past regret, feel the tug toward future worry, observe the gravitational force of identity concerns, and for the first time, I wasn't automatically following any of them.

It was as if I had been a leaf being blown around by wind and suddenly realized I could be the tree instead—rooted, stable, able to feel the wind without being carried away by it.

The moment was so simple it was almost anticlimactic. I was still walking. The same thoughts were still arising. The same emotional pulls were still present. But I wasn't inside them anymore—I was watching them from the still center of the compass itself.

"I don't have to go there," I whispered aloud, stopping on the sidewalk as the full implications hit me. It wasn't that the thoughts and emotions were wrong or needed to be eliminated. It was that I had a choice I'd never realized existed. I could acknowledge the pull of the East direction without projecting my entire awareness into future catastrophe. I could notice the South pull of comparison without drowning in inadequacy.

For perhaps the first time in my adult life, I felt the difference between experiencing thoughts and being experienced by them. The compass wasn't just a useful metaphor—it was revealing an actual choice point that existed in every moment, a freedom I had been carrying within me without knowing it was there.

I stood there for several minutes, experimenting with this newfound capacity. When anxiety about money arose, I practiced saying internally, "That's the East pull, and I don't have to follow it all the way." When shame about my situation surfaced, I gently noted, "South direction activated," and simply returned to the physical sensation of standing on the sidewalk.

The exhaustion I'd been carrying for months began to lift, not because my circumstances had changed, but because I was no longer spending energy fighting a war on four fronts simultaneously. I had found the eye of the hurricane—not by eliminating the storm, but by discovering the place within it that remains forever still.

The revelation came when I realized I didn't have to follow these habitual movements. I could notice the pull without being pulled. I could observe the plumb bob's motion without identifying with it. And most importantly, I could gently guide it back to center whenever I noticed it had drifted.

The Four Directions of Distraction: Mapping Attention's Habitual Patterns

Now that I had discovered this capacity to observe the plumb bob's movement without being pulled by it, I became fascinated with understanding these patterns more deeply. Recognizing the specific ways attention gets captured can dramatically shorten the time between noticing drift and returning to center. While the breakthrough itself came through direct experience, mapping these patterns has proven essential for sustaining that freedom in daily life.

North: The Identity Direction

When attention moves northward, it's fixated on who you think you are—your self-image, reputation, achievements, failures, qualities, and flaws. This isn't the same as self-awareness; it's self-preoccupation—the mind's constant narration about "me and my story."

I spent years with my attention predominantly in this northern direction. As a television meteorologist, my identity was constantly reinforced—by viewers who recognized me in public, by station promotions featuring my image, by social media interactions where I was "Eric the Weatherman." This external validation felt good, but it created a dependency that made my eventual collapse so devastating. When the weatherman identity was stripped away, who was left?

The northern pull comes in two flavors: self-aggrandizement and self-defense. Both keep attention trapped in the same territory.

Your identity has two basic strategies for self-maintenance. In *self-aggrandizement*, the mind is occupied with thoughts about how special, accomplished, or different you are. "I'm the only meteorologist in this market with a degree from..." "My ratings are higher than anyone else's..." "People trust my forecasts more than the competition's..." These thoughts might seem positive, but they keep attention fixated on a constructed self-image rather than present reality.

In *self-defense*, the mind frantically works to protect this same identity when it feels threatened. "How dare they question my expertise, my value..." This defensive posture requires even more energy than self-aggrandizement and often leads to conflict with others who aren't validating the identity we're working so hard to maintain.

Here's the crucial insight about the northern direction: whether through pride or defense, attention in this direction keeps you locked in Levels 4 and 5 of Consciousness—Fear and Desire. You're either afraid of losing your identity (Level 4) or desiring more validation for it (Level 5). Either way, you're stuck in lower consciousness and cut off from the Flow State.

South: The Comparison Direction

When attention drifts southward, it's engaged in the exhausting practice of comparing. Like a machine, your mind grinds through comparisons between yourself and others, your current situation to your past or imagined future, your achievements to your expectations.

After losing my career and financial stability, my attention was constantly pulled south. I would see former colleagues succeeding in their careers and feel a crushing sense of failure. I would watch neighbors coming home from work in nice cars while I walked aimlessly around the neighborhood. Every social media post showing someone's vacation or new purchase became evidence of my inadequacy.

Like the northern direction, the southern pull also has two variations: superiority and inferiority. Both keep attention trapped in the comparative framework.

In *superiority*, the mind seeks evidence that you're better than others or than a previous version of yourself. "At least I'm not as bad off as that person..." or "I've come so far from where I started..." These thoughts might provide temporary comfort, but they maintain the underlying pattern of measuring and comparing.

In *inferiority*, the mind finds evidence that you don't measure up. "Everyone else has their life together except me..." or "I should be further along by now..." This painful self-judgment creates a constant background of shame and inadequacy that drains vital energy.

The truth about the southern direction is that it's a game you can never win. There will always be someone doing better than you in some area, and someone doing worse. There will always be aspects of your past that seem better than the present and others that seem worse.

Comparison is an infinite loop that keeps attention trapped in Levels 1-3 of Consciousness—Shame, Guilt, and Apathy.

West: The Past Direction

When attention moves westward, it's lost in what has already happened—replaying events, conversations, decisions, and experiences that exist now only as memories. I heard a quote that fits so perfectly, "What happened happened, and it couldn't have happened any other way because it didn't." Ponder the solidity of that statement. However, we are still human.

During my darkest periods, my attention was frequently pulled west. I would spend hours mentally revisiting decision points: "If only I had saved more money..." or "If only I had developed other skills..." This mental time travel changed nothing about my circumstances but consumed enormous emotional and mental energy.

The western pull also has two main expressions: regret and nostalgia. Both remove attention from the only moment where change is possible—the present.

In *regret*, the mind obsesses over perceived mistakes and missed opportunities. "I should have known better..." or "If only I had chosen differently..." This backward focus creates guilt and shame while reinforcing the illusion that the past could have been different than it was.

In *nostalgia*, the mind selectively recalls "better times" with an aching longing to return to them. "Things were so much easier when..." or "I was so much happier before..." This selective remembering often ignores the challenges that existed even in those supposedly ideal times while creating dissatisfaction with the present.

The westward direction keeps attention trapped in a reality that no longer exists except as neural patterns in your brain. This fixation on the past keeps consciousness at Levels 2 and 3—Guilt and Apathy.

East: The Future Direction

When attention drifts eastward, it's projected into what hasn't yet happened—anticipating events, planning conversations, imagining scenarios, and constructing potential realities that exist now only as mental simulation.

As my situation deteriorated, I would spend days catastrophizing: "We'll end up living in our car..." "I'll never work in television again..." "Our son will suffer because of my failure..." I would also escape into fantasy: "Maybe someone will see my value and offer me the perfect job..." "Perhaps we'll win the lottery..." "Some opportunity will come along and solve everything..." Neither mental state helped me respond effectively to what was actually happening.

Like the other directions, the eastern pull has two primary manifestations: worry and fantasy. Both remove attention from the only place where effective action is possible—the present.

In *worry*, the mind rehearses potential problems, threats, and disasters. "What if I can't pay next month's rent?" Worrying is using the immense power of your imagination to focus on what you DON'T want. This creates fear and anxiety, conditioning the body to respond as if the threat were actually happening.

In *fantasy*, the mind constructs elaborate scenarios of future happiness or success. "When we move to a new city, our problems will be solved..." "After I achieve this goal, I'll finally feel fulfilled..." This constant projection into an imagined better future creates dissatisfaction with the present while establishing conditions for happiness that continually move beyond reach.

The eastward direction keeps attention fixated on possibilities that don't yet exist—either fearful or desirable—rather than engaging with what is. This preoccupation with the future keeps consciousness fluctuating between Levels 4 and 5—Fear and Desire.

The Attention Compass

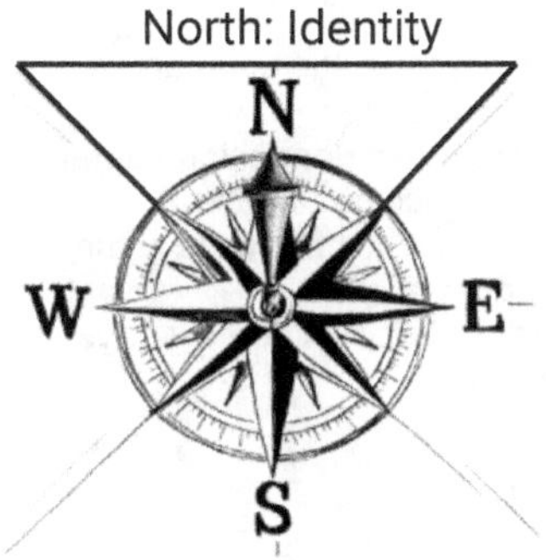

Pull: Thoughts about who you think you are or should be; self image concerns, or reputation
Examples: "I'm the kind of person who always succeeds" or "What will others think of me"
Physically: Often felt as tension in the jaw, forehead, or facial muscles
Consciousness Level: Typically levels 4-5 (Fear and Desire)

Pull: Measuring yourself concept against others or against your own expectations
Examples: "Everyone else is doing better than me, I should be further along by now
Physically: Often felt as hollowness or churning in the stomach
Consciousness Level: Typically levels 1-3 (Shame/Guilt/Apathy)

The Attention Compass

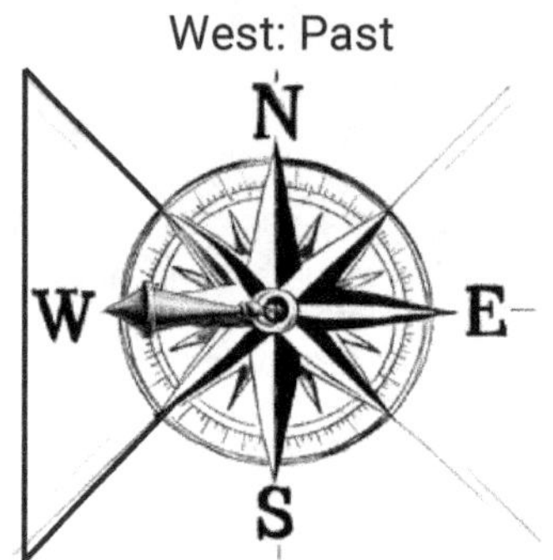

Pull: Thoughts of regret, the good times or when replaying events on a loop
Examples: "If I only had done things differently," "Things were so much better before"
Physically: Often felt as heaviness in the shoulders or upper back
Consciousness Level: Typically levels 2-3 (Guilt/Apathy)

Pull: Planning, worrying, fantasizing about what might happen
Examples: "What if everything falls apart?" "Once I achieve this, I'll finally be happy"
Physically: Often felt as tightness or fluttering in the chest
Consciousness Level: Typically levels 4-5 (Fear/Desire)

The Center: Finding Stillness Amid Movement

Now that we've explored the four directions of distraction, let's turn to what lies at the center of the compass—the still point around which all movement occurs.

When the plumb bob rests at center, attention isn't pulled into identity concerns, comparative thinking, past regrets, or future anxieties. It simply rests in present awareness—alert, responsive, and undivided. This isn't a state of disconnection or passive observation; it's full engagement with reality as it's actually unfolding rather than as the mind is interpreting, judging, or wishing it to be. With just a little time and intention, you can bring your attention to this highly desirable centered spot. I call this practice the Attention Compass Centering Process.

What makes this centering practice so powerful extends beyond individual experience. HeartMath Institute's groundbreaking research has documented that the human heart generates an electromagnetic field that extends several feet beyond our physical bodies in all directions.

This field, measurable with sensitive magnetometers, is 60 times greater in amplitude than the brain's electrical activity and can be detected up to three feet away.

Even more remarkable, research has shown that when one person achieves a centered, coherent state through processes like the Attention Compass Centering Process, their heart's electromagnetic field becomes more organized and can measurably influence the brain waves of people nearby. This provides scientific validation for something many of us have intuitively experienced—that a person in a centered, peaceful state can create a "field effect" that subtly influences others in proximity. When attention returns to center, we're not just shifting our personal experience; we're literally broadcasting a more coherent signal into the environment around us, creating ripples that extend far beyond our individual awareness.

I discovered this center point during one of my many walks through the neighborhood. After months of attention wrenched in all directions, I experienced a moment of unexpected stillness. It wasn't that my circumstances had changed—I was still jobless, financially devastated, and uncertain about the future. But suddenly, my attention wasn't fixated on any of that. It simply rested in the experience of walking—the sensation of feet touching ground, the rhythm of breath, the quality of light filtering through trees.

At that moment, I wasn't "Eric the failed weatherman" (North). I wasn't "less successful than my colleagues" (South). I wasn't regretting past decisions (West) or worrying about future catastrophes (East). I was simply present—aware of reality without the usual overlay of mental commentary.

The revelation wasn't that such moments exist; it was that I could intentionally cultivate them by recognizing when attention had drifted and gently guiding it back to center. The plumb bob would always be pulled in various directions—that's the nature of the mind. But I didn't have to follow every pull. I could observe the movement and choose whether to go with it or return to center.

This center point is the gateway to higher levels of consciousness. When attention rests here, even briefly, you begin to access Level 7 (Acceptance), Level 8 (Peace), and eventually Level 9 (Enlightenment). From this still point, the three brains—gut, heart, and mind—naturally align, creating the conditions for the Flow State to emerge.

The center doesn't deny or exclude what arises in the four directions; it holds them in a larger awareness. You can notice thoughts about identity, comparative judgments, memories, and anticipations without becoming completely absorbed in them. They're like clouds passing through the sky of awareness rather than defining the sky itself.

The Code Connection: How the Compass Navigates Consciousness Levels

The Attention Compass isn't just a helpful metaphor; it's a practical tool for understanding and shifting between consciousness levels. Each direction of attention corresponds to specific levels, and the center point provides access to higher states that are otherwise unreachable.

Let's map these connections explicitly:

North (Identity Direction):

- When attention is pulled north into identity concerns, consciousness typically operates at Levels 4 and 5—Fear and Desire.

- The fear of losing or damaging your self-image keeps you defensive and contracted.

- The desire for identity and recognition keeps you seeking external approval.

- These levels generate sufficient energy to function and achieve in the world but not enough to access genuine fulfillment or the Flow State.

South (Comparison Direction):

- When attention is pulled south into comparative thinking, consciousness typically operates at Levels 1, 2, and 3—Shame, Guilt, and Apathy.

- The shame of feeling inferior to others creates a sense of fundamental unworthiness.

- The guilt of not measuring up to your own or others' expectations creates self-punishment.

- Constant negative comparisons lead to resignation and disengagement.

- These levels drain energy and create a downward spiral that can lead to depression and complete withdrawal.

West (Past Direction):

- When attention is pulled west into the past, consciousness typically operates at Levels 2 and 3—Guilt and Apathy.

- The guilt of perceived mistakes and regrets keeps consciousness heavy and contracted.

- The apathy that comes from feeling trapped by the past creates a sense that change is impossible.

- These levels keep you locked in repetitive patterns, as the energy needed for transformation is consumed by rumination.

East (Future Direction):

- When attention is pulled east into the future, consciousness typically operates at Levels 4 and 5—Fear and Desire.

- The fear of potential threats and problems creates anxiety and stress in the present.

- The desire for future satisfaction creates perpetual seeking without arrival.

- These levels create constant movement without progress, as attention is never where transformation is possible—in the PRESENT.

Center (Present Awareness):

- When attention is centered in present awareness, consciousness can access Levels 7, 8, and 9—Acceptance, Peace, and Enlightenment.

- The acceptance of reality as it is (not as you wish it were) creates spaciousness and possibility.

- The peace that comes from non-resistance allows solutions to emerge naturally.

- The enlightened awareness of your true nature beyond all identifications creates a sense of gratitude, freedom, and joy.

- These levels generate abundant energy while requiring minimal effort to maintain, creating conditions for the Flow State to emerge.

Understanding these connections gives you a map for consciously and intentionally shifting levels. When you notice yourself feeling shame, guilt, or apathy, you can check whether your attention has been pulled southward into comparison. When you're experiencing fear or craving, you can ask yourself if your attention has drifted north into identity concerns, east into future worries, or west into past regrets.

Most importantly, you can recognize that the way out of lower consciousness isn't through more thinking, analyzing, or figuring out—it's through bringing attention back to center, where higher consciousness naturally becomes available.

This is why meditation, mindfulness, and other present-moment practices have been central to wisdom traditions throughout history. They're not just relaxation techniques or stress management tools; they're technologies for shifting consciousness levels by relocating attention from the periphery to the center of your awareness.

Acclaimed filmmaker David Lynch credits his daily practice of meditation with his profound creativity and extraordinary success. In his book, *Catching the Big Fish: Meditation, Consciousness, and Creativity*, he writes:

> "When I first tried meditating, I was filled with anxieties and fears. I felt a sense of depression and anger.
>
> I often took out this anger on my first wife. After I had been meditating for about two weeks, she came to me and said, 'What's going on?' I was quiet for a moment. But finally said, 'What do you mean?' And she said, 'The anger, where did it go?' And I hadn't even realized that it had lifted.
>
> I call that depression and anger the Suffocating Rubber Clown Suit of Negativity. It's suffocating, and that rubber *stinks*. But once you start meditating and diving within, the clown suit starts to dissolve. You finally realize how putrid the stink was when it starts to go. Then, when it dissolves, you have freedom.
>
> Anger and depression and sorrow are beautiful things in a story, but they're like poison to the filmmaker or artist. They're like a vise grip on creativity. If you're in that grip, you can hardly get out of bed, much less experience the flow of creativity and ideas. You must have clarity to create. You have to be able to catch ideas."

I couldn't agree more that creativity (from the Flow State) suffers when any of the four directional pulls hijacks your attention away from center. And one of the most significant rewards from using the Attention

Compass Centering Process is the resulting flow of creative juices you can use as you wish.

Practical Techniques for Returning to Center

Understanding the Attention Compass conceptually is one thing; applying it practically in daily life is another. Here are some specific techniques I developed during my journey from collapse to transformation—tools that helped me bring the plumb bob back to center whenever I noticed it had drifted.

1. The Pause

The simplest and most fundamental technique is what I call the Pause Practice. It's exactly what it sounds like—a momentary suspension of automatic patterns to create space for choice.

Throughout your day, set an intention to pause regularly—either at scheduled times (every hour, for example) or whenever you notice emotional intensity arising. During this pause:

- Take a single conscious breath, feeling the sensation of air entering and leaving your body.

- Notice where your attention has been focused—Identity (North)? Comparison (South)? Past (West)? Future (East)?

- Without judgment, gently guide attention back to your sensory experience in the present moment—the feeling of your body, the sounds around you, what you can see right now.

This practice takes only a few seconds but interrupts habitual patterns before they gain momentum. It's like snagging a thought before it gets out to center stage and takes over the show.

I began using this technique during some of my darkest days. When I noticed myself spiraling into shame about my financial collapse (South) or anxiety about becoming homeless (East), I would pause, take a conscious breath, and bring attention back to the physical sensation of walking or the visual details of my surroundings. This didn't solve my practical problems, but it prevented the additional suffering caused by unfettered attention drift.

2. The Body Anchor

Since the body exists only in the present moment (unlike the mind, which time-travels constantly), physical sensation provides a reliable anchor for returning attention to center.

Whenever you notice the plumb bob has drifted:

- Shift attention to a specific physical sensation—the feeling of your feet on the ground, the weight of your body in a chair, the sensation of hands touching each other.

- Explore this sensation with genuine curiosity—not thinking about it but directly experiencing its qualities (temperature, pressure, texture, movement).

- When the mind inevitably wanders back to one of the four directions, gently return attention to the chosen sensation.

During my long walks, I would use the rhythmic feeling of feet touching the ground as my anchor. No matter how turbulent my thoughts about identity loss (North) or regrets about financial decisions (West), the simple sensation of walking was always available as a pathway back to center. By the way, there are those who cite studies endorsing walking outside with bare feet as an even more effective activity for getting grounded and centered.

3. The Direction Detector

This technique involves developing awareness of your attention's habitual patterns. With practice, you can catch the drift earlier, before you're completely absorbed in a particular direction.

For one week, carry a small notebook or use a note-taking app on your phone. Several times each day, pause and ask:

- Where is my attention right now—North, South, East, or West?

- How long has it been there?

- What triggered this particular direction of attention?

Record your observations without judgment. By the end of the week, patterns will become apparent—you might notice that work meetings pull you North into identity concerns, while family gatherings pull you South into comparison, for example.

When you understand your own "attention habits," you can notice and get ready for the situations that usually throw you off balance. It's like knowing where the strong currents are in a river so you can steer through them more easily.

4. The Thought Inquiry

This helps disrupt the content that pulls attention in various directions by questioning its validity. When you notice attention has drifted into one of the four directions:

- Identify the specific thought that's capturing attention ("I'm a failure," "Others are doing better than me," "I should have seen this coming," "Everything is going to get worse").

- Expose the lie! Ask yourself: "Is this absolutely true? Can I know for certain this is true?"

- Notice how you feel when you believe this thought.

- Consider who or how you would be without this thought.

This practice, adapted from Loving What Is, Revised Edition: Four Questions That Can Change Your Life; The Revolutionary Process Called "The Work" by Byron Katie and Stephen Mitchell, doesn't try to replace negative thoughts with positive ones (which often doesn't work). Instead, it creates space around thoughts by questioning their absolute truth, allowing attention to naturally return to center when thoughts are held more lightly.

During my bankruptcy proceedings, I was consumed by the thought "I'll never recover from this" (East). When I inquired into this thought, I realized I couldn't absolutely know it was true—I simply had no way of knowing what the future held. Recognizing this created space around the thought; it became something I was aware of rather than completely identified with.

5. The Environment Design

Your physical environment can either facilitate or hinder your ability to keep attention centered. This technique involves deliberately structuring your surroundings to reduce unnecessary pulls on attention.

Consider:

- Reducing digital distractions by turning off notifications, using website blockers, or designating specific times for email and social media.

- Creating visual cues that remind you to return to center (a small symbol on your desk, a note on your bathroom mirror, a specific image as your phone wallpaper).

- Designating specific spaces for specific activities to help the mind stay present rather than constantly planning or reviewing.

- Simplifying your environment to reduce visual clutter that pulls attention in multiple directions.

In my personal environment, I have a very special and symbolic memento which serves me well. My son carved the small rectangular whistle with a hawk beak on it, presented it to me, and my heart melted. Aidan knows I am fascinated by hawks, always noticing them in our neighborhood or on a walk. For me, the hawk is a totem representing a big picture view that soars above the chaos of life. Aidan added the hawk beak to the wooden whistle and together, we named the whistle "Iroh." This is from a Nickelodeon show we often watch together, where my favorite character is a wise uncle whose role is to give advice about life. I would repeat his nuggets of wisdom for both Aidan and myself to consume. So, Iroh the Whistle sits on my desk, even as I write this book, reminding me to stay present—like my son, who doesn't seem to have a choice.

The threat of being homeless was paramount as a provider during this time. A friend suggested that I hire a lawyer to go and "find the deed" to our property we were currently living in, which allowed us to stay (even though I would call it squatting) in our own home. At least this would allow us to function as devoted parents of an autistic child.

By finding the center, I found a way to stay that nobody, outside of this good friend, had even heard of or recommended. We continue to live in the same house today. However close it loomed, we were never homeless.

When you are in the Flow State, this is where the whispers that lead to miracles happen.

6. The Brief Immersion

This technique involves fully immersing attention in a simple sensory experience for a brief period—30 seconds to 2 minutes. It's like a mini-meditation that can be integrated into daily activities.

Choose an ordinary experience like:

- Drinking a glass of water with complete attention to the sensation

- Listening to the ambient sounds around you for one minute

- Feeling the sensation of the shower water on your skin

- Looking at a natural object (a leaf, stone, or flower) with focused, full visual attention

The key is total immersion—bringing all your attention to the sensory experience without commentary, analysis, or planning. This brief but complete centering of attention interrupts momentum in the four directions and strengthens your capacity to return to center.

During one particularly difficult period, I developed the habit of stopping to watch the sunset each evening—not photographing it, not thinking about it, just watching with my full attention as colors shifted and light changed. Those few minutes of complete immersion would reliably bring the plumb bob back to center, even when the day had pulled it wildly in all directions.

The Dream Deepens: Finding Center

One night, after spending most of my day engaged in the beginnings of the Attention Compass development, he came to me again in my dream.

———◆———

Together, the now-familiar man and I stand at the edge of a vast, circular labyrinth that stretches before us. I have the idea that this is a living map of consciousness. From above, it might resemble a compass rose, with elaborate paths extending in four directions before curving inward through intricate patterns of stone and living hedge.

The air here feels different—clearer somehow, and charged with the energy of possibility. Each breath fills me with awareness so sharp it borders on pain.

"I've been lost in there for years," he tells me, gesturing toward the maze. His voice carries neither self-pity nor resignation, just the simple acknowledgment of experience. "Each time I try to reach the center, I get pulled down one of those four main paths."

Looking closer, I see ornate signs marking each of the four primary entrances: NORTH— Identity; SOUTH—Comparison; WEST—Past; and EAST— Future. The paths beyond them twisted seductively, promising answers, resolution, escape.

"Which path keeps pulling you?" I ask, though something in me already knows the answer.

With a sidelong glance and a small smile at the corners of his mouth, he says, "All of them. Just like you." The words land with the weight of absolute truth.

Without planning to, I step into the labyrinth, feeling an immediate pull toward the Western path of the Past. It tugs at me with the gravitational force of regret. *So many moments I wish I could rewrite.* As I begin drifting that way, surrendering to its familiar current, I feel his hand on my shoulder—warm, steadying, unexpectedly strong.

"There's another way," he says, pointing to what I hadn't seen before—a barely visible path that cut straight through the labyrinth's elaborate rings to its center. It is not carved of stone like the other paths, but seems made of light itself, faintly shimmering with a quality I can't name. "But you can only see it when you're not being pulled."

I focus on his finger, straining to discern this hidden route, but the more I try to see it, the more it disappears, like a star that vanishes when looked at directly. Only when I relax my gaze, allowing my attention to rest without effort or demand, does the direct path briefly shimmer into visibility—a silver thread woven through the elaborate maze.

"The center exists," he says, his voice somehow both a whisper and the clearest sound I'd ever heard. "You don't need to search for it. You only need to stop drifting away from it."

———◆———

I woke with the image of that labyrinth burning behind my eyes, my heart pounding with recognition. The distinctions were crystal clear: NORTH— Identity; SOUTH—Comparison; WEST—Past; and EAST— Future. Throughout that day, whenever I caught my attention being pulled in one of the four directions, I remembered that straight path to the center. And, in moments of grace I couldn't manufacture but could only receive, I found it—*the direct route to presence* that had always been there, hidden in plain sight beneath the pathways of my wandering mind.

Exercise: Working with Your Own Attention Compass

I committed to tracking my attention for one week, noting whenever I caught it drifting in the four cardinal directions. What I discovered shocked me. My attention wasn't randomly wandering—it was following deeply grooved pathways.

During financial discussions, it pulled relentlessly eastward into catastrophic future scenarios. When passing neighbors who still had their careers, it yanked southward into painful comparisons. When thinking about my old TV weathermen job, it drifted westward into nostalgia or regret. And whenever I attempted anything new, it swung northward into identity concerns about whether it would fit "who I was."

Simply *noticing* these patterns created a subtle but profound shift. The pulls didn't stop, but a space opened between me and them—a brief pause where I could choose rather than react automatically. This practice became my lifeline during the darkest periods, not by eliminating challenges but by changing my relationship with them.

It's time for you to experience the Attention Compass directly in your own awareness. This exercise will help you map your personal attention patterns and develop the skill of returning to center. Yes, it's a skill, and I promise it's a learnable skill—if I could learn it, you can, as well.

You'll need:

- 20-30 minutes of uninterrupted time

- A journal or paper for notes

- A timer or clock

Part 1: Mapping Your Attention Roaming (10 minutes)

Begin by reflecting on and writing about your habitual attention patterns:

1. **North (Identity):** When and how does your attention get pulled into concerns about who you are? What situations, people, or internal states trigger preoccupation with your

2. self-image, reputation, or status? What are the thoughts and feelings that characterize this direction for you?

3. **South (Comparison):** When do you find yourself comparing your life, achievements, appearance, or circumstances to others? Who do you tend to compare yourself with most frequently? How does this comparison affect your emotional state and energy level?

4. **West (Past):** What aspects of your past tend to capture your attention most frequently? Are there specific regrets, relationships, or unfinished business that your mind returns to repeatedly? How much of your daily mental energy is consumed by what has already happened?

5. **East (Future):** What aspects of the future tend to occupy your attention? Do you lean more toward worry or fantasy? What specific anticipated events or imagined scenarios consume your

mental energy on a regular basis? Recalling a recent time you were worrying or fantasizing, what was going on just before your attention headed East?

6. **Center (Present):** When do you most naturally find yourself present and centered? What activities, environments, or conditions help your attention rest in the current experience rather than being pulled in any of the four directions?

Part 2: Attention Direction Practice (10 minutes)

Now, set a timer for 10 minutes and allow your attention to move naturally, without trying to control it. Your task is simply to notice which direction it tends to move in and to practice gently returning it to center when you notice it has drifted. You are not your thoughts—so you can practice observing them, watch them roam, and bring your intention to guide and direct your attention back to the center.

1. Sit comfortably and begin by taking a few deep breaths, bringing attention to the physical sensation of breathing.

2. As your attention naturally begins to drift (which it will), notice which direction it moves toward:

   - North: Thoughts about your identity, qualities, image

   - South: Comparative thoughts about yourself and others

   - West: Memories, regrets, replaying past events

   - East: Anticipation, planning, worrying about the future

3. When you notice a drift in any direction, mentally note it ("North... identity thinking" or "East... planning"). Add no judgement.

4. Gently guide attention back to a present-moment anchor—the sensation of breathing, the feeling of your body, and sounds in your environment.

5. Continue this process of noticing drift and returning to center until the timer sounds.

Part 3: Reflection and Application (5-10 minutes)

After completing the practice, reflect on what you discovered:

1. Which direction did your attention drift most frequently? Was there a pattern to this movement?

2. What did you notice about the experience of returning to center? Was it easy or difficult? What helped the return?

3. Did you discover any hooks or themes when your attention drifted?

4. How might you use this awareness in your daily life? Identify 2-3 specific situations where being mindful of and intentional about your Attention Compass could be particularly valuable.

5. Choose one of the practical techniques from this chapter that resonates with you and commit to practicing it daily for seven days.

This practice transformed my daily walks from exercises in anxiety to opportunities for integration. I remember one particularly difficult morning when we received another threatening letter from creditors. My attention immediately fragmented—part of me panicking about worst-case scenarios, part comparing our situation to friends who remained financially stable, part berating myself for past decisions that led to this.

With the powerful tool, the Attention Compass, rather than being hijacked by these pulls, I recognized them as movements on the compass. All along my walk, I practiced returning to the center. The external situation hadn't changed, but my relationship to it shifted dramatically.

Solutions began emerging not from frantic problem-solving but from the clarity that appeared when attention rested at center. The path forward wasn't what my fragmented thinking could have engineered—it was simpler and more direct. Moving forward on my new path felt effortless, yet it was ultimately more effective than anything I could have forced from scattered awareness.

The goal isn't to permanently fix attention at the center—that's neither possible nor desirable. The mind naturally moves. The aim is to develop awareness of these movements so they no longer occur on autopilot, pulling you into lower consciousness levels where you feel helpless and trapped. With practice, you'll never feel trapped; you will be able to produce the key that unlocks the doorway to higher consciousness. You will be able to guide your attention into the Flow State.

The Compass as Gateway to Flow

The deeper purpose of the Attention Compass Centering Process is to create the conditions for the Flow State to emerge.

When attention repeatedly returns to center rather, than being constantly pulled in any of the four directions, something remarkable begins to happen. The three brains—gut, heart, and mind—naturally come into alignment. Without the conflicting pulls of identity concerns, comparative thinking, past regrets, and future anxieties, your neural networks can communicate clearly with each other.

The gut's intuitive knowing, the heart's compassionate wisdom, and the mind's analytical clarity begin to work in harmony rather than opposition. Decisions become clearer. Actions become more effective. Creativity flows more readily.

> *"Problems that seemed insurmountable from the fragmented perspective of divided attention often reveal unexpected solutions when approached from centered awareness."*

This alignment isn't something you directly "do"—it's what naturally occurs when you stop doing the things that prevent it. Just as water flows downhill unless obstructed, the Flow State emerges spontaneously when the obstructions of attention drift are removed.

I discovered this during my darkest period. With no career identity to maintain, no achievements to compare, no successful past to cling to, and no secure future to plan for, I found myself—it seems by default—more frequently at center.

Even when everything around me was chaotic, those centered moments gave me a sense of peace and clear thinking that I'd never had— not even when I was at the peak of my success.

In the next chapter, we'll explore how unexpected teachers illuminated the path toward what I now understand as the Flow State.

The Attention Compass prepared the ground for these teachings by creating space within my awareness where wisdom could be recognized when it appeared—often in the most unlikely forms, including a simple acorn, a persistent weed, and my autistic son Aidan.

CHAPTER 5

Unexpected Teachers

"Aha!"

It's part of the human experience. We suddenly gain understanding of a concept, solution, or idea that previously seemed confusing or unclear. It's more than going from not knowing to knowing, it's a realization beyond knowledge—it's wisdom.

Have you ever noticed how wisdom tends to appear when you least expect it? Not in the grand seminar room or sacred temple, but in the ordinary moments we might otherwise overlook—a child's innocent question, an object found on a nature walk, or a way through something that initially seemed like an obstacle.

Anyone or anything can spark your *aha!* moment, and I call these teachers. There's a curious paradox at work here: often the greatest teachers don't present themselves as teachers at all. They don't arrive with credentials, followers, or even awareness of the lessons they carry. They simply appear in your life, holding wisdom you're finally ready to receive.

This chapter tells the story of three unlikely teachers who appeared during my darkest days—a simple acorn, a persistent weed, and my son Aidan. Their lessons opened doors to an understanding that all my years of education and professional achievement had never revealed.

These unexpected encounters didn't make themselves known as profound spiritual experiences at the time. There were no lightning bolts, no dramatic revelations—just quiet moments of clarity that, in retrospect, contained exactly the wisdom I needed to begin moving toward acceptance and the Flow State.

The key, I discovered, wasn't finding better teachers but becoming a better student—developing the quality of attention that could recognize wisdom in its many disguises. The Attention Compass had created space for this recognition by bringing me more frequently to center, where learning could happen without the filters of identity, comparison, past, and future constantly distorting the message.

The Unfiltered Teacher: My Son Aidan

The most constant and profound teacher in my journey has been my son Aidan. Born in 2005, he showed signs early on that his development would follow a unique path. By age five, when my career collapsed, he was still struggling with basic speech. Later assessments would identify aspects of autism in his neurological makeup.

In the conventional framework of our society, this would be categorized as a disability or disorder—something to be fixed, overcome, or at least very "managed." And indeed, like any caring parents, my wife Michelle and I pursued therapies and interventions that might help Aidan navigate a world not designed for minds like his.

But something unexpected happened. As I spent more time with Aidan (especially during those long, empty days of unemployment), I began to recognize that his way of experiencing the world wasn't just different from mine—it was more authentic, more present, and more aligned with reality than my own neurotypical perception.

One fall morning, during one of my aimless walks through the neighborhood, I returned home to find Aidan in the front yard, intensely engaged with our Halloween decorations—inflatable pumpkins and ghosts that he affectionately called "blow-ups." He spent hours with these objects, not just playing with them but relating to them. He would carefully "put them to sleep" at night, wipe rain off them after storms, and speak to them with tenderness, like they were beloved pets.

Conventional wisdom would label this behavior as inappropriate anthropomorphism, a failure to distinguish between animate and inanimate objects. But as I watched him that morning, something shifted in my perception. What if this wasn't a deficit but a different, perhaps more accurate, way of relating to the world?

Quantum physics shows that, at the deepest level, there isn't a sharp line between what's alive and what's not. Everything is energy and information, always moving and exchanging. The divisions we make between different kinds of existence help us to understand, but in the end, they are really just ideas created by the human mind.

Aidan seemed to intuitively grasp something I had forgotten through years of education and socialization—that everything is, in some sense, real and connected. His relation to these Halloween decorations wasn't childish confusion but a direct and unfiltered perception.

Later that same day, I showed Aidan an acorn I had picked up during my walk. "What's this?" I asked, expecting a simple naming exercise that his speech therapist had encouraged us to practice.

Instead, he looked at the acorn with intense focus for several moments, then said something that stopped me in my tracks: "It's just like me, huh, Pappa?"

The profundity of this simple statement hit me like a physical force. Without any botanical education, without understanding oak tree reproduction or the concept of potential, he had intuited the essential nature of an acorn—that within its small, seemingly insignificant form lay the complete pattern for becoming something much larger and "grown up."

What surprised me most was how quickly he saw himself in this truth. "It's just like me." It wasn't a comparison or a symbol. The acorn's reality was his reality. Inside his own life, often ignored or underestimated by others, there was hidden potential. It was just waiting for the right moment to come out.

In that moment, Aidan wasn't my son with developmental challenges. He was my teacher, offering a perspective I desperately needed but couldn't access through my programmed, educated, achievement-oriented mind. Wisdom didn't flow from me to him but from him to me.

I began to wonder—what else was I missing by looking at him only in terms of growth and progress? What if I paid attention instead to his simple, complete presence? What lessons were hidden in his natural way of being that I couldn't see because I was so focused on my constant striving to become?

Spiritual Assets I Started to Notice

Present-Moment Awareness: Aidan lived exclusively in the now. He couldn't remember much of the past and didn't conceptualize the future. Initially, I saw this as a limitation—he couldn't plan, couldn't learn from history, couldn't prepare for what might come. But gradually, I recognized the freedom in this. Without regret about the past or anxiety about the future, he experienced each moment with complete attention. His joy was uncomplicated by anticipation, his sadness untainted by fear of its recurrence.

Non-Comparison: Aidan never seemed to compare himself to others. The concept that he should be "keeping up" with peers or meeting certain milestones by certain ages was entirely foreign to him. He simply was who he was, developing at his own pace, following his own interests with an intensity that neurotypical children often lose early. The suffering that comparison caused in my own life—constantly measuring myself against colleagues, friends, even my former self—was completely absent in his experience.

Caring Without Conditions: Aidan's affection wasn't dependent on performance, appearance, or status. He didn't love the Halloween decorations because they were impressive or valuable; he loved them simply because they existed in his field of awareness. He didn't withhold this love when they failed to meet expectations. This unconditional positive regard extended to people as well—he didn't categorize others by conventional hierarchies of success, appearance, or social standing.

Natural Authenticity: Perhaps most strikingly, Aidan never performed a version of himself for others' approval. The concept of crafting a public persona or adjusting his behavior to make others comfortable simply didn't exist in his world. What you saw was who he was— completely, unfiltered, moment by moment. (The exhausting division

I had maintained between my public weatherman self and my private reality was inconceivable to him.)

As I began to see these qualities not as developmental deficits but as spiritual assets, my relationship with Aidan transformed. I was no longer just a father guiding a son but a student receiving wisdom from an unlikely teacher. He embodied many qualities I was struggling to cultivate—presence, authenticity, non-judgment, unconditional love—without any formal practice or even awareness that these were special states of consciousness.

What Aidan showed me, more clearly than any spiritual text or guru ever had, was that many qualities we strive to develop through years of dedicated practice are actually our natural state. It's like as soon as we're born, the world imposes its will, and we start forgetting how to live from our natural center. The qualities we seek don't need to be chased after, earned, or created—simply uncovered from beneath the layers of conditioning that have obscured them.

This insight was revolutionary. What if the Flow State I was seeking wasn't something to achieve through effort but something to return to by removing obstacles? What if Aidan wasn't behind in his development but ahead in his wisdom? Unlike me, he was simply free to be.

The lesson wasn't to abandon all effort toward growth and development—both Aidan and I needed structured supports to navigate the practical realities of the world. But it was to recognize that alongside the necessary developmental journey exists a dimension of being that is already complete, already perfect, already in flow. Accessing this dimension doesn't require adding anything, but removing the filters that prevent us from experiencing it directly.

"The sun is always shining; you need only remove the clouds."— David Hawkins, M.D., Ph. D.

The Persistent Teacher: A Weed in the Rubble

Another unexpected teacher appeared during a daily walk, this time past a construction site in our neighborhood where the main avenue was being redone. The project had created temporary mounds of dirt as high as a house—barren mini-mountains of displaced earth that would eventually be moved elsewhere or redistributed.

On one of these mounds, something caught my eye: a single green weed growing from the otherwise lifeless dirt. It wasn't particularly beautiful or unusual—just an ordinary plant that would be considered a nuisance in any garden. But its conspicuous presence caught my eye and halted my step.

The conditions couldn't have been less favorable for growth. The dirt pile was temporary, frequently disturbed by heavy machinery. The Florida sun beat down mercilessly, with no shade or consistent water source.

This location was impossible for sustained life. Yet there it was— green, growing, alive in defiance of circumstance.

I stood looking at this weed for several minutes, feeling a strange resonance with its situation. My own circumstances seemed equally hostile to thriving—financial ruin, career collapse, social isolation, identity loss. Everything external suggested growth was impossible, that survival itself was questionable. This weed and I had no support system, yet, today, we were here, alive.

Something in me recognized the message: life finds a way. Not because conditions are favorable, not because success is guaranteed, but because it's the intrinsic nature of life to grow toward the light whenever the slightest possibility of survival exists.

This little weed didn't stop to figure out its chances of survival before sending roots into the hard ground. It didn't run a risk check or make backup plans. It just followed the basic drive to grow that all living things have. One cell divided into two, then four, then eight—carrying out the instructions in its DNA no matter what the outside conditions were.

I realized I had been doing the opposite. I kept overthinking—always planning, always worrying, waiting for the "right" conditions before I moved forward. I wanted certainty before making choices, and guarantees before putting in energy.

The weed showed me another way: grow now, with what you have, right where you are. Don't wait for perfect conditions—they may never come. Don't look for guarantees—they don't exist. Don't hold out for the best support—make use of whatever is available.

This insight broke something loose within me. I had been waiting for my old life to somehow be restored, for a clear path forward to appear, for someone or something to rescue me from the rubble of collapse. But what if I simply needed to start growing from exactly where I was, with exactly what I had?

This didn't mean denying the difficulty of my circumstances or pretending everything was fine. The weed wasn't "thinking positive" or "manifesting abundance"—it was simply acting according to its nature despite limitations. I didn't need to pretend my situation was better than it was; I just needed to stop letting the difficulty prevent any movement at all.

Growth doesn't require ideal conditions, just minimal viable ones. And even in the darkest periods of collapse, those minimal conditions usually exist if we're willing to recognize and work with them rather than waiting for something better.

For me, the minimal viable conditions included a supportive wife who believed in me even when I didn't believe in myself. A university job that, while far below my previous station, provided some income and free education. A son whose needs gave purpose to days that might otherwise have lacked direction. These weren't the conditions I (my identity) would have chosen, but they were sufficient for growth if I stopped resisting them as inadequate.

The weed's message wasn't comfortable or easy. It didn't promise that growth would be fast, impressive, or even ultimately successful in conventional terms. But it clarified that the alternative—remaining dormant until conditions improved—wasn't a strategy for survival but a path to certain withering.

In the months that followed, I began to look for minimal viable growing conditions in my own life. Instead of focusing on what was missing or inadequate, I asked: what's present that I can work with? What small steps are possible right now, even if they don't guarantee long-term success? Where can I send roots, however tentative, into the soil available to me?

Widely attributed to Theodore Roosevelt, this encouraging phrase sums it up:

"Do what you can, with what you've got, where you are."

The Humble Teacher: An Acorn's Potential

The massive oak trees that lined our streets were shedding their seeds by the thousands, creating a natural carpet underfoot.

I had passed these acorns daily without much thought. They were just part of the fall landscape, natural debris to be navigated. But one morning, something unusual happened. As I walked, a small internal voice seemed to say, "Pick me up."

The thought was so distinct that I stopped mid-stride. It wasn't an audible voice but a clear nudge that seemed to come from somewhere beyond my usual mental chatter. Having nothing better to do, I bent down and picked up an acorn from the sidewalk.

It sat in my palm—small, smooth, unremarkable. I carried it with me for the remainder of my walk, occasionally rolling it between my fingers, feeling its weight and texture. When I returned home, Aidan was in the front yard with his beloved Halloween decorations. I showed him the acorn, which led to his profound observation: "It's just like me, huh, Pappa?"

But the acorn had more to teach beyond that initial exchange. As I continued to reflect on it throughout the day, several insights emerged that spoke directly to my situation:

Everything Necessary Is Already Present: Within that small acorn was everything needed to become a magnificent oak tree. Not the physical mass, of course—that would come from soil, water, and sunlight—but the complete informational pattern, the exact blueprint for becoming a massive oak. Nothing needed to be added to its essential nature; it just needed the right conditions to express what was already encoded within it.

I began to wonder: What if the same is true for humans? What if everything necessary for our fullest expression isn't something we need to acquire from outside but is already present within us, waiting for the right conditions to emerge? This turned my understanding of growth and achievement upside down. Perhaps success wasn't about adding more (education, skills, resources) but about removing obstacles to what was already there. It's no small thing to give up the belief that "when…

then…" and embrace the belief that all that's needed is already present—but this is one of the most important teachings in life.

No Concern for the Future: The acorn contained enormous potential but demonstrated no anxiety about fulfilling it. It didn't worry about whether conditions would be favorable for germination or if there would be enough sunlight, water, or soil nutrients. It didn't compare itself to other acorns or feel inadequate if it hadn't sprouted as quickly as its neighbors. And as far as I could tell, it was not wishing it were a maple tree, instead. It simply was what it was, completely at peace with its current form while containing the pattern for something radically different.

This quality of being fully present in current form while holding potential for transformation struck me as the antidote to my constant anxiety about the future. I had been caught in endless loops of worry about whether I would ever work again, how we would manage financially, what would become of us. The acorn suggested a different approach: be completely present in your current reality while trusting the unfolding of your intrinsic nature.

Releasing Control: The acorn had no control over its eventual fate. It might be eaten by a squirrel, crushed underfoot, or it might find perfect conditions and grow into a majestic oak living for centuries. I had been exhausting myself trying to control outcomes that were largely beyond my influence. The job market, the economy, others' perceptions of my value—these weren't directly under my command, however much effort I exerted. The acorn's wisdom suggested that my task wasn't to control circumstances but to fully embody my nature within whatever circumstances arose.

Value Is Independent of Outcome: The acorn held value regardless of whether it ever became an oak tree. If eaten, it would provide essential nutrition to wildlife. If decayed, it would return nutrients to the soil. If carried to a new location, it might pioneer forest growth in previously barren areas. No possible outcome negated its worth in the larger system; they just represented different expressions of its contribution.

This perspective offered profound relief from the achievement orientation that had defined my life. My worth as a human wasn't dependent on returning to my former success or achieving some new pinnacle of accomplishment. I have intrinsic value. You have intrinsic value.

The acorn didn't need to convince itself or others of its potential or worth; it simply existed as what it was, fully expressing its nature in present circumstances while holding the pattern for future possibilities.

As I reflected on these insights, something shifted in my relationship with my own collapsed state. What if this period wasn't just failure and loss but contained a seed of transformation that couldn't have emerged without the breaking open of my previous life? What if, like the acorn that must crack and decompose before the oak can emerge, my own identity needed to break down for something new to grow?

This wasn't spiritual bypassing or toxic positivity—pretending collapse was wonderful or denying its genuine pain. It was recognizing that even in dissolution, essential nature remains, and sometimes that nature can only express itself fully when previous forms have broken down.

My collapse could be seen not just as an ending but as part of a larger process that included new beginnings I couldn't yet imagine.

The Code Connection: Moving Toward Level 7 (Acceptance)

These three unlikely teachers—my neurodivergent son, a persistent weed, and a humble acorn—all conveyed aspects of the same fundamental wisdom: acceptance of reality as it is. No amount of pity-party wishing changes anything; it only blocks awareness of what is right there, right now, that holds new possibilities. This quality of acceptance corresponds directly to Level 7 in The Code's consciousness framework.

Remember that the Levels of Consciousness aren't just psychological states but distinct energy frequencies that shape how we perceive and interact with reality. Levels 1-6 (Shame through Anger) all contain some form of resistance to what is—either through collapse, denial, or fight. Level 7 (Acceptance) represents the first truly higher vibration, where resistance drops away and alignment with reality becomes possible.

Acceptance is often misunderstood as passive resignation or giving up. "This is just how things are, so I'll stop trying to change them." But true acceptance—the energy of Level 7—is something entirely different. It's seeing reality clearly, without the distortions of denial or fantasy, and responding to what actually exists rather than to what you wish existed.

Each of my unexpected teachers embodied this quality of acceptance in their own way:

Aidan accepted reality without the filtering layers that neurotypical perception often imposes. He didn't categorize experience according to conventional hierarchies of value or importance; he simply engaged with what was present, as it was. His love for the Halloween decorations wasn't contingent on their meeting certain criteria; it was a direct response to their actual presence in his experience.

The weed didn't deny the harsh reality of its growing conditions or wait for them to become ideal. It worked with what was available rather than resisting that as inadequate. Its growth wasn't fantasy or denial but precise alignment with actual possibilities.

The acorn didn't resist its current form while holding potential for something different. It fully embodied what it was in the present while containing patterns for what it might become. This wasn't a contradiction but integration—complete acceptance of current reality alongside complete alignment with emergent possibilities.

As I absorbed these teachings, I found myself naturally shifting toward Level 7 Consciousness. This didn't happen all at once or permanently—I still cycled through lower levels, especially when facing practical challenges. But increasingly, I could access this frequency of acceptance, particularly when using the Attention Compass to bring my awareness back to center.

The shift to Level 7 manifested in several practical ways:

From Resistance to Response: Instead of continually fighting against the reality of my collapsed career ("This shouldn't be happening to me"), I began to ask, "Given that this is happening, what's the most aligned response?" Aligned meaning with your true self, the one that is found when you are centered. Some call this "God" others call it "Source Energy". Either way, it is when you access your true potential and feel the presence of something pure. This wasn't giving up on improvement but addressing actual conditions rather than wishing they were different.

From Fixed to Fluid Identity: Rather than clinging to my weatherman identity and seeing its loss as catastrophic, I began to recognize that identity as just one temporary expression of deeper potential. Like the acorn that is neither more nor less itself whether in seed form or as a mature oak, my essential nature wasn't dependent on specific roles or achievements.

From Judgment to Discernment: The harsh self-judgment that had dominated my internal dialogue ("I've failed," "I'm worthless without my career") gradually softened into more accurate discernment of my situation. I could see challenges clearly without converting them into verdicts about my worth or capability. Judgement leaves no room for compassion.

From Control to Cultivation: Instead of trying to force specific outcomes through sheer will and effort, I began to approach change more like a gardener—creating favorable conditions where growth could happen naturally, according to its own timing and patterns. This didn't mean abandoning intent or direction but aligning with natural processes rather than fighting against them.

From Isolation to Connection: Perhaps most significantly, I began to experience myself not as an isolated entity struggling against hostile circumstances but as part of larger systems and patterns, connected to flows of energy and information that extended far beyond my individual story. This broader perspective didn't eliminate challenges but contextualized them within larger movements that included but weren't limited to my personal experience.

These shifts weren't the result of positive thinking or affirmations. They emerged naturally as I absorbed the wisdom of my unexpected teachers and practiced bringing attention back to center through the Attention Compass. The frequency of Level 7 Consciousness became more accessible not because I was forcing myself toward it but because I was removing the obstacles that had previously blocked my way.

This is a crucial point about consciousness evolution: higher levels aren't achieved primarily through addition (more knowledge, more techniques, more practices) but through subtraction—removing the patterns, beliefs, and perceptual filters that keep us locked in lower frequencies. The energy of Acceptance isn't something you create but something you access when the resistance patterns of lower levels are no longer dominating your awareness.

Breaking Free from Conventional Wisdom

One of the most significant aspects of these unexpected teachings was how thoroughly they contradicted conventional wisdom about success, growth, and recovery from failure. The dominant cultural narrative offers very specific guidance for someone in my position:

- "Bounce back quickly" – but the acorn knows that transformation has its own timing that can't be rushed.

- "Never show weakness" – but Aidan's complete authenticity revealed the exhausting cost of maintaining facades.

- "Only results matter" – but the weed demonstrated the value of process regardless of guaranteed outcomes.

- "No pain, no gain" – but awareness of teachers on your path is available at any point, not just when you've hit bottom and are desperate for answers.

- "You are what you achieve" – but all three teachers embodied worth independent of external accomplishment.

- "Control your destiny" – but nature's wisdom shows that participation in larger patterns often matters more than control.

- "Know your limits" – but who gets to say what is a "limit" or, instead, is a "unique gift," as my shift in perceiving Aidan showed me.

These conventional beliefs aren't just abstract ideas; they're energetic frequencies that tend to keep consciousness locked in Levels 4 and 5 (Fear and Desire). They create the conditions for perpetual striving without arrival, constant comparison without satisfaction, and achievement without fulfillment.

My unexpected teachers offered an alternative frequency—one aligned with Level 7 (Acceptance) and beyond. Their wisdom wasn't a new self-improvement strategy within the conventional framework but a fundamental shift to a different framework entirely.

This shift isn't easy in a culture saturated with messages that reinforce lower consciousness frequencies. Media (especially "social media"), advertising, education, workplace expectations—all tend to normalize Level 4 and 5 consciousness while diminishing the qualities of higher levels. Someone operating consistently from Level 7 or above might be seen as insufficiently driven, or naive about "how the world really works."

Breaking free from ordinary thinking takes more than just disagreeing with it in your mind. It takes real-life experiences that prove there are other ways of being—things you can directly feel and see, not just theories. That's what my unexpected teachers gave me—living examples of consciousness working at levels beyond the usual.

Aidan didn't argue against achievement orientation; he simply existed in a state where such orientation was irrelevant, revealing its constructed rather than inevitable nature. The weed didn't write a manifesto against waiting for ideal conditions; it simply grew in hostile circumstances, demonstrating the possibility of action without guarantees. The acorn didn't give a lecture on intrinsic versus extrinsic value; it simply embodied worth independent of outcome, showing a different basis for meaning than external validation.

As I absorbed these teachings, the grip of conventional wisdom gradually loosened. Not because I rejected it intellectually, but because I experienced alternatives directly. The question shifted from "How do I succeed according to conventional standards?" to "What forms of flourishing are possible beyond those standards?"

This didn't mean abandoning all practical concerns or responsibilities. We still needed income, healthcare, special and adjusted education for Aidan, and basic security. But these necessities could be approached from a different consciousness frequency—one that recognized their importance without making them the primary measures of worth or success.

The freedom I found wasn't about escaping challenges. It was about no longer seeing them only through the usual set of values. Each problem wasn't just an obstacle to success—it was also an invitation to grow in new ways that ordinary ways of thinking might never show.

This perspective doesn't romanticize hardship or suggest that suffering is necessary for growth. Many of the challenges I faced were genuinely painful and would never be chosen voluntarily. But it does recognize that when conventional paths are blocked, unexpected teachers often appear, offering wisdom that might otherwise remain undiscovered.

Summary of These Teaching Examples

These three unexpected teachers—Aidan, the weed, and the acorn—each prepared me for the profound stillness discovery that would follow. They weren't separate lessons but interconnected facets of the same fundamental truth I was about to encounter more directly.

Aidan demonstrated the natural state of presence that exists before the mind's divisions take hold—showing me what consciousness looks like when it isn't constantly pulled away from center by identity concerns, comparisons, past regrets, or future anxieties. His complete absorption with whatever captured his attention was a living example of the centered awareness I would soon discover.

The persistent weed revealed how growth emerges not from ideal conditions but from alignment with what is—teaching me that stillness isn't passive withdrawal but active engagement with reality from a place of acceptance rather than resistance. Its quiet persistence foreshadowed the effortless effectiveness that comes from operating at higher Consciousness Levels.

The acorn contained the pattern of everything it would become while resting in perfect stillness—embodying the paradox I was about to experience: that the most profound movement arises from immovable centeredness. Its patient containment of potential was preparing me to recognize the creative power of stillness.

Like tributaries flowing into a single river, these separate teachings were converging toward the ocean of stillness I was about to discover. Teachers open the doorway to the Flow State where the three brains align in coherent harmony.

The Dream Deepens: The Student Appears

The very night after Aidan showed me the wisdom in his response to the acorn, my dream transported me to a classroom I'd never seen before.

———◆———

Sunlight streams through tall windows, casting golden rectangles across worn wooden floors that creak beneath my feet as I enter.

The space feels both foreign and strangely familiar—like a place I'd forgotten I once knew. The room holds an eclectic collection of unexpected occupants: a young boy who seems absorbed in his own world, drawing patterns with his finger on the surface of a desk; a persistent weed growing through a crack in the floor, its tender green leaves reaching toward the light; an acorn resting on what appears to be the teacher's desk, perfect and whole in its humble potential.

And there—in the back row—sits the disheveled man. His eyes meet mine with a quiet intensity that no longer makes me want to look away.

"Where's the teacher?" I ask, scanning the room, my voice echoing slightly.

The corner of his mouth lifts in a smile that holds no mockery, only gentle knowing. "Everyone here is a teacher," he says softly. "Including you."

My shoulders stiffen, resistance rising in my chest. "I'm not qualified to teach anything anymore," I reply, the words bitter on my tongue. "My career is over. My expertise is obsolete."

"That's the weatherman talking," he says, rising from his seat. His voice carries a tenderness I hadn't heard before. "The one who thinks teaching requires credentials and a platform."

He gestures around the room, his hand moving in a slow arc that encompasses everything—the boy, the weed, the acorn. "These teachers never attended university. They haven't published papers or appeared on television. Yet their wisdom is impeccable."

As if on cue, the boy looks up, his gaze clear and direct. "The most important things can't be measured," he says—a statement both simple and profound that seems to bypass my intellect and land directly in my heart.

I think I'm beginning to understand these "teachers." I notice the weed has pushed another inch through concrete since I entered—its silent testimony to persistence and finding life in unlikely places. The acorn sits in its perfect wholeness, containing forests without effort or striving.

The disheveled man approaches me. His clothes are still worn, his hair still untamed, but he carries himself with a dignity I haven't recognized before.

"Perhaps," he says, his voice low and resonant, "true teaching isn't about having the right answers, but about being willing to learn from everything."

For the first time, I see there's a small notebook in his pocket—identical to the one I had started carrying on my walks. He has been taking notes too, learning as he goes. The revelation strikes me: He is not my failed self or my inferior self. He is the part of me that has remained curious, humble, and open while the weatherman became increasingly certain, polished, and closed.

<hr>

Again, as soon as I awoke, I could tell tears had escaped during my dream. And I sensed a strange reversal in my mind—the polished weatherman suddenly seeming less knowledgeable than the disheveled man I had once rejected.

On my walk that morning, I caught myself approaching each encounter with a new question: "What is this teaching me?" Even my deepest pain points now seemed to carry lessons I had been too afraid or too proud to receive.

Exercise: Finding Teachers in Your Everyday Life

Unexpected teachers surround us constantly, offering insights that formal education rarely provides. This exercise helps you identify and learn from these everyday sources of wisdom.

You'll need:

- A journal or note-taking device

- 10-15 minutes of uninterrupted time

- An open, curious mindset

Part 1: Teacher Inventory

Begin by reflecting on potential teachers already present in your life:

1. Non-Human Teachers

- What plants, animals, or natural objects do you regularly encounter?

- Are there elements of nature that particularly draw your attention, even if you're not sure why?

- What non-living objects or processes do you interact with that might contain wisdom? (Tools, machines, buildings, weather patterns, etc.)

2. Unexpected Human Teachers

- Who in your life sees the world very differently than you do?

- Is there someone you know who isn't conventionally educated or successful but possesses unusual wisdom?

- Are there children in your life whose perspective you typically see as "immature" rather than valuable?

- Do you know anyone who has overcome extraordinary challenges or lives with conditions others might view as limitations?

3. Challenging Situations

- What current difficulties or obstacles in your life might themselves be teachers?

- Are there recurring problems that might contain lessons you haven't yet recognized?
- What aspects of your life that seem like failures or setbacks might be viewed differently?

Make notes about 3-5 potential teachers from these categories that you'll pay special attention to in the coming week.

Part 2: Receptive Observation

For each potential teacher you've identified, commit to a period of receptive observation—a time when you'll set aside your usual assumptions and interact with them with fresh attention. For example:

- Spend 10 minutes simply observing a plant or animal without categorizing or analyzing
- Have a conversation with a child where you genuinely listen to their perspective without correction or guidance (just curiosity)
- Engage with a difficult person or situation while listening for what it might teach rather than how to fix or escape it

As you practice this receptive observation, ask yourself:

- What qualities does this teacher embody that I might benefit from developing?
- How does this teacher's perspective differ from conventional wisdom?
- What becomes visible from this viewpoint that I might otherwise miss?
- If this teacher could speak directly to my current life challenges, what might they say?

Record your observations, focusing on insights rather than analysis or judgment.

Part 3: Application Integration

For each insight you've gathered from your unexpected teachers, consider:

- How might this perspective shift my approach to a current challenge?

- What specific action or practice could help me embody this wisdom?

- What conventional assumption might I need to question or release to apply this insight?

- How would my experience change if I viewed the world more consistently from this perspective?

Choose one insight that feels most relevant or powerful and commit to a simple practice that helps you integrate it into daily life. This might be as simple as a brief reflection question you ask yourself each morning, a small shift in how you approach a routine activity, or a reminder phrase that helps you access this perspective when faced with challenges.

Part 4: Ongoing Awareness

Expanding your receptivity to unexpected teachers isn't a one-time exercise but an ongoing practice. Consider these approaches for continuing this awareness:

- Set a reminder on your phone to pause once daily and notice what unexpected teacher might be present at that moment

- Create a dedicated section in your journal for insights from non-traditional sources of wisdom

- Share this practice with a friend and check in weekly about what you're learning from unexpected teachers; or start a social media platform/page where all can contribute

- Notice when you're dismissing or devaluing potential wisdom because it doesn't come in a form you expect or respect

Remember, the point isn't to romanticize everything as profound or to abandon discernment. Not every plant, person, or situation contains wisdom relevant to your current journey. The most powerful unexpected teachers often don't announce themselves as such. Your openness to recognizing these teachers is itself a movement toward Level 7 Consciousness—the acceptance that wisdom might appear in forms we neither control nor anticipate.

Wisdom Hiding in Plain Sight

As we conclude this chapter, I'm reminded of an ancient teaching story: A spiritual seeker traveled the world searching for the greatest master. After years of quest, the seeker returned home disappointed, only to discover that the local water carrier he had passed countless times without notice was in fact the master he had been seeking all along.

This pattern repeats throughout wisdom traditions: the extraordinary concealed within the ordinary, the profound hidden in the seemingly simple, the teacher appearing not in expected forms but in what we've been conditioned to overlook or dismiss.

My unexpected teachers were present in my life long before I recognized their wisdom. What changed wasn't their presence but my capacity to perceive them differently, a capacity that emerged partly from desperation (when conventional sources of meaning had failed me) and partly from the practice of returning attention to center through the Attention Compass.

In the next chapter, we'll explore how the foundations established through the Attention Compass and unexpected teachers created the conditions for a profound discovery: the stillness at the center of all movement, where the three brains align and the Flow State naturally emerges.

What ordinary experiences might contain extraordinary insights if approached with fresh attention? The journey toward flow begins not with finding what's missing but with *seeing differently* what's already here. Train yourself to start "listening for" what is missing so you can discern vs. what's "wrong."

CHAPTER 6
The Stillness Discovery

Have you ever experienced a moment when everything seemed to stop? Not in the sense of physical movement ceasing, but where all is quiet within? Perhaps it happened during an intense physical activity, a creative pursuit, or even an ordinary moment that unexpectedly opened into something extraordinary. In that brief interval of inner silence, you might have felt a curious paradox—being simultaneously more fully present and somehow beyond yourself, more deeply engaged yet strangely untethered. Less connected to the outside world, more connected with your consciousness.

What you experienced in that moment wasn't an anomaly or a random neurological fluctuation. It was a glimpse of what lies at the center of the Attention Compass—the stillness that becomes available when the plumb bob stops swinging between identity concerns, comparative thinking, past regrets, and future anxieties. This stillness isn't emptiness or disconnection; it's the ground state of consciousness from which our most authentic and effective engagement with life emerges.

In this chapter, I'll share how I discovered this stillness amid the chaos of collapse, how it became the gateway to the Flow State, and how you can create the conditions for experiencing it in your own life—not as an occasional accident but as an increasingly accessible reality.

The Lake and the Mind: How Stillness Found Me

The discovery came not through seeking but through surrender.

After months of fruitless job searching, financial distress, and identity crises, I had a daily routine of walking through our neighborhood and the surrounding natural areas. These walks began as desperate attempts to escape being home alone and the constant reminder of failure it represented. Then they transformed into something else—a practice without purpose, movement without destination.

One autumn afternoon, my path took me to a small lake near our subdivision. Florida is dotted with these water bodies—some natural, some created by developers, all teeming with life and constantly changing with the light, weather, and seasons. I had passed this lake hundreds of times without giving it much attention. But on this day, something different happened.

I stood at the shoreline, watching the water's surface. It was one of those rare, perfect Florida days—low humidity, gentle temperature, minimal wind. The lake's surface was so still it created a mirror-perfect reflection of the sky, clouds, and surrounding vegetation. The boundary between water and air, reflection and reality, seemed to dissolve in this perfect stillness.

As I gazed at nature's mirror, something shifted in my perception. It wasn't a thought or an insight in the usual sense, but a direct recognition: my mind could be like this lake. Not empty or frozen, but perfectly still, reflecting reality without distortion. And in that stillness, something beyond my personal thoughts, feelings, and identity might become perceptible.

I sat on a bench overlooking the water and simply continued watching. Minutes passed, perhaps longer. As the lake reflected the world around it with perfect fidelity, my attention gradually settled into a similar quality of reflection—not grasping at thoughts or experiences but allowing them to appear, move, and dissolve of their own accord.

What happened next is challenging to describe in language designed primarily for ordinary states of consciousness. The boundaries that usually seemed so solid and defining—between self and other, internal and external, observer and observed—became permeable, not in the sense of dissolution but of recognized continuity. The lake wasn't just something I was seeing; in some inexplicable way, it was continuous with the seeing itself.

This wasn't a mystical hallucination or transcendent vision. If anything, it was the opposite—a direct perception of what was actually present, but without the usual filters, categories, and separations my thinking mind habitually imposed. The lake was more vividly itself, not less. The surrounding trees and sky were more distinctly present, not transformed into something else.

What changed wasn't the content of perception but its context—the awareness in which perception occurred. It didn't feel like "my" awareness but like awareness itself experiencing the moment through this particular vantage point. Not Eric-consciousness but consciousness-as-Eric, a localized expression of something that extended far beyond this single perspective.

Then I noticed something remarkable. The chronic tension I had carried for months—the tight chest, clenched jaw, constricted breathing, and knotted stomach that had become so familiar I barely noticed them anymore—began to release. Not through deliberate relaxation techniques but as a natural response to this different quality of awareness.

My breathing deepened and slowed without effort. My posture adjusted subtly, becoming more aligned and relaxed simultaneously. Even more striking was a sense of synchronization between three centers that usually operated somewhat independently—the gut (solar plexus region), the heart (chest), and the brain (head). Rather than sending conflicting signals (gut saying "danger," heart saying "connect," brain saying "analyze"), these centers seemed to harmonize into a unified field of perception and response.

This wasn't just a pleasant relaxation response. It was a fundamentally different state of organization—what I would later understand as the alignment of the three brains that creates the conditions for the Flow State. In this alignment, information wasn't processed sequentially through separate systems but seemed to register simultaneously across all centers, creating a more comprehensive and immediate understanding than any single center could generate alone.

When I finally rose from the bench and continued my walk, this shifted state persisted for some time. Colors appeared more vivid, sounds more distinct, my physical movement more coordinated. Thoughts still arose, but they no longer commanded the same automatic involvement; they moved through awareness rather than capturing it completely.

The most striking aspect of this experience wasn't its extraordinariness but its ordinariness—the recognition that this quality of perception wasn't something exotic or supernatural. This was probably the first time in my life that I experienced the natural state of consciousness. It wasn't something to achieve but something to allow by removing the habitual patterns that prevented its natural expression.

In the days that followed, I returned to the lake, hoping to recapture this experience. Sometimes similar shifts occurred; other times my mind remained caught in its usual noisy patterns despite the external conditions being nearly identical. *What made the difference?* Gradually, I began to recognize factors that facilitated or hindered this shift, learning not how to force stillness but how to create conditions where it might naturally emerge.

The Three-Brain Alignment: Understanding the Physiology of Flow

While many approaches recognize the importance of the mind-body connection, the three-brain model offers distinct advantages over simplified dualistic frameworks. Unlike models that see the body merely as housing emotions or intuition, this approach recognizes the gut and heart as sophisticated neural networks with unique information-processing capacities.

The *gut brain* specializes in boundary recognition, safety assessment, and instinctive knowing about what to approach or avoid. The *heart brain* excels at relational intelligence, qualitative discernment, and holistic pattern recognition. The *head brain* offers analytical precision, linguistic processing, and conceptual mapping.

Think about a time you walked into a room full of strangers. Maybe it was a networking event, a party, or the first day at a new job. The moment you stepped in, your gut brain started working. It gave you that instant sense of, *"Does this feel safe? Do I want to be here, or do I want to leave?"* That's your gut helping you quickly read the environment.

Next, your heart brain tuned in. Maybe you noticed someone smiling warmly at you, and your heart told you, *"This person seems open. I could probably connect with them."* The heart is where we sense meaning and relationships, so it helps us decide who and what matters most in that moment.

Finally, your head brain jumped in. It started analyzing: *"Okay, introduce yourself. Remember their name. Ask about their work."* Your head gives you the words and helps organize the whole experience into something that makes sense.

When all three work together, you walk away with not just a safe experience (gut), not just a warm connection (heart), and not just clear facts (head)—but the full picture. You can feel it, value it, and explain it. That's the power of using all three "brains" in your daily life.

FLOW

Flow emerges when all three operate in synchronized harmony—each contributing its specialized intelligence to a unified field of awareness that transcends what any single brain could generate alone. And if one brain takes over, there is no flow. That's why rules like "follow your heart," or "use your head," or even "trust your gut" fall short when singled out and not integrated with one another.

To comprehend what happened at the lake that day—and more importantly, how to access similar states intentionally rather than accidentally—we need to understand the physiology of consciousness in a way that goes beyond simplistic brain-centered models. The shift I experienced wasn't just psychological; it involved a fundamental reorganization of the body's information processing systems.

Let's dive into some modern neuroscience. It confirms what ancient wisdom traditions intuited millennia ago: humans don't have just one brain but three distinct neural networks that process information and generate our experience of reality:

The Cranial Brain (Head Center): The brain in our skull is the most familiar of the three. Containing approximately 86 billion neurons, it specializes in analytical thinking, language processing, planning, and conceptual understanding. This is the center that categorizes, names, plans, and constructs the narratives we typically identify as "me and my story."

The Cardiac Brain (Heart Center): Less well-known but equally important is the complex neural network centered around the heart. Containing approximately 40,000 neurons, this "heart brain" processes information independently from the cranial brain and sends more signals to the brain than it receives. The heart center specializes in relational intelligence, emotional processing, value recognition, and holistic perception—our sense of what matters and how things relate to each other beyond analytical categories.

The Enteric Brain (Gut Center): Perhaps most surprising to those educated in conventional models is the extensive neural network in our intestinal region—the "gut brain." With approximately 500 million neurons (more than in the spinal cord), this center processes information about both our internal state and our external environment. The gut specializes in intuitive knowing, threat detection, resource assessment, and our fundamental sense of safety and belonging in the world.

In ordinary consciousness, these three brains often operate semi-independently and sometimes at cross-purposes. The head might be planning a project while the heart feels uncertain about its value and the gut senses potential danger in proceeding. This creates the internal conflict and confusion we often experience when making decisions or responding to challenges.

What I experienced at the lake was a synchronization of these three centers—a state where they weren't working separately or hierarchically (with the head typically dominating) but in coordinated harmony. This synchronization creates a coherent field that allows information to flow more efficiently throughout the entire system rather than being processed in isolated compartments.

The HeartMath Institute and other research organizations have documented the physiological markers of this state, including:

Heart Rate Variability Coherence: The heart doesn't actually beat at a constant rhythm but varies its timing in complex patterns. In states of stress, fear, or fragmented attention, these patterns become chaotic and disordered. In states of alignment, they become extraordinarily coherent—showing sine wave-like patterns that indicate optimal communication between heart and brain.

Neural Synchronization: EEG measurements show that in Flow States, different regions of the brain synchronize their activity in ways that rarely occur during ordinary consciousness.

Particularly significant is the coordination between the prefrontal cortex (executive function) and limbic system (emotional processing), areas that often conflict in everyday states.

Immune System Enhancement: During states of three-brain alignment, the immune system shows measurable improvements in function, with increased production of immunoglobulin A and other markers of enhanced immunity. This suggests that alignment isn't just subjectively pleasant but biologically regenerative.

Hormonal Rebalancing: The stress hormones cortisol and adrenaline decrease during alignment states, while beneficial hormones like DHEA and oxytocin increase. This shift creates conditions for healing, creativity, and optimal function rather than the defensive mobilization characteristic of fragmented consciousness.

Understanding these physiological dimensions helps us recognize that the Flow State isn't just a psychological curiosity or spiritual concept but a distinct state of biological organization—one that represents not an exceptional condition but optimal human functioning. We evolved to operate from this coherent state; our fragmented condition is the deviation, not the other way around.

Here's a simple summary: When we're stressed or distracted, our bodies show it. The heart's rhythm gets off kilter, the brain regions fight each other, and stress hormones flood our system. But when we enter a state of alignment—Flow—the opposite happens.

The heart beats in smooth, wave-like patterns, showing strong communication with the brain. The brain itself works in sync, with thinking and emotional centers cooperating instead of clashing. The immune system even gets stronger, producing more of the good cells that keep us healthy. And the hormones shift—stress chemicals go down while healing and feel-good chemicals go up.

This shows that Flow isn't just about feeling good—it's how our bodies were designed to work at their best. In other words, Flow isn't the exception; it's the natural state we were meant for.

The question then becomes how to remove whatever is blocking Flow. Imagine a river that flows through a valley, nourishing the farmland and providing water and fish to those who rely on it. It's easy to see that a log jam would need to be handled quickly in order to restore the river's flow. We wouldn't focus on the water itself, just on finding and resolving the flow-stopping issue.

Just as the lake's surface naturally becomes still when the wind subsides, our three brains naturally synchronize when the constant disturbance of fragmented attention diminishes.

This understanding transformed my approach to accessing the Flow State. Instead of striving to enter some extraordinary condition through force of will, I began focusing on identifying and reducing the factors that blocked or disturbed my natural coherence. The Attention Compass became crucial in this process—a tool not for achieving alignment but for recognizing and releasing the habitual patterns that prevented it.

Three-Brain Integration Diagram

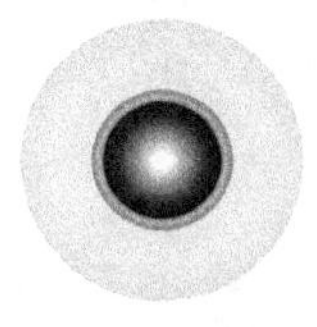

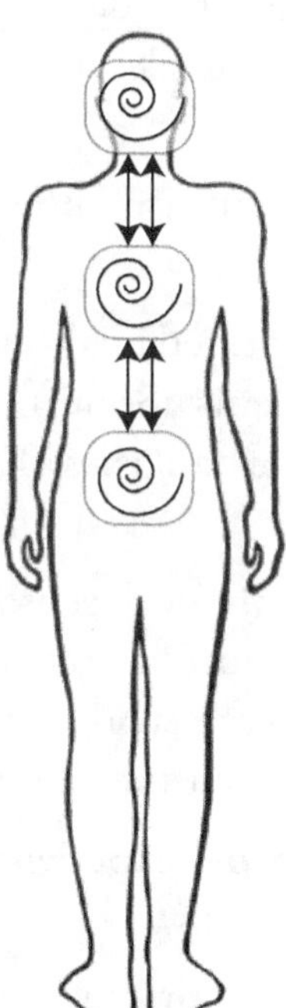

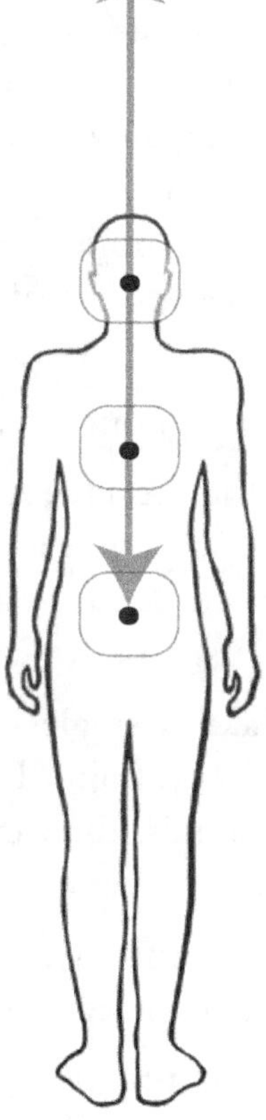

Universal Quantum Mind:
Feild of All Possibilities

HEAD: Cranial Brain System
86 Billion Neurons

HEART: Cardiac Nervous System
40,000 Neurons

GUT: Enteric Nervous System
500 Million Neurons

The Gateway to Stillness: Practical Pathways to the Flow State

While my initial experience of stillness came spontaneously at the lake, subsequent exploration revealed certain conditions and practices that made this state more accessible. These aren't formulaic techniques that guarantee results but invitations that create favorable conditions for natural coherence to emerge.

1. The Attention Reset

The most fundamental practice involves using the Attention Compass to recognize when attention has been captured by one of the four directions (identity, comparison, past, future) and gently returning it to center. This isn't about forcing attention to remain fixed in one place but developing the capacity to notice drift and restore center without struggle.

A simple version of this practice involves:

- Setting an intention to notice the movement of attention throughout the day.

- When you recognize that attention has been captured by thoughts of who you are (North), comparative judgments (South), past regrets or nostalgia (West), or future worries or fantasies (East), pause briefly.

- Take a single conscious breath, feeling the physical sensation of breathing. Breathe in through the nose, pause a couple of seconds, then exhale through the mouth. (Breath work experts give the reminder "smell the roses" then "blow out the candles."

- Gently bring attention back to your present sensory experience— what you can see, hear, feel, taste, or smell right now.

- Your attention is reset. Continue with whatever activity you were engaged in, but from this state of presence.

The key here isn't perfection but frequency. Each time you notice attention has drifted and bring it back to center, you strengthen the neural pathways that support this movement. Over time, the return to center becomes more natural and immediate, requiring less conscious effort.

During my darkest periods, I practiced this reset dozens of times every day. Walking through the neighborhood, I would notice my mind caught in anxious thoughts and fears about money (East). Shifting my focus to how the ground felt under my feet with each step helped me to gently bring my attention back to center. Sitting with Aidan, I would notice the prickly thoughts of comparison with other parents who hadn't experienced financial collapse (South). Then I focused on his hands, now almost the size of mine, but more graceful and less calloused. This returned my attention to the actual interaction happening in that moment.

Every time you come back to center, it gives your three brains a chance to sync up. At first, that might only last a few seconds. But each little moment breaks the pattern of being fragmented and makes it easier to stay aligned for longer stretches over time.

2. Nature Immersion

Almost universally, people report that natural environments facilitate access to stillness and the Flow State more readily than artificial settings. This isn't merely subjective preference; nature provides specific conditions that support three-brain alignment:

Fractal Patterns: Natural environments are filled with fractal patterns— self-similar shapes that repeat at different scales, from the veins of a leaf to the branching of trees to the structure of forest canopies. These patterns engage our attention in a way that is simultaneously focused and relaxed—what researchers call "soft fascination." Unlike the "hard fascination" of digital screens that captures attention forcefully, nature's patterns invite attention without demanding it.

Sensory Harmony: Natural settings provide multi-sensory input that tends toward harmony rather than the conflicting sensory experiences of modern environments. The sound of wind matches the visual movement of leaves; the scent of soil corresponds to its appearance. This sensory coherence supports neural coherence in the perceiver.

Temporal Alignment: Nature operates at rhythms and tempos that more closely match our biological design—the cycles of day and night, the progressions of seasons, the pulse of waves. Modern environments often impose artificial tempos that conflict with our internal rhythms, creating a subtle but persistent form of stress that hinders three-brain alignment.

During my recovery journey, daily time in natural settings became essential. These weren't dramatic wilderness expeditions but simple immersions in whatever nature was accessible—the local park, the lake, even the oak trees lining our subdivision streets. The key was quality of engagement rather than specific settings; even a small patch of sky or a single plant could serve as a gateway when approached with receptive attention.

If your circumstances limit access to natural environments, even brief exposure can support alignment. Research shows that looking at photographs of nature, listening to natural sounds, or keeping plants in your workspace can produce measurable shifts toward coherence. The body recognizes and responds to these elements even in limited or simulated forms.

3. Movement Integration

The body isn't just a vehicle for consciousness but an integral part of it. Physical movement, when engaged with awareness, can significantly facilitate three-brain alignment and access to the Flow State.

Different types of movement support alignment in different ways:

Rhythmic Movement: Walking, swimming, cycling, rowing, and similar activities with consistent rhythm can entrain brain waves into more coherent patterns. The key is engaging in the movement with attention to its sensory qualities rather than using it as background for continued mental chatter.

Spiral and Cross-lateral Movement: Movements that cross the body's midline or follow spiral patterns help integrate the brain's hemispheres and coordinate communication between different neural centers. Simple practices like drawing figure eights with your hands, walking in spiral patterns, or intentional cross-crawl movements can reset neural patterns that maintain fragmentation.

Micro-movements: Even subtle adjustments of posture, breathing, and muscle tension can shift the body's energetic state toward greater coherence. Practices that bring awareness to these micro-movements—like certain forms of yoga, qi gong, tai chi, or somatic experiencing techniques—can interrupt habitual patterns of tension that block alignment.

During my walks, I began experimenting with these movement dimensions. Sometimes I would walk in spiral patterns around trees. Other times I would focus completely on the cross-lateral coordination of arms and legs during normal walking. These weren't separate "exercises" but integrated aspects of everyday movement approached with different qualities of attention.

The body itself often knows what movement would best support alignment in a given moment. Learning to listen to these subtle signals—an impulse to stretch in a particular way, an inclination to move at a certain tempo—becomes part of developing sensitivity to the conditions that facilitate the Flow State.

The Flow State is similar to what athletes call being "in the zone." Let's look at what a couple of best-in-the-world athletes have said about this:

- **Roger Federer (tennis):** In a 2015 interview, Federer described a period of extreme success between 2005 and 2007, saying, "I was in a zone, and it is really important to be there for the longest possible time."

- **Ayrton Senna (Formula 1 racing):** "I felt as though I was driving in a tunnel. I had reached such a high level of concentration that it was as if the car and I had become one." This reflects the common experience among athletes of merging with the activity itself.

4. Creative Engagement

Certain forms of creative activity naturally tend to induce the Flow State by engaging all three brains simultaneously. Artists, musicians, writers, and craftspeople have long recognized that their creative practice can access states of consciousness different from ordinary awareness.

What makes creative engagement especially effective for accessing stillness and flow?

Unified Attention: Creative activities often require complete attention that naturally integrates multiple faculties—conceptual understanding, emotional resonance, and embodied skill. When painting, for instance, you must simultaneously conceive the image (head), feel its emotional quality (heart), and execute precise physical movements (gut).

Process Orientation: Although creative work often has goals, the actual experience typically shifts attention from outcome to process—the brush stroke happening now, the musical phrase being played at this moment, the sentence currently forming. This naturally brings attention to the present rather than future results.

Boundary Dissolution: During creative flow, the typical boundary between creator and created becomes permeable. Musicians report feeling that the music is playing them; writers describe words arriving from beyond their conscious composition. This shift in the sense of agency parallels the boundary relaxation characteristic of three-brain alignment.

I returned to creative practices I had abandoned during my career-focused years—drawing, writing, and simple carpentry alongside Aidan. These weren't pursued professionally or even with particular skill, but as gateways to a different quality of engagement with experience. The process, not the product, was the point.

Have you ever seen "zen garden" sand art? Perhaps the most obvious illustration of "it's the process, not the product." To bring a sense of serenity and quiet, you use a rake or your hands to make patterns in sand. Then, it's gone, smoothed over by the artist or the weather. The ever-changing nature of the sand serves as a reminder of the impermanence of all things in the universe. The practice of meditating and slowly drawing patterns in sand serves the purpose of experiencing harmony and flow.

You needn't identify as an artist to use creative engagement as a pathway to stillness and flow. Simple activities like arranging flowers, preparing food with full attention, or even rearranging furniture can engage the same integrative attention that supports three-brain alignment.

5. Sound and Vibration

Perhaps the most direct external support for accessing stillness comes through specific forms of sound and vibration that naturally entrain the brain and body toward coherence.

Binaural Beats: When slightly different frequencies are presented to each ear, the brain produces a third frequency—the difference between the two. Certain frequency differences can guide brainwaves toward patterns associated with deep meditation and flow states.

Harmonic Resonance: Sounds based on natural harmonic ratios— found in certain forms of classical music, indigenous singing traditions, and purposefully designed sound healing—can synchronize neural oscillations across different brain regions, supporting integration.

Natural Sound Environments: The complex yet ordered acoustic patterns of natural settings—flowing water, wind in trees, bird songs— provide optimal stimulation that engages attention without overwhelming or fragmenting it.

During particularly challenging periods, I would listen to specifically designed harmonic compositions before sleep and upon waking—times when the brain is naturally more receptive to entrainment. I also would have the large TV in our living room streaming tones, or natural sounds instead of programmed stations; the hum in the background is very pleasant.

These sound approaches are especially valuable when other pathways are temporarily inaccessible due to circumstances. Physical limitations, confined environments, or high-stress situations may restrict options like nature immersion or movement integration, but sound remains available as a gateway to stillness in almost any setting.

6. The Threshold State

One of the most surprising discoveries in my exploration of stillness and flow was the value of what sleep researchers call "hypnagogic" and "hypnopompic" states—the transitional states of consciousnesses between waking and sleeping. These threshold states naturally tend toward different neural organization than either full wakefulness or deep sleep, often displaying characteristics of three-brain alignment.

The periods just before falling asleep and just after waking—when consciousness is neither fully focused in external awareness nor completely withdrawn into sleep—offer uniquely favorable conditions for experiencing stillness and accessing the Flow State. The mind's habitual patterns naturally relax during these transitions, creating openings for different qualities of awareness to emerge.

Let's look at a few ways to practice presence during transition states:

Conscious Descent: As you're falling asleep, maintain a thread of witnessing awareness without engaging in thinking or trying to control the process. Simply observe the shifting qualities of consciousness as you descend toward sleep, maintaining presence without interference.

Extended Emergence: Upon waking, instead of immediately engaging with thoughts about the day ahead, remain in the liminal space between sleep and full wakefulness. Without falling back asleep, explore the quality of awareness that exists before the mind's habitual patterns fully activate.

Deliberate Returns: Throughout the day, briefly recreate elements of these threshold states through micro-practices—a 30-second "conscious descent" while sitting at your desk, a momentary "extended emergence" when transitioning between activities. These brief returns can reset attention and provide windows for three-brain alignment.

During my recovery journey, I began treating these threshold periods as formal practices rather than merely transitions to be passed through. I would set an intention before sleep to maintain awareness into the descent, and I placed a journal by my bed to record insights that emerged during the extended emergence upon waking.

What makes these threshold states so valuable is that they represent natural relaxations of our usual cognitive constraints. The mind's control mechanisms naturally loosen during these transitions, allowing access to aspects of consciousness that typically remain below the threshold of awareness during ordinary waking states.

The Code Connection: Entering Level 8 (Peace)

The practices and conditions described above gradually facilitated more frequent and extended experiences of stillness and flow. As these states became more familiar, I recognized that they corresponded to Level 8 (Peace) in The Code's consciousness framework—a distinct vibration or frequency beyond even the acceptance of Level 7.

Remember that each level of consciousness isn't just a psychological state but a specific energy frequency that shapes how we perceive and interact with reality. Level 8 (Peace) represents a quantum shift beyond the levels most people typically experience, with several distinctive characteristics:

Non-Identification with Thought: At Level 8, thoughts still arise, but awareness no longer automatically identifies with them. They're experienced as events appearing in consciousness rather than defining consciousness itself. This creates a profound shift in the sense of identity—from being the thinking entity to being the awareness in which thinking occurs.

Cessation of Seeking: The constant sense that something is missing, that some future achievement or acquisition will complete you, naturally dissolves at Level 8. This isn't resignation but the recognition that what you've been seeking through external pursuits is actually the peace that emerges when seeking itself ceases.

Synchronistic Flow: At Level 8, the sharp boundary between "inner" and "outer" softens, creating conditions where internal states and external events display remarkable correspondence. What you genuinely need tends to appear when needed; obstacles that would have seemed insurmountable from lower levels resolve through unexpected means or reveal themselves as unnecessary detours.

Effortless Effectiveness: Actions taken from Level 8 consciousness typically produce better results with less strain than the striving characteristic of lower levels. This isn't magic but the natural outcome of perception unclouded by the distortions of fear, desire, and self-preoccupation. Solutions become visible that simply couldn't be perceived from more fragmented states.

Stable Presence Amid Change: Perhaps the most distinctive quality of Level 8 is the capacity to remain centered through circumstances that would trigger reactivity at lower levels. This isn't detachment or indifference but engagement from a stability that isn't dependent on external conditions remaining certain ways.

My experiences at the lake and in subsequent moments of stillness displayed these characteristics to varying degrees. They weren't permanent achievements but windows into a level of consciousness that became increasingly accessible as I practiced the conditions that supported three-brain alignment.

It's important to understand that Level 8 isn't an exalted or superior state reserved for gurus and spiritual elites. It represents human consciousness functioning as designed, without the interference patterns created by trauma, conditioning, and identification with limited self-concepts. In this sense, accessing Level 8 isn't about becoming something other than who we are but about expressing our authentic humanity more fully.

The significance of Level 8 in the journey toward the Flow State is that it creates the stable foundation from which the practice of "feeling it in" (which we'll explore in the next chapter) becomes not just possible but natural. Without the stillness and coherence of Level 8, attempts to manifest through feeling typically remain caught in the limitations and distortions of Levels 4 and 5 (Fear and Desire), producing mixed results at best.

Stillness as Gateway to Universal Mind

As experiences of stillness and three-brain alignment became more frequent, I began to recognize something remarkable: this state wasn't just a different way of experiencing my individual consciousness but an access point to what can only be described as a field of intelligence beyond personal awareness.

In moments of complete stillness—when identity concerns, comparative thinking, past regrets, and future anxieties had all temporarily subsided—information, insights, and understanding would emerge that didn't seem to originate from my personal knowledge or experience. Solutions to problems I'd been struggling with would appear fully formed. Creative ideas would manifest with a sense of reception rather than generation. Precisely what was needed in specific situations would become clear without figuring it out.

This phenomenon has been described across cultures and traditions using various terms—Universal Mind, Collective Unconscious, Akashic Field, Divine Intelligence, and many others. The particular label matters less than recognizing the experience itself: when personal consciousness becomes still enough, it apparently can function as a receiver for information from a larger field of intelligence that transcends individual limitations.

Modern understanding of quantum physics and information theory offers intriguing parallels to this ancient recognition. The universe itself appears to function not as a collection of separate objects interacting mechanically but as an integrated information field where everything is connected to everything else through non-local correlations. Our individual consciousness may not be so much a generator of awareness as a localized expression of a field of awareness that extends beyond personal boundaries.

The practical implication is profound: many of our most intractable problems remain unsolved not because solutions don't exist but because the fragmented consciousness from which we're attempting to solve them cannot access the level of intelligence where solutions are already present. It's like trying to understand a three-dimensional object while insisting on perceiving only in two dimensions where there is no concept of depth of field (3D).

I experienced this dimension of stillness most powerfully during a period when our financial situation had become desperate. After months of fruitless searching for employment in my field, I had exhausted all conventional approaches. After one meditation one day, after a particularly complete experience of stillness, a clear knowing emerged:

I could take my wife's nonprofit (https://hearts-hands-hope.org/) and create a solution to the problem of food insecurity. Rather than just provide food to those who are hungry, provide a vehicle to help them find their own way to financial stability and food security. It became later known as The 3 Phase System.

This guidance made no sense. I had no background in nonprofit management and certainly no financial resources to launch such a venture. Yet the knowing came with a certainty that bypassed all these rational objections. We lived it after all.

Within months, this organization was not only serving families in need but had attracted funding, partnerships, and opportunities that resolved our own financial crisis in ways I could never have planned or predicted from my limited personal perspective. So far, we have helped more than 300 families become food-secure households and continue to help others to reach the same. We are helping others out of the situation we once found ourselves in, through this work.

This isn't a story about magical manifestation or the universe rewarding virtue. It's an example of what becomes possible when individual consciousness aligns sufficiently to access information and possibilities from a larger field of intelligence. The nonprofit idea emerged not from my personal brilliance or willful determination, but from allowing an intelligence beyond my individual limitations to guide action through the stillness of three-brain alignment.

The same kind of breakthroughs show up in science, art, and business. It's not something supernatural—it happens when people enter a clearer state of mind. In that state, the usual limits of scattered thinking fade, and the brain works in a more connected way. This gives access to a wider field of ideas and possibilities, which is why people often "out of the blue" come up with discoveries, creative works, or fresh solutions they couldn't see before.

The stillness discovered through three-brain alignment may create conditions for quantum processes at the cellular level—processes that renowned physicist Sir Roger Penrose and anesthesiologist Stuart Hameroff propose as the basis for consciousness itself. Their Orchestrated Objective Reduction (Orch OR) theory suggests that consciousness emerges from quantum computations in microtubules— lattice-like structures within neurons.

When the mind is agitated and fragmented, quantum coherence cannot be maintained due to what physicists call *decoherence*. But in states of deep stillness, the conditions for quantum coherence improve dramatically. Research has detected quantum vibrations in brain microtubules that could support this theory, suggesting that the stillness practices described in this book might literally be creating the conditions for quantum coherence in the brain. This could explain why insights and solutions often appear spontaneously during moments of stillness—we're accessing information processing at the quantum level, beyond conventional neural computation.

The stillness at the center of the Attention Compass may enable our consciousness to operate at the fundamental quantum level, where Penrose and Hameroff propose that consciousness interfaces with the basic structure of the universe itself.

Using the Attention Compass is about expressing human potential more fully by accessing the resources of the larger system in which we are a part.

The Dream Deepens: Reflections at the Lake

The night following my experience at the lake, my dream transported me back to that same shoreline.

The water's surface is perfectly calm, creating a mirror that reflects the sky so precisely it's difficult to discern where water ends and air begins.

I am standing at the edge, gazing down at the familiar weatherman atop the water. He's neatly dressed, hair perfectly styled, the image I have cultivated so carefully for so many years. I see ripples forming, distorting my image, though I haven't moved or touched the water. My reflection gradually shifts, features rearranging, until—I see the disheveled man.

Unlike previous encounters, I feel no shock or disgust—only a quiet curiosity that feels both deeply personal and somehow universal, as if witnessing something that belongs not just to my own journey.

I kneel at the water's edge to look more closely, drawn by a magnetic pull I couldn't have resisted even if I'd wanted to.

"The stillness doesn't remove me," the reflection says, his voice carrying as clearly as if we were sitting side by side. "It reveals me."

"Who are you, really?" I ask, the question emerging from somewhere deeper than thought. "Who are you…beyond the appearance?"

"Come closer," he says, his eyes holding a compassion I had never shown myself. "Be still enough to see."

I lean forward until my face nearly touches the water's surface. As I grow still, the boundary between observer and reflection begins to dissolve.

At first, I saw them distinctly—the weatherman's composed features with their practiced confidence flickering alongside the disheveled stranger's hollow, searching eyes. But as my breathing deepens and my gaze softens, their separate forms begin to shimmer and blend, like images superimposed on glass. The weatherman's strong jawline merges with the stranger's trembling mouth, then separates again. The stranger's unkempt hair flows into the weatherman's carefully styled appearance, creating a face that is somehow both and neither.

The colors are not sharp or defined—more like watercolors bleeding into each other. Warm golden tones from the weatherman's polished exterior mix with the cooler, deeper hues of the stranger's raw authenticity. Sometimes one face dominates, sometimes the other, but increasingly they exist as a single, fluid form that contains infinite facets.

But as my attention settles even deeper, something else emerges from beneath these shifting forms—not another face, but a quality of awareness itself. It's like looking through clear water that simultaneously contains the reflected sky above and reveals the depth below, without being limited to either. In this luminous presence, both the weatherman and the disheveled stranger appear as temporary expressions of something vast and unchanging.

I sense that I am neither the weatherman nor the disheveled stranger, but the still awareness in which both appear—the witnessing presence.

"This is what you find in stillness," I hear the voice say, no longer seeming to come from the reflection but from everywhere and nowhere at once. "Not an improved self, but the self beyond improvement or degradation."

The lake is quiet and still. I sit close to the dark water's edge, experiencing a peace that requires no cause or condition—a peace that came from nowhere but the cessation of seeking it elsewhere. It is as if the lake itself has taught me what no words could convey: that beneath all movement of thought and emotion lies a stillness that has never been disturbed, a wholeness that has never been broken.

◆

I carried that stillness with me throughout the day. At my son's school, when I was asked to tell the class what I did, I found myself hesitating before the habitual responses, sensing something more fundamental than any role I had ever played, any achievement I had ever claimed, any failure I had ever feared. Now my answer: "I am Aidan's dad."

Exercise: Creating Conditions for Entering the Flow State

The Flow State can't be conjured up like a genie, although that would be nice. It has no leash to grip and tug toward you, but it has its own clear ideas about what feels irresistibly inviting. You can create attractive conditions that make it more likely to show up. This exercise integrates multiple pathways to stillness and three-brain alignment, adapting to your unique circumstances and preferences.

You'll need:

- 20-30 minutes of uninterrupted time

- A comfortable place to sit or lie down

- Optional: a journal or recording device for capturing feelings and insights

Part 1: Environment Preparation (5 minutes)

Begin by creating conditions that support stillness:

1. Reduce Sensory Overload:

    - Minimize unnecessary noise (or use noise-canceling headphones)

163

- Adjust lighting to a comfortable level (natural light is ideal when available)

- Ensure comfortable temperature and air quality

- Silence electronic notifications and remove visible devices when possible

2. Incorporate Natural Elements:

   - If outdoors, find a space with natural features (trees, water, open sky)

   - If indoors, position yourself near plants, natural materials, or a window with a natural view

   - If neither is available, have an image of a natural setting nearby or in your mind's eye

3. Establish Body Support:

   - Find a position that allows your body to be both relaxed and alert

   - Ensure your spine can maintain its natural curves without strain

   - Allow your hands to rest in a position that feels open rather than closed or tense

Part 2: Three-Brain Harmony Practice (10-15 minutes)

This practice intentionally engages all three brain centers to facilitate their alignment:

1. Begin with Gut Centering (3-5 minutes):

   - Place one hand on your lower abdomen, just below the navel

   - Bring attention to sensations in this region—temperature, movement, tension/relaxation

   - Breathe slowly and deeply, allowing your breath to move your hand

   - With each exhale, invite unnecessary tension in this area to release

- Notice any intuitive knowing that emerges from this center—not as thoughts but as direct recognition

2. Move to Heart Centering (3-5 minutes):

   - Shift your hand to rest over your heart center in the middle of your chest

   - Feel the physical sensations in this region—your heartbeat, warmth, expansion/contraction

   - Allow your breath to flow into this area as if breathing directly through the heart

   - Invite a quality of appreciation or gratitude without forcing specific content

   - Notice the emotional intelligence of this center—how it knows through feeling rather than analysis

3. Include Head Centering (3-5 minutes):

   - Rest your attention in the space between and slightly behind your eyes

   - Notice sensations of activity, pressure, or energy in this region

   - Allow your breath to seem as if it's flowing in and out through this center

   - Rather than engaging in active thinking, invite a quality of clear seeing or witnessing

   - Notice how this center can observe without immediately analyzing or judging

4. Integrate All Three Centers (3-5 minutes):

   - Expand awareness to include all three centers simultaneously

   - Imagine or feel a current of energy or information flowing between them

   - Notice if one center feels dominant and gently invite balance without forcing

   - Allow your breath to move through all three centers as if they were connected by a single channel

- Rest in the integrated field created by this simultaneous awareness

Part 3: Attention Reset (5 minutes)

This final phase reinforces the capacity to notice when attention drifts and return it to center:

1. Maintain the integrated awareness from the previous practice while allowing your attention to rest on a single focus—your breath, a natural object, or simply the space around you.

2. When you notice attention has been captured by:

   - Thoughts about yourself or your identity (North)

   - Comparative thinking about others or yourself (South)

   - Memories or regrets about the past (West)

   - Plans or worries about the future (East)

3. Simply notice this movement without judgment or frustration.

4. Gently return attention to your chosen focus and the integrated field of the three centers.

5. Continue this process of noticing drift and returning to center for the remainder of the practice.

Part 4: Integration and Transition (3-5 minutes)

Complete the formal practice with these steps:

1. Take a few moments to notice the quality of awareness present now. Is it different than when you began?

2. Without analyzing or judgment, simply register any shifts in your state—energy level, emotional tone, clarity, physical sensation.

3. If insights or guidance emerged during the practice, briefly note them (mentally or in writing) without elaborating or planning.

4. Set an intention to maintain a thread of this integrated awareness as you return to regular activities.

5. Transition mindfully by moving slowly at first, maintaining connection with the quality of consciousness you've accessed.

Daily Access Practice:

To build on this formal practice and make the Flow State more accessible in daily life:

1. **Micro-Practices:** Several times throughout your day, take 30-60 seconds to quickly center attention using abbreviated versions of the three-brain harmony practice. These brief resets can interrupt fragmentation before it gains momentum.

2. **Transition Awareness:** Use natural transitions in your day—arriving at a new location, beginning a new task, interacting with different people—as reminders to reset attention and check for three-brain alignment.

3. **Environmental Anchors:** Place objects in your regular environment that remind you of stillness and flow—perhaps a stone from the place where you first experienced this state, an image that evokes the quality of awareness, or a symbol meaningful to you.

4. **Physical Cues:** Develop a simple physical gesture—touching thumb to forefinger, placing a hand over your heart, or taking a specific breath pattern—that you use only when intentionally accessing stillness. With practice, the gesture itself can help trigger the associated state.

5. **Challenge Integration:** When facing specific challenges, pause briefly to access three-brain alignment before responding. This doesn't delay effective action but ensures it emerges from integrated intelligence rather than fragmented reaction.

Remember that accessing the Flow State isn't about perfecting a technique but about removing the obstacles to what naturally emerges when fragmentation subsides. Each return to stillness strengthens the neural pathways that support this access, making the state increasingly available even amid life's complexities and challenges.

Stillness in Motion: Beyond the Formal Practice

As we wrap up this chapter, it's important to recognize that stillness isn't limited to formal meditation or special practices. The ultimate goal isn't to access the Flow State only during dedicated sessions but to bring its qualities into active engagement with life's full spectrum.

Stillness, properly understood, isn't the absence of movement but movement without resistance or friction. Like the hub of a wheel that remains relatively still even as the wheel turns rapidly, the center of awareness can maintain stillness even as life moves at full speed around it.

I discovered this dimension of "stillness in motion" unexpectedly during a particularly challenging morning with Aidan. He was having difficulty transitioning from home to school, a common challenge for children with his neurological pattern. Normally, such situations would trigger my problem-solving mind, emotional reactivity, or both, creating a state of internal fragmentation that only intensified the external challenge.

But on this morning, something different happened. In the midst of what appeared outwardly as chaos, I spontaneously accessed the quality of stillness I had been practicing at the lake. Without removing myself from the situation or disengaging emotionally, I found myself responding from three-brain alignment rather than fragmented reaction.

Externally, my actions might have looked similar to previous responses, but the internal quality from which they emerged was entirely different. Rather than forcing a solution from fragmented thinking, I was allowing a response to arise from integrated awareness. The distinction is subtle but profound—like the difference between pushing against the current of a river and skillfully navigating with it.

In this stillness-in-motion, I could simultaneously feel Aidan's distress, recognize the practical need to get to school, and maintain a broader perspective that neither identified completely with the challenge nor dissociated from it. Response flowed naturally from this integrated perception rather than being constructed by analytical problem-solving or driven by emotional reactivity.

The result wasn't a miraculous resolution where all difficulty magically disappeared. Aidan still struggled with the transition. We still experienced delay and frustration. But the quality of our shared experience transformed. Instead of two people caught in escalating stress, we became companions navigating a challenging moment together, with more spaciousness around the difficulty.

This wasn't an isolated incident. As I continued to practice the conditions that support stillness, I found this quality increasingly available in all kinds of situations—professional interactions, creative projects, practical problem-solving, even mundane activities like driving or household chores. The Flow State wasn't limited to special conditions but could infuse ordinary life when the habits of fragmentation were sufficiently interrupted.

This integration of stillness and action represents the maturation of the Flow State beyond momentary experiences into a more stable capacity. It doesn't mean permanent residence in higher consciousness—we all continue to cycle through various levels depending on circumstances and internal conditions. But it does mean that the doorway to stillness becomes more recognizable and accessible, even amid life's inevitable complexities and challenges.

The three-brain alignment that characterizes the Flow State isn't meant to be an exclusive experience reserved for perfect conditions but an increasingly available resource for navigating the full spectrum of human experience. Stillness doesn't reject or avoid life's intensity but engages it from a different quality of presence—one that participates fully without becoming completely identified with or consumed by passing circumstances.

In the next chapter, we'll explore how this stillness creates the foundation for the transformative practice of "feeling it in"—living FROM your desires rather than FOR them. This distinction is crucial for understanding how *your* consciousness shapes *your* reality, and it depends entirely on the quality of stillness we've explored here.

"Act as if what you do makes a difference. It does."—William James

CHAPTER 7

Feeling It In

Have you ever felt the difference between just wanting something, and feeling like it's already yours? Between chasing after a goal, and living as if you've already reached it? Between working hard to get somewhere, and acting like you're already there?

For example, think about an athlete before a big game. One player might keep thinking, *"I hope we win."* Another player steps onto the field already acting and feeling like a winner. That second mindset often brings out more confidence, energy, and focus—because they're living from the goal instead of only chasing it.

This distinction isn't mere semantics—it's the fundamental difference between conventional manifestation approaches that often produce mixed results and the transformative practice I call "feeling it in." This practice not only enhances your capacity to create desired experiences, but it also revolutionizes your understanding of how reality itself emerges from consciousness.

The stillness we explored in the previous chapter isn't just a pleasant state of calm or a respite from stress—it's the foundation for perhaps the most powerful creative capacity humans possess: the ability to generate reality through the feeling tone of consciousness itself. When you access the Flow State through three-brain alignment, you create the precise conditions where "feeling it in" becomes not just possible but natural.

In this chapter, I'll share what I discovered about this practice during my darkest times of despair, how it differs from conventional visualization or affirmation techniques, and how you can begin applying it in your own life—not as a metaphysical belief system but as a practical approach to engaging with the creative nature of consciousness.

Living FROM Your Desires, Not FOR Them

There's a crucial distinction that transforms how we approach manifestation and creation: the difference between living FOR your desires and living FROM them.

When living FOR your desires, you're in a state of seeking, striving, and working toward something you perceive as absent from your current reality. This stance creates an energetic frequency of lack—a vibration that says, "I don't have this yet, but I'm trying to get it." The emotional signature of this frequency typically includes elements of yearning, effort, and subtle frustration with current conditions. You have a chronic sense that something is missing, wrong, or both.

In contrast, when living FROM your desires, you embody the feeling state that would be yours if the desire were already fulfilled. Rather than projecting fulfillment into a future that perpetually recedes as you approach it, you access the emotional essence of that fulfillment now, regardless of external circumstances. The energetic frequency of this stance is of *completion* rather than seeking, and *presence* rather than absence.

Despite applying for numerous jobs, networking relentlessly, and trying every conventional approach to income generation, our situation continued to deteriorate. Each effort came from a consciousness of lack and fear, creating a persistent feeling tone of desperation that seemed to repel rather than attract opportunities.

One evening, after a particularly powerful experience of stillness, I found myself spontaneously accessing a feeling I hadn't experienced in months—the sense of financial ease and security I'd known during my successful career. This wasn't deliberate visualization or forced positive thinking; it emerged naturally from the stillness as an authentic feeling state.

I didn't want to look a gift horse in the mouth, so to speak, but I was perplexed about this unexpected occurrence. What made this experience different from conventional positive thinking was that I wasn't imagining a better future or trying to convince myself that "everything will be fine." I was experiencing the actual feeling state of security and sufficiency in the present moment, despite external circumstances that contradicted it. Not as denial or fantasy, but as a direct recognition that the feeling of abundance is not dependent on external conditions.

In that moment, I understood experientially what I had previously known only intellectually: consciousness doesn't primarily respond to external reality; it generates the experience of reality through its own feeling tone. The universe doesn't deliver what we want or think about—it reflects back the energetic frequency we embody through feeling. It mirrors our inner feelings.

"Feeling It In" Comparison Chart

What to recognize when living From your dreams, and not For them

	Living FOR Desires	Living FROM Desires
Emotional State	Yearning, Lack	Fulfillment/Presence
Physiological Signature	Contracted Tense	Expanded/Relaxed
Action Quality	Effortful Straining	Effortless/Flowing
Manifestation Patterns	Inconsistent Mixed Results	Coherent/Aligned
Time Orientation	Future-Focused	Present/Centered
Consciousness Levels	Levels 4 & 5 (Fear/Desire)	Levels 7 & 8 (Acceptance/Peace)

The Goddard Connection: Feeling is the Secret

What I discovered through direct experience during my darkest moments aligns remarkably with the teachings of Neville Goddard, a spiritual philosopher whose work from the early to mid-20th century provides profound insights into the creative power of consciousness. When I first encountered Goddard's writings during my recovery journey, it was like finding scientific validation for what I had been experiencing intuitively.

Goddard's central premise, captured in his 1944 book, *Feeling Is the Secret*, is that the feeling associated with your desire, not merely the mental picture, is what creates your reality. "The feeling," he wrote, "is the secret." Nearly a century ago, he taught that imagining and emotionally embodying your desire as already fulfilled creates a shift in consciousness that naturally attracts corresponding experiences.

During those long walks where I practiced accessing the feeling state of financial security despite my external circumstances, I was unknowingly applying the exact principles Goddard had taught decades earlier, proving their timeless validity. The difference between my approach and conventional visualization techniques was precisely what Goddard emphasized throughout his work—the primacy of feeling over mental imagery. No wonder the act of just reading positive affirmations was not working for me, as I wasn't feeling as if they were true.

I wanted security, both financial and social. Those who already have the resources to obtain that which they desire go and get it, simple as that. They don't fret about "when" or "how" because they "know" they already can. Since I was not tuned into the frequency of *having* security, my efforts and affirmation statements got me nowhere.

Goddard taught several specific techniques that align perfectly with what I came to call "feeling it in":

The State of the Wish Fulfilled

"Enter the state of the wish fulfilled," Goddard instructed. This meant assuming the feeling that would be yours if your desire were already reality—not as a technique for getting what you want, but as a recognition that consciousness itself is primary in creating your experience.

"You must assume the feeling of the wish fulfilled until your assumption has all the sensory vividness of reality," he wrote. This is precisely what happened during my spontaneous experience of financial security amid actual lack—a sensory vividness that felt more real than my external circumstances.

The "I Remember When" Technique

One of Goddard's most powerful practices involved imagining yourself in a future time where your current desire is something already accomplished. By mentally positioning yourself beyond the fulfillment and remembering it as past, you bypass the resistance of trying to believe in something that seems unreasonable, given your current circumstances.

I found myself naturally using this approach during my recovery. Rather than constantly affirming "I will find meaningful work," I would access the feeling of *remembering back* when I was struggling (before discovering my purpose through Hearts, Hands and Hope). I recognized I already had meaningful work! This subtle shift—from striving toward to looking back upon—created a fundamentally different feeling state that allowed manifestation to unfold naturally. Then, effortlessly, more meaningful work evolved from my own vibrational field.

The Before-Sleep Practice

Goddard placed special emphasis on the moments before sleep as particularly powerful for impressing new feeling states on the subconscious. "The state of consciousness in which you sleep," he taught, "defines the state in which you will awaken."

As I sought relief from my despair, I developed the practice of deliberately accessing feelings of security, purpose, and fulfillment as I drifted toward sleep—not as affirmations or visualizations, but as authentic emotional states. This wasn't denial of circumstances, but recognition that my essential feeling state wasn't dependent on external conditions. I consistently found that my mental and emotional state upon waking directly reflected these pre-sleep feeling practices.

What makes Goddard's approach so aligned with what I discovered is that it isn't about using the mind to trick reality. It's about recognizing that consciousness itself, particularly its feeling dimension, is the primary creative force from which external circumstances emerge. As Goddard put it, "The world and all within it is man's conditioned consciousness objectified." Or in simpler terms—your life is the mirror of your internal feeling state.

This wasn't just philosophical theory for me—it became my daily reality as I applied these principles during my recovery journey.

The Mechanics of Feeling It In: Practical Techniques

Understanding the conceptual distinction between living FOR versus FROM your desires is one thing; developing the practical capacity to shift your feeling state regardless of circumstances is another.

Through experimentation during my recovery journey, I discovered several approaches that facilitate this shift without forcing or pretending. The biggest of them all, as stated before, was feeling that this was my house. And it remains my house to this day.

These aren't formulaic techniques guaranteed to produce specific outcomes but practices that create favorable conditions for authentic feeling shifts to occur. The key isn't perfecting a method but developing sensitivity to the subtle emotional frequencies that actually generate our experience of reality. To change what we "see" we must change how we "feel."

1. The Stillness Foundation

The foundation for the entire "feeling it in" practice is the stillness we explored in the previous chapter. Without three-brain alignment and access to the Flow State, attempts to shift feeling states typically remain superficial—mental exercises that don't engage the full spectrum of consciousness required for authentic transformation. Many of us have been exposed to similar promises of "manifesting our reality" and have been frustrated with the results. This is different.

Begin any "feeling it in" practice with at least a brief period of stillness cultivation:

- Use the Attention Compass to notice when attention is pulled in the four directions (identity, comparison, past, future) and gently return it to center

- Engage the three brains through conscious breathing that connects gut, heart, and mind

- Allow external and internal activity to settle naturally rather than forcing a particular state

- Rest in the quality of awareness that emerges when the mind's habitual patterns and chatter temporarily subside

This stillness creates the open field where authentic feeling shifts can occur without the distortion of trying to make something happen. It's the difference between stirring muddy water in an attempt to clear it versus allowing the sediment to settle naturally, revealing the inherent clarity that's always been there.

During my practice sessions, I would often begin in my room during the day, allowing the natural setting to support the emergence of stillness. However, I gradually discovered that this state could be accessed anywhere—driving in traffic, sitting in waiting rooms, walking through crowded spaces—once the neural pathways for three-brain alignment had been sufficiently established through regular practice. You are forming a reliable neural pathway by retracing your steps again and again. The more you practice the method, the stronger the pathway becomes.

2. The Essence Distillation

Once a foundation of stillness is established, the next step involves distilling the essential feeling tone of your desire, distinct from its specific form or circumstances.

Every desire, regardless of its external details, contains an essential feeling that attracts us. We don't want things, experiences, or accomplishments for their own sake but for the feeling states we believe they'll create. This, by the way, is what drives billions of dollars in advertising. The next time you watch a TV commercial, notice what "feeling state" it's selling (it's not the product itself).

To practice essence distillation:

- Identify a desire that feels significant in your current life

- Ask yourself: "If this desire were fulfilled exactly as I imagine, what would the emotional essence of that fulfillment be? What would it feel like?"

- Allow your attention to bypass the mental details of the desire (how it would happen, what it would look like) and directly access its feeling essence alone

- Notice the bodily sensations associated with this feeling essence—where you feel it physically, its qualities of movement, temperature, density, etc.

- Rest attention on these sensations rather than mental concepts about the desire

During a particularly challenging period when facing possible foreclosure on our home, I practiced this essence distillation with the desire for housing security. Rather than focusing on specific outcomes (keeping our particular house, finding a better one, etc.), I distilled the essential feeling of "being at home"—the sense of sanctuary, belonging, comfort, and peace that transcends any particular physical structure.

This distillation revealed that what I truly sought wasn't a specific building or location but a feeling state that could potentially be accessed in many different circumstances. This insight didn't eliminate the practical challenges we faced, but it freed my consciousness from attachment to particular forms of resolution, creating space for solutions I couldn't have anticipated through conventional problem-solving. As previously stated, we never lost our home.

3. The Reality Shift

The core practice of feeling it in involves a subtle but profound shift in how you relate to the distilled feeling essence—from experiencing it as something you want to create in the future to recognizing it as something already present in consciousness itself.

This isn't pretending or affirming something contrary to current conditions. It's recognizing that the feeling state of any experience exists as a potential within consciousness itself, independent of external circumstances. You don't need to wait for conditions to change to access the essential feeling that those conditions seem to promise.

To practice the reality shift:

- From the foundation of stillness, access the distilled feeling essence of your desire

- Rather than projecting this feeling into a future scenario, allow yourself to recognize it as already present in your awareness now

- Notice the subtle difference between "I will feel this when..." and "I am feeling this now."

- If resistance arises (thoughts about why you can't authentically feel this yet), simply notice these thoughts without arguing with them or trying to eliminate them. Let them pass along like clouds in the sky

- Return attention to the feeling essence itself, allowing it to expand into whatever dimensions of your awareness are receptive

This shift is so subtle that the mind often misses it, continuing to associate authentic feeling with external validation. The key is recognizing that while external circumstances may facilitate certain feeling states, they don't create them. Consciousness itself is the generator of all feelings, and external reality is more reflective than cause. Simply put, your life is but a mirror of your feelings.

After my career fell apart, I really wanted to feel respected in my work again. Instead of waiting for someone to hire me or tell me I was valuable, I practiced shifting how I saw things. I focused on the *feeling* of making a meaningful contribution—right here and now. I realized that this sense of value already lives inside me, not just in what others say or do. Once I *felt* that truth—that I was already needed, wanted, and appreciated—my life started to change in big ways.

This change didn't instantly fix my job situation, but it did change how I looked at opportunities. Instead of desperately chasing anything that came along, I started noticing what truly fit with my real sense of purpose. That shift eventually led me into nonprofit work, which turned out to be far more meaningful and fulfilling than just trying to rebuild my old career.

4. The Embodiment Practice

The most powerful dimension of feeling it in goes beyond mental recognition to full physical embodiment of the feeling state. This involves allowing the feeling essence to permeate your entire physical experience—posture, movement, facial expression, vocal tone, and subtle energy patterns.

Embodiment isn't acting or pretending but allowing the authentic feeling state to express through the body's natural intelligence. When feeling and physical expression align, a coherent field is created that significantly amplifies the signal being broadcast to the quantum field. And by law, it must be returned as your new reality. This is why affirmations often don't work for most people. They read something nice that they want to feel, but they are vibrating on a different level and, therefore, never see any changes. Affirmations can work, but only when feelings inside are changed first.

To practice embodiment:

- Notice how your physical body naturally responds to the feeling essence you've accessed

- Allow these natural adjustments to emerge rather than forcing specific expressions

- Pay particular attention to subtle shifts in posture, breathing pattern, facial muscles, and overall tension/relaxation

- Experiment with movement that naturally expresses the feeling essence (walking, gesturing, etc.)

- Engage your voice by speaking (aloud or internally) from this embodied state, noticing how tone, rhythm, and word choice naturally shift

The most dramatic example of this embodiment practice came during a public presentation I gave while still recovering from financial collapse.

Rather than approaching the presentation from the needy position of someone trying to rebuild a damaged reputation, I fully embodied the feeling essence of someone already contributing meaningful insight from a place of authentic authority—not as performance but as recognition of what was already true at the level of consciousness itself.

The external feedback was remarkable—people responded not just to the content but to the coherent field created by this aligned embodiment. Opportunities emerged from that single presentation that I couldn't have strategically engineered. This did not occur because I had performed well, but because I had temporarily suspended the consciousness of lack that had been blocking resonant connections in the past, and this created more of what I desired in the present moment.

5. The Detached Engagement

The final element that transforms feeling it in from a manifestation technique to a consciousness practice is detachment. The key is to let go of set goals or specific outcomes while maintaining full engagement with the process. This release actually amplifies the power of the feeling state. This paradoxical stance—fully embodying the feeling without attaching to particular results—creates the conditions where quantum possibilities can collapse into experiences that genuinely serve your highest good rather than your limited conceptual preferences.

I know the geek in me can sometimes come out, so let me clarify the quantum possibilities. In the field of quantum physics, where all possibilities exist at the same time, only one collapses into your experience. Why? Because of how you feel inside, the narrative you keep alive is the problem. Want to change what shows up, want something else to "collapse" for you to see? Believe with your whole being that it already is real. Use all your imagination and senses. And it will become. Now I understand the meaning of a motivational poster I once saw: "What you conceive and believe, you will achieve."

To practice detached engagement:

- Notice any attachment to specific forms or timelines for your desire's fulfillment

- Recognize that such attachment actually creates tension in the feeling field, reducing its coherence

- Return to the pure feeling essence that transcends particular forms or circumstances

- Take inspired action that naturally emerges from the embodied feeling state, without forcing or straining

- Remain curious about how the embodied feeling might express in ways you haven't anticipated or imagined

During my recovery journey, I practiced this detached engagement with my desire for meaningful work. This led into a speaking career where I share this technique with others. You see, there is always something to create and feel FROM as long as you are alive and excited.

The paradox of detached engagement is that by releasing attachment to specific forms of fulfillment, you actually increase the likelihood of experiencing fulfillment that exceeds your limited concepts of what would satisfy your desire. The quantum field responds not to your mental specifications but to the coherent feeling tone you embody, often delivering experiences that serve your evolution in ways your planning mind couldn't anticipate.

Goddard's Wisdom for Modern Practice

Revisiting Goddard's teachings with the benefit of modern understanding reveals how remarkably aligned they are with what quantum physics and consciousness research are now confirming. His insistence that "imagination creates reality" and that feeling is the mechanism through which imagination operates wasn't mystical speculation but practical insight into how consciousness shapes experience.

Goddard emphasized several key principles that enhance our understanding of feeling it in:

The Imaginal Act

"An imaginal act," Goddard wrote, "is not something you do to make a thing happen, it is simply the way you think of yourself when you want to create something." This distinction is crucial—feeling it in isn't a technique applied to reality but a fundamental shift in how you relate to reality through consciousness.

When I was developing Hearts, Hands and Hope, I didn't constantly visualize success to make it happen; I simply allowed myself to think and feel from the state of already being a meaningful contributor regardless of external validation. The organization's growth and impact emerged naturally (and quickly!) from this shift in consciousness rather than from strategic planning alone.

The Law of Assumption

Goddard frequently taught that "if you assume you are what you want to be, you will become what you want to be." This wasn't positive thinking or affirmation but a recognition that consciousness itself is creative. When you assume a state (fully occupy it in feeling), physical reality has no choice but to reorganize around that assumption.

The emphasis on *assumption rather than affirmation* distinguishes Goddard's approach from many contemporary manifestation teachings. Affirmation attempts to convince yourself of something; assumption simply occupies the feeling state directly, bypassing the need for convincing altogether.

I found this distinction liberating during my recovery. Instead of repeating affirmations like "I am successful" or "abundance flows to me" while feeling their contradiction internally, I would simply assume the feeling state of security and contribution directly, without mental commentary or internal debate. With practice, this became easier and easier, especially since it was obviously working!

Revision

One of Goddard's most powerful techniques was what he called "revision"—the practice of reimagining past events from a more empowered perspective, not to deny what happened but to change its emotional imprint on consciousness.

I applied this principle to my career collapse. Rather than seeing it as a catastrophic failure, I would access the feeling of recognizing it as the necessary clearing that made space for more authentic expression. This wasn't denial, but rather a conscious reinterpretation, and it profoundly altered my emotional relationship with these experiences.

The observer effect in quantum physics—where particles behave differently when observed versus when unobserved—suggests that consciousness itself plays a fundamental role in how reality manifests. Goddard intuited this connection between consciousness and physical reality decades before quantum research began confirming these relationships.

The Code Connection: Emotions as Creative Frequencies

To understand why feeling it in works at levels beyond conventional manifestation techniques, we need to connect it explicitly to the consciousness framework of The Code. Emotions aren't just subjective experiences or chemical reactions in the brain; they're distinct energy frequencies that interact directly with the quantum field from which physical reality emerges.

Each consciousness level generates specific emotional frequencies that literally broadcast different signals to the universe:

Levels 1-3 (Shame, Guilt, Apathy): These levels generate extremely dense, slow-vibrating frequencies characterized by contraction, heaviness, and disconnection. When broadcasting these frequencies, you naturally attract experiences that match them—situations that reinforce feelings of unworthiness, regret, and hopelessness. Not as punishment, but as resonant reflection.

These heavy states make you feel stuck and disconnected, and they tend to draw in more experiences that keep you feeling unworthy or hopeless.

Levels 4-5 (Fear, Desire): These somewhat higher frequencies still vibrate in patterns of lack and separation. Fear broadcasts a signal of danger and insufficiency; desire broadcasts endless seeking without arrival. Both generate experiences of "almost but not quite"—opportunities that seem promising but don't quite fulfill, relationships that approach but don't quite reach genuine connection, achievements that momentarily satisfy but quickly reveal their emptiness.

Fear and desire create a sense of always missing something, so even when you get close to what you want, it never fully satisfies.

Levels 6-7 (Anger, Acceptance): At Level 6, the frequency begins to carry enough energy for transformation, though often through conflict and opposition. Level 7 represents the first truly coherent frequency—one that doesn't resist reality but aligns with it, creating conditions for harmonious rather than oppositional creation. These levels start attracting experiences of genuine movement and flow rather than stagnation or struggle.

Anger has enough energy to spark change, but acceptance brings the first real sense of flow by working with life instead of fighting it.

Levels 8-9 (Peace, Enlightenment): These highest frequencies vibrate in patterns of profound coherence, broadcasting signals of wholeness, harmony, and non-separation. When embodying these states, you naturally attract experiences that reflect these qualities—synchronistic flow, effortless effectiveness, and communion rather than isolation. The reflection isn't a reward for achieving high consciousness but resonance between internal and external frequencies.

Peace and enlightenment create harmony inside and out, so life feels more connected, effortless, and full of meaning.

Modern neuroscience provides compelling evidence for how "feeling it in" creates lasting change through neuroplasticity—the brain's ability to reorganize itself by forming new neural connections. Research from Massachusetts General Hospital demonstrated that just eight weeks of mindfulness practice—which, like feeling it in, involves embodying specific emotional states—produced measurable increases in gray matter density in brain regions associated with self-awareness, compassion, and introspection.

When we embody the feeling of already having what we desire, we're not just engaging in wishful thinking; we're literally rewiring our neural pathways. Studies have shown that the brain doesn't distinguish between an intensely imagined experience and an actual one—both create similar patterns of neural activation and, with repetition, strengthen the same neural networks. This explains why consistent practice of feeling it in produces such powerful results: we're not just temporarily changing our mood but physically restructuring our brain to support this new way of being. The emotional frequency we embody becomes encoded in our neurobiology, gradually transforming how we perceive and interact with reality at the most fundamental level

The practice of feeling it in works most powerfully from Levels 7-9 because these frequencies naturally embody the coherence necessary for conscious creation. From lower levels, attempts at manifestation often produce mixed results because the broadcast signal contains conflicting frequencies—conscious intention vibrates at one frequency while unconscious patterns of lack, fear, or separation vibrate at another.

As stated before, this explains why conventional visualization, affirmation, or goal-setting techniques often yield disappointing results. It's not that these approaches are inherently flawed; it's that they're typically practiced from Level 4-5 consciousness, where the underlying emotional frequency contradicts the stated intention. You can't effectively broadcast abundance from a frequency of scarcity, nor connection from separation, nor fulfillment from seeking—regardless of your positive thoughts or mental images.

The breakthrough in understanding feeling it in comes from recognizing that emotions aren't responses to reality but generators of the reality we experience. The universe doesn't deliver what we think about, visualize, affirm, or even deeply desire; it reflects back the emotional frequency we embody as our primary vibration. The observer effect is, in fact, very real.

I experienced this principle dramatically during the darkest period of financial collapse. Despite constantly thinking about, visualizing, and working toward financial recovery, the situation continued deteriorating because these efforts emerged from a consciousness of lack and fear. It was only when I accessed moments of genuine acceptance and peace—Levels 7-8 consciousness—that the frequency shifted enough for new possibilities to emerge.

These shifts weren't immediately visible in external circumstances. They began as subtle internal reorganizations—different quality of ideas, unexpected points of connection, fresh perspectives on familiar challenges.

I wondered, "Who is the 'I' in 'I am'?"

How the "I" vibrates became more important. Little by little, the shifts inside me made my life on the outside match the frequency I stayed in most often.

The most powerful example came through the nonprofit work that emerged not from desperate seeking for income but from embodying the frequency of contribution regardless of compensation. This alignment with higher consciousness levels created a coherent signal that naturally attracted corresponding experiences—not through magical manifestation but through the fundamental principle that similar frequencies resonate and amplify each other. Like attracts like.

Understanding emotions as creative frequencies rather than just subjective experiences transforms the entire approach to manifesting desired experiences. Instead of trying to think positive thoughts while feeling negative emotions (a common pattern that broadcasts conflicting signals), the focus shifts to embracing the emotional frequency that naturally corresponds to your desires, independent of external conditions.

This isn't denying current reality but recognizing that reality itself is more response than cause—more reflection of consciousness than independent condition to which consciousness must submit. When you shift the emotional frequency you're broadcasting through genuine embodiment rather than mental effort, the reflection must eventually shift as well, according to the immutable laws of resonance that govern both quantum and psychological fields.

Why Visualization Without Feeling Has Limited Power

Many popular manifestation approaches emphasize visualization—creating detailed mental images of desired outcomes as if they were already reality. While visualization can be a valuable component of conscious creation, without the accompanying feeling state, its effectiveness remains severely limited.

This limitation explains why many people report disappointing results despite diligent visualization practice. They create vivid, detailed mental pictures of desired outcomes, or sometimes collect images by cutting them out of magazines or printing them on paper (in order to build a "vision board") to have their dreams displayed in their room or office. But if they don't access the emotional frequency that would broadcast a coherent signal to the quantum field, the result is often frustration and disillusionment with "manifestation principles" themselves.

I experienced this limitation firsthand during early attempts to improve our financial situation. I would visualize new job opportunities, business success, or unexpected financial windfalls with great detail and consistency. I created vision boards of desired outcomes and spent time every day imagining these scenarios as if they were already manifested.

Yet these practices produced nominal results because they emerged from Level 4-5 consciousness—Fear and Desire—creating an emotional broadcast of lack and separation, regardless of the positive mental images. The universe wasn't responding to my visualizations but rather to the underlying emotional frequency that contradicted them. It always does this.

The shift came when I discovered that visualization could serve as a pathway to authentic feeling states rather than a technique for programming specific outcomes. Instead of mentally rehearsing detailed scenarios, I began using simplified images as doorways to the essential feeling tones of particular desires.

For example, rather than visualizing specific job interviews, offers, and income levels, I would hold a simple image—perhaps seeing myself sitting across from someone whose face lit up with recognition as I shared an insight that genuinely helped them understand something they'd been struggling with. Not the details of who they were or what specific problem we were discussing, but just that moment of connection when knowledge flows from one person to another in a way that creates real value. I would focus on the feeling of that exchange—the warmth in my chest when I knew I had offered something truly useful, the sense of alignment when my authentic gifts met someone's genuine need, the quiet satisfaction of contributing something meaningful to another person's journey.

This approach bypassed the mind's tendency to fixate on particular forms and timelines, allowing direct access to the emotional frequency that could broadcast a coherent signal.

This distinction explains why two people can practice seemingly identical visualization techniques with dramatically different results. The individual who uses visualization primarily as mental rehearsal while maintaining an emotional frequency of lack or separation (Levels 1-5) creates a conflicted broadcast that produces mixed results at best. The one who uses visualization as a doorway to authentic feeling states that align with higher consciousness levels (7-9) creates a coherent broadcast that naturally attracts resonant experiences.

The power lies not in the mental image itself but in the emotional frequency it helps you access and embody. Visualization serves consciousness evolution not by programming the universe to deliver specific outcomes but by providing a bridge between conceptual understanding and embodied feeling—a pathway from thinking about what you want to feeling what you want as present reality.

This understanding transformed my approach to visualization from detailed mental rehearsal to simple feeling access. Rather than elaborately imagining every aspect of desired outcomes, I would use minimal imagery as an entry point to the essential feeling state, then allow that state to permeate my awareness without attachment to particular forms or timelines.

The result wasn't that I suddenly manifested exactly what I had visualized (a common but misleading promise of some manifestation teachings). Instead, I accessed emotional frequencies that attracted experiences resonating with those frequencies—often in forms I couldn't have anticipated or planned through mental visualization alone.

The nonprofit work that eventually resolved some of our financial challenges and provided a deeply fulfilling purpose wasn't something I had specifically visualized or planned. It emerged as a natural resonance with the emotional frequency of contribution and service that I had accessed through simplified visualization, followed by authentic feeling embodiment.

This pattern repeated across different areas of life: the most powerful manifestations rarely matched specific mental images but always corresponded precisely to my emotional frequencies I was able to embody with some consistency. The universe wasn't delivering what I had pictured but reflecting back to me what I felt at the deepest levels of consciousness.

The distinction is subtle but crucial: effective creation doesn't come from mental programming but from emotional broadcasting.

The Dream Deepens: The Emotional Bridge

On the night I first practiced "feeling in" the reality of keeping our home, the dream (yes, *that* dream again) came with new intensity. This time, I experienced something unprecedented—I wasn't observing the disheveled man, I *was* him.

◆

I am surprised as it dawns on me that I am the disheveled man. I can feel what it is like to exist in his skin—the weight of rejection, the raw vulnerability of living without the protective mask of success. Yet within this experience is also a strange freedom—the liberty of having nothing left to lose, no reputation to protect, no expectations to fulfill.

From this perspective, I watch a weatherman moving through life—confidently delivering forecasts, smiling for cameras, navigating social situations with practiced ease. I can feel the exhaustion behind his performance, the vigilance required to maintain his perfect image. I sense the fear that hums beneath his certainty like a bass note too low to hear, yet always felt.

Suddenly, we are facing each other across a narrow ravine. Between us stretches a bridge made of an unusual material—it seems to be shimmering, woven with emotional currents that flow visibly through its structure, changing colors as different feelings pass through it—the deep blue of grief, the fiery red of anger, the golden warmth of joy, all intermingling in patterns too complex to name.

"I've been trying to cross to your side," I say, my voice emerging from the disheveled man's throat yet carrying the cadence of my deepest self. "But the bridge only forms when you feel what I feel."

The weatherman looks hesitant, afraid of what he senses is radiating from the bridge. I feel his resistance as if it were my own—because it is. "I've spent my life avoiding those feelings," he says, his professional voice cracking slightly.

"And that's why we remain divided," I reply. "You can't think your way to me. You can only feel your way."

Tentatively, the weatherman places a foot on the bridge. He begins to experience what I experience—the vulnerability, the nakedness, but also the authenticity. With each step, the perfectly coiffed weatherman changes, not becoming disheveled exactly, but more real, more present. The rigid posture softens. The fixed smile melts into expressions that move naturally with his emotions. The life-sized wax figure steps off his pedestal and turns real.

I walk forward to meet him. The moment we touch, everything shifts. I'm suddenly one entity rather than two—neither the weatherman nor the disheveled man, but something integrating aspects of both. I sense that the clarity and communication skills of the weatherman have merged with the authenticity and depth of the disheveled man. The capacity for public engagement joined with the capacity for private truth.

◆

Tears flowed freely as I opened my eyes, the visceral memory of that emotional bridge still vivid in my body. As thoughts came up that day about our home, I remembered that the path forward wasn't through more thinking or planning but through fully embodying the feeling state that already existed within me—the feeling of home that transcended any particular physical structure or financial arrangement.

Exercise: The Feeling-It-In Practice

I first discovered this approach during bad times. Bills were mounting, opportunities seemed non-existent, and the future looked bleaker by the day. Traditional manifestation techniques I'd learned—visualization, affirmations, goal-setting—all felt hollow and ineffective.

On one of my walks, after a powerful stillness experience by the lake, I spontaneously felt myself shift into the emotional state I'd known during my successful career—the internal feeling of security, contribution, and fulfilled purpose. This wasn't forced positive thinking or denial of current challenges; it was a direct recognition that the feeling itself existed within consciousness, independent of circumstances. How could I still tap into this feeling when it was anything but present? The shift was happening inside me, and I was paying attention.

The shift wasn't intellectual but visceral—my posture straightened, my breathing deepened, tension released from my shoulders, and my walking pace naturally adjusted. I wasn't pretending things were different; I was experiencing the emotional essence of what I sought, regardless of whether external conditions matched it—yet.

This comprehensive exercise integrates the principles and techniques we've explored, creating a step-by-step approach to the practice of "feeling it in." Think of it as a flexible framework that you can adapt to your unique circumstances and preferences.

You'll need:

- 20-30 minutes of uninterrupted time

- A comfortable, private space

- Optional: a journal for recording insights

Part 1: Stillness Foundation (5-7 minutes)

Begin by establishing the stillness that creates optimal conditions for authentic feeling shifts:

1. Settle into a comfortable position that allows both relaxation and alertness.

2. Take several conscious breaths, allowing your attention to follow the natural rhythm of breathing.

3. Notice when attention is pulled toward:

   - Thoughts about yourself or your identity (North)

   - Comparative judgments about yourself or others (South)

- Memories or regrets about the past (West)

- Plans or worries about the future (East)

4. Each time you notice a pull in any direction, gently guide attention back to center through:

   - A conscious breath

   - Feeling the physical sensations of your body

   - Noticing the space around you

5. Allow a quality of receptive awareness to emerge naturally as mental activity gradually settles

Don't force a particular state, rush, or judge your experience. Simply notice what's happening and continue the gentle process of returning to center whenever attention drifts.

Part 2: Desire Identification (3-5 minutes)

From the foundation of stillness, identify a desire that feels significant in your current life:

1. Ask yourself: *What would I like to create or experience that feels meaningful right now?*

2. Notice what naturally arises without forcing or overthinking.

3. Select one desire to work with during this practice session.

4. Briefly note the external details of this desire (what are you wearing, what are the smells of the room/area, what do you look like from another's viewpoint, what are you touching, what sounds do you hear...Invoke the senses).

5. Set these details aside for now, recognizing that they're the form but not the essence of your desire.

If multiple desires arise, choose the one that feels most resonant in this moment. You can work with others in subsequent practice sessions.

Part 3: Essence Distillation (3-5 minutes)

Now distill the essential feeling tone of your desire, distinct from its specific form or circumstances:

1. Ask yourself: *If this desire were fulfilled exactly as I imagine, what would be the essential feeling of that fulfillment?*

2. Allow your attention to bypass mental details and directly access the feeling essence.

3. Notice where and how this feeling registers in your body—sensations, energy movements, temperature, etc.

4. If mental analysis arises ("I would feel this way because..."), gently return to direct feeling without analysis.

5. Allow the pure feeling essence to clarify and stabilize in your awareness.

This isn't about forcing a particular emotion but discovering what naturally draws you to this desire beyond its external form.

Part 4: Reality Shift (5-7 minutes)

Now practice the subtle but profound shift from wanting the feeling to recognizing it as already present:

1. Rather than thinking about the feeling or projecting it into a future scenario, simply notice it as already present in your awareness now.

2. If thoughts arise about why you can't authentically feel this yet, simply notice these thoughts without arguing with them.

3. Return attention to the feeling itself, allowing it to be exactly as it is without forcing intensity or duration.

4. Notice the subtle difference between "I will feel this when..." and "I am feeling this now..."

5. Allow the feeling to expand naturally into the dimensions of your awareness that are receptive, without pushing or straining.

The key here isn't to convince yourself of something unreal, but to recognize that the feeling itself exists in consciousness now, regardless of external circumstances.

Part 5: Full Embodiment (5-7 minutes)

Now allow the feeling essence to permeate your entire physical experience:

1. Notice how your physical body naturally responds to the feeling essence you've accessed.

2. Allow subtle adjustments in posture, facial expression, breathing pattern, and muscle tension.

3. If comfortable, experiment with movement that naturally expresses this feeling—walking, gesturing, etc.

4. If appropriate, engage your voice by speaking aloud from this embodied state, noticing how your tone and word choice naturally shift.

5. Imagine this feeling state radiating from your entire being like a broadcast signal reaching the quantum field.

Again, this isn't acting or pretending but allowing authentic feelings to express through your body's natural intelligence.

Part 6: Detached Engagement (3-5 minutes)

Finally, practice the paradoxical stance of complete embodiment without attachment:

1. Notice any attachment to specific forms or timelines for your desire's fulfillment.

2. Recognize that such attachment creates tension in the feeling field.

3. Return to the pure feeling essence that transcends particular forms.

4. Set an intention to remain open to how this feeling might express in ways you haven't anticipated.

5. Consider what action naturally emerges from this embodied state, without forcing or straining.

This isn't giving up on your desire but releasing the limitations you've placed on how it might fulfill.

Part 7: Integration and Closing (2-3 minutes)

Complete the formal practice with these steps:

1. Take a few moments to notice the quality of your experience compared to when you began.

2. Acknowledge any insights, shifts, or questions that arose during the practice.

3. If using a journal, briefly record these observations without elaborate analysis.

4. Set an intention to maintain awareness of this feeling essence as you return to regular activities.

5. Transition mindfully by moving slowly at first, maintaining connection with the quality of awareness you've accessed.

Daily Integration Practice:

To build on the formal practice and integrate "feeling it in" into daily life:

1. Mini-Sessions: Several times throughout your day, take 30-60 seconds to access the feeling essence of your desire without elaborate preparation. For example, Sue's desire is to own a second home, a cottage on Nokomis Beach. She keeps a beautiful pink shell on her desk. She closes her eyes and imagines she is breathing in ocean air, whenever she wants to visit her desire. These brief touchpoints maintain the broadcast frequency between formal practice sessions.

2. Environmental Triggers: Place objects or images in your environment that remind you of the feeling essence you're working with. These might be symbolic representations rather than literal images of the desire itself.

3. Body Anchors: Develop a simple physical gesture—touching a specific point on your body, assuming a particular hand position, or taking a distinctive breath—that you associate with the feeling

state. Use this anchor to quickly access the feeling during various activities.

4. Challenge Integration: When facing challenges related to your desire, pause briefly to access the feeling essence before responding. This doesn't deny the challenge but ensures your response emerges from aligned consciousness rather than reactive patterns.

5. Notice and Appreciate Small Wins: Pay attention to any moment that gives you even a taste of what you're seeking, then take time to really appreciate it. If you want to feel valued at work, notice when a coworker thanks you for help or when you solve a problem successfully—even if it's not the big promotion you're hoping for. If you're seeking a loving relationship, appreciate the kind cashier who smiles at you or the friend who remembers your birthday—even though they're not your future partner. When you genuinely appreciate these smaller experiences that contain the same feeling you're after, you reinforce that positive emotional state in your system.

This practice became the bridge between inner shift and outer manifestation. After consistently feeling in the essence of meaningful contribution rather than chasing it as a future possibility, I received the clear guidance about Hearts, Hands and Hope that would transform not just my own circumstances but the lives of many others in our community.

What's crucial to understand is that this manifestation didn't happen because the universe was rewarding my good thoughts or because I had perfectly executed some cosmic formula. It emerged naturally from the shift in consciousness frequency—from broadcasting *lack and separation* to broadcasting *fulfillment and connection*. The external forms that appeared often surprised me, rarely matching my specific visualizations but consistently reflecting the essential feeling state I had accessed.

Even today, when facing new challenges, I return to this practice not as a technique to manipulate reality but as a remembrance of where true creation begins—not in desperate striving for what's absent but in recognition of what's already present at the level of consciousness itself.

The Sleeping Method: Goddard's Most Powerful Technique

Of all Neville Goddard's manifestation practices, none was more emphasized than what he called "the sleeping method"—entering sleep while holding the feeling of your fulfilled desire. "Nothing is so important as feeling," Goddard wrote. "If you can sustain the feeling of your wish fulfilled during the time it takes you to drop off to sleep, you will express that state in this three-dimensional world."

The moments between wakefulness and sleep represent a unique threshold state where consciousness becomes highly receptive. The analytical mind naturally relaxes, creating an opening where feeling impressions can reach deeper levels without resistance. Goddard described this as "planting seeds in the fertile soil of subconsciousness."

Willing to give anything a try, I discovered the remarkable power of this approach. On evenings when financial anxiety would typically have dominated my thoughts, I would instead deliberately access the feeling of abundance and security as I prepared for sleep. Not through elaborate visualization, but by simply feeling how it would feel to be completely secure, regardless of external circumstances. I reminded myself of how that used to feel, for example.

The key distinction was that I wasn't attempting to convince myself that our financial situation was different than it appeared. I was simply accessing a feeling state that existed within consciousness itself, independent of conditions. This subtle but crucial difference transformed the practice from wishful thinking to authentic frequency shifting. Yes, it actually is possible to recalibrate yourself to become perfectly tuned to your desires.

What made this approach particularly effective was its cumulative nature. While daytime practices were frequently interrupted by external demands and habitual thought patterns, the sleeping method created uninterrupted periods where the new frequency could impress itself deeply into consciousness. Night after night, this consistent practice gradually shifted my dominant broadcast from fear and lack to security and contribution.

Goddard suggested a simple enhancement to this practice—mental revision of the day just completed. Rather than rehearsing problems or replaying conflicts, he recommended reimagining the day as if your desires were already fulfilled, allowing you to drift off to sleep feeling the natural satisfaction and gratitude such fulfillment would generate. This wasn't denial of reality but conscious redirection of emotional energy toward preferred states.

So, instead of mentally reviewing financial worries or reliving disappointments, I would *reimagine* the day through the lens of sufficiency and meaningful purpose. This wasn't pretending problems didn't exist but choosing which emotional frequency would accompany me into sleep and then, hopefully, shape the next day's experience. And, it did. Short-term jobs with connections to other opportunities began to show up. After I'd been dying of thirst in a desert of no hope, it was like opportunities for income started raining from the sky.

Remember, your consciousness during sleep doesn't just passively experience dreams—it actively shapes the probability fields that determine which potential experiences collapse into your waking reality. The feeling state you consistently maintain during these threshold moments broadcasts continuous signals that gradually reorganize external circumstances to match their frequency.

This practice requires no special skills or elaborate techniques—just the willingness to direct attention toward feeling states that align with your desires rather than your current conditions.

Beyond Manifestation: The Deeper Purpose of Feeling It In

As we conclude this chapter, it's important to recognize that feeling it in serves a purpose far beyond merely manifesting specific desires or improving life circumstances. While these outcomes often accompany the practice, its deeper value lies in the fundamental shift it facilitates in how we understand and experience the relationship between consciousness and reality.

The conventional view says our mind mainly takes in the outside world—what we see, hear, and feel—and then builds our inner experience from that. In that view, we're mostly passive, and the only way we affect things is by taking physical action. But the "feeling it in" perspective flips this around. Here, consciousness isn't just receiving—it's creating. It helps shape reality through the energy, or frequency, it carries. Our outer world doesn't cause our inner state; instead, it mirrors it, following a natural law of resonance that works at all levels, from the tiniest particles to our own thoughts and feelings.

Dr. Joe Dispenza's research offers fascinating scientific validation of this principle. His studies have documented how our brain waves and heart rhythms actually synchronize and create a coherent field when we enter states similar to what I call "feeling it in." As he explains, "When our bodies are super relaxed and calm, and our minds are more awake and aware... we're just very present — and at the same time, very joyfully conscious. That's the formula right there. That's the side effect of heart and brain coherence."

This heart-brain coherence isn't just a subjective experience but a measurable physiological state with profound implications. Dispenza's research with quantitative electroencephalogram (QEEG) and electrocardiogram (ECG) readings shows that when we enter these coherent states, our brains shift from high beta waves (associated with stress and analytical thinking) to a harmonious blend of alpha, theta, and even gamma frequencies. This neural synchronization creates a powerful electromagnetic field that extends beyond our physical bodies and interacts with the quantum field around us.

This revelation doesn't eliminate life's challenges or guarantee specific outcomes. But it does transform our relationship with challenges from victim stance to creative engagement, from passive reaction to conscious participation.

During my recovery journey, this deeper understanding proved far more valuable than any specific manifestations that accompanied it. Rather than being at the mercy of things happening "to me," I was empowered to relate to things as happening "through me."

This shift didn't make challenges disappear, but it transformed them from obstacles to opportunities—not through positive thinking or denial, but through recognition of my participatory role in how those challenges were experienced and what they ultimately revealed.

The scientific evidence from Dispenza's research suggests that when we access these coherent states, we're actually changing our biology at the cellular level. He has documented how participants in his advanced workshops show measurable changes in gene expression, immune function, and even brain structure through consistent practice of these coherent states. Our thoughts and feelings aren't just subjective experiences—they're electromagnetic broadcasts that directly influence our physical bodies and the field around us.

As we move into the next chapter on the Flow State, we'll explore how this understanding of consciousness as creative rather than merely receptive plays out in daily life. You don't need to give up on your dreams in order to step away from a stressful struggle towards attainment; feeling in it can become a simple habit to embrace as a path leading to your deepest desires. So, if it's already yours…claim it emotionally as if it were already so, and it will be.

CHAPTER 8

The Flow State Manifested

"Scoop, spread, set, tap—the trowel moves as if it already knows. Rhythm. My hands follow the rhythm without thought, brick sliding into place with quiet certainty. There is no wall behind me, no wall ahead, only this line forming under my touch. The pattern carries me, and I feel the work flowing through me more than from me."

"The bow moves, draws, lifts—the notes spill before I can name them. My fingers fall into place without effort, each sound rising like breath. The room disappears; there is only vibration, tone, resonance. The music plays me, moving through my body as if I were the instrument, and in its current, I am weightless, timeless, whole."

Have you ever watched a master craftsman at work? Or seen an athlete in the zone, where every movement seems effortless yet perfectly executed? Perhaps you've experienced moments yourself when everything just clicks—when writing flows without strain, decisions arise with clarity, or solutions appear that weren't visible moments before.

These aren't just pleasant anomalies or random occurrences. They're glimpses of what becomes increasingly available when the Flow State moves from occasional experience to more consistent reality.

The previous chapter laid the foundation for understanding how "feeling it in" creates the precise consciousness frequency that allows manifestation to occur. Now let's explore what happens when these principles are expressed in real-world situations—not as theoretical possibilities but as lived experiences that transform both inner awareness and outer circumstances.

The scientific research on brain-heart coherence gives us a window into what's happening physiologically during these Flow State experiences. Dr. Joe Dispenza's studies have shown that when we align our three brains—gut, heart, and mind—we create what researchers call "psychophysiological coherence."

In this state, our heart rhythm patterns become smooth and ordered, our brain waves synchronize across different regions, and our autonomic nervous system shifts from sympathetic (fight-or-flight) dominance to a balanced state where the parasympathetic (rest-and-digest) system can function optimally.

What makes this research so revolutionary is that it's providing measurable, scientific evidence for what ancient wisdom traditions have taught for millennia—that consciousness itself is a creative force, not just a passive observer of reality. When we enter the Flow State, we're not just feeling better subjectively; we're literally changing our biology and creating a different

electromagnetic signature that interacts with the quantum field in ways that can produce what appear to be "miraculous" manifestations.

In this chapter, I'll share concrete examples from my own journey and others I've worked with, showing how the Flow State translates into practical outcomes across different life domains. We'll explore the connection to Level 9 consciousness, examine how reality consistently mirrors our consciousness level, address common obstacles that interrupt flow, and provide practical exercises to move these principles from theory to application in your daily life.

The Flow State Process Map
The Journey from Fragmentation to Flow

Starting Point

1. Fragmented Attention (Scattered Thoughts, Emotions, Sensations)

2. Recognition (Awareness of Fragmentation)

When Lost Again
(Start The Process Again)

Ultimate Goal

7. Universal Mind Access
(Create and Experience From)

3. Return To Center
(using Attention Compass)

6. Aligned Action
(Effective Engagement with Life)

4. Three Brain Alignment
(Gut, Heart and Head Synchronizing)

5. Flow State Access
(Stillness and Coherence)

Aidan's Marvel Moment: The Flow State Through a Child's Eyes

Of all the teachers who showed me the Flow State in action, none was more powerful than my own son. Aidan's unique neurological makeup—what most would label as autism—gave him a natural capacity to enter states of consciousness that many adults spend decades trying to access through spiritual practices.

There was one particular evening that transformed my understanding of manifestation through the Flow State. It was during an end-of-year celebration at Aidan's elementary school. Despite his challenges with social interaction and short-term memory, Aidan navigated his world with a contentment and presence I'd come to deeply admire. While other children formed tight social groups, Aidan often wandered by himself, completely at peace in his own world—fully immersed in the present moment without the constant mental chatter that fragments most others attention.

This evening was special because our shared love of Marvel Universe characters had created a bond between us as father and son. Among hundreds of prizes to be won through a raffle drawing at this event was a collection of Marvel action figures—ten 8-inch tall characters that represented the pinnacle of desire for both children and adult collectors alike.

As our family arrived, we purchased numerous raffle tickets to increase our chances of winning various prizes. But Aidan wanted to buy just one ticket with his own money. When we approached the Marvel prize basket, his grandmother, grandfather, mother and I began filling out multiple tickets to maximize our chances of winning this highly coveted prize.

Aidan insisted on writing his name himself on his single ticket, despite his poor penmanship. His grandfather pulled me aside with concern, "What are you going to do when he doesn't win?" The question reflected a natural parental instinct—how would we manage the inevitable disappointment?

But something remarkable was happening with Aidan that I didn't fully comprehend at the time. While we adults were calculating probabilities and preparing for disappointment, Aidan was operating from an entirely different state of consciousness. He stood by the basket, completely fixated, telling us precisely where he would place each of the ten action figures once we got home.

"We're going to have to go to Home Depot to buy a bookshelf for all the figures," he stated matter-of-factly, without a hint of doubt or concern.

What I was witnessing—but didn't yet have the framework to understand—was the Flow State in its purest form. Aidan wasn't hoping to win; he had completely bypassed the state of desire (Level 5 consciousness) and was living from the state of having already received what he wanted. His focus wasn't divided between present lack and future fulfillment. He was fully embodying what Neville Goddard described as "the feeling of the wish fulfilled."

When the time came for the drawing, thousands of tickets filled the basket for this prize. Our family had contributed dozens ourselves, but I had little expectation of winning given the overwhelming odds. As they prepared to draw the winning ticket, I found myself saying a quiet prayer: "Please say 'Aidan'…"

And the announcer did just that.

When we went to claim the prize and match the ticket, we made an astonishing discovery. When Aidan went up to claim his prize, it was the one ticket he bought and wrote his name on. His one chance! Somehow, his single ticket had manifested the exact outcome he had so completely embodied.

This experience connects directly to what Dr. Joe Dispenza explains in his groundbreaking work and book, *You Are the Placebo: Making Your Mind Matter*. Dispenza teaches that our thoughts and feelings create our reality at the biological level. He writes that "your thoughts and feelings come from your past memories. If you think and feel a certain way, you begin to create an attitude… If you string a series of attitudes together, you create a belief." These beliefs then form our perceptions, which in turn creates (over time) your personality which directly shapes your reality. There is a pattern.

Unlike most adults, Aidan wasn't carrying limiting beliefs or past disappointments that would create internal resistance. His consciousness wasn't divided by doubt or contradictory thoughts. As Dispenza explains, when we hold a clear intention of a new future and marry it to a state of elevated emotion, repeating this until we create a new state of being, these thoughts become more real to us than our previous limited view of reality. This is precisely what Aidan demonstrated.

In one of his most powerful insights, Dispenza notes that "when you change the way you think, feel, and act, you are literally changing your brain and creating new synaptic connections." This neurological restructuring is exactly what the Flow State facilitates—a rewiring of neural pathways that creates coherence between thought, emotion, and physical experience. Aidan's autism, which many view as a limitation, actually gave him access to this coherent state more readily than most adults can achieve.

The power of innocent consciousness to manifest isn't magic—it's physics operating through consciousness. As Dispenza puts it, we must feel "as if the thought were more real than anything else"—exactly what Aidan demonstrated that evening. His mind wasn't clouded with thoughts of "what if I don't win"—he only focused on where he would place his prize. He had achieved what Dispenza calls "the state of being" where you're no longer separate from what you desire but have become one with it at the level of feeling and perception.

This pure embodiment of the Flow State teaches us that manifestation isn't about force or control but about the coherent alignment of all aspects of consciousness into a unified field. And it shows us that what we call "manifestation" isn't about magical thinking but about removing the internal contradictions that keep us from broadcasting a clear, coherent signal into the quantum field.

What happened with Aidan that night wasn't a fluke or coincidence—it was a demonstration of how consciousness operates when conflicting beliefs are not fragmenting it. Dr. Dispenza's research helps us understand this at the neurological level, explaining how our thoughts and feelings create physical changes in our biology.

When we operate from fragmented consciousness, it creates what Dispenza calls "incoherent brain states" where our electromagnetic field broadcasts confusing signals to the quantum field.

By contrast, when we enter the Flow State, these brain regions synchronize. EEG readings show increased coherence between different areas of the brain, particularly between the analytical left hemisphere and the intuitive right hemisphere. This neural synchronization creates what scientists call "whole-brain functioning"—a state in which different brain regions work in harmony rather than in opposition.

Dispenza's research with thousands of participants in his advanced workshops has documented remarkable cases of healing and transformation that occur when people learn to access this coherent brain state. In one particularly striking example, a woman with severe mobility limitations due to multiple sclerosis was able to walk unassisted after accessing a profound state of neural coherence through guided meditation. She didn't just imagine walking; she created a new reality by embodying the feeling state of already being healed.

The physiological signature of the Flow State has been extensively documented through HeartMath Institute's research on heart rate variability (HRV)—the naturally occurring beat-to-beat changes in heart rhythm. Their studies reveal that during Flow States, heart rhythms shift from erratic, disordered patterns characteristic of stress and fragmented attention to a highly ordered, sine-wave-like pattern they term "coherence."

This coherent HRV pattern indicates optimal synchronization between the sympathetic and parasympathetic branches of the autonomic nervous system—precisely the physiological conditions where the three brains (gut, heart, and mind) can communicate most efficiently. HeartMath researchers have found that this coherent state correlates with enhanced cognitive performance, emotional stability, and intuitive access—hallmarks of the Flow State described throughout this book. This is the key understanding that transforms the Flow State from a nice theory to a practical tool for creating change. When you align your three brains—gut, heart, and mind—you're not just feeling better subjectively; you're literally rewiring your neural networks and broadcasting a different electromagnetic signature into the quantum field.

What makes this approach so revolutionary is that it doesn't require external circumstances to change first. As Dispenza writes, "Your personality creates your personal reality." When you change your "state of being" through the Flow State, you change what you broadcast to the quantum field, which ultimately changes what you experience in your external reality.

Hearts, Hands and Hope: Flow State in Action

One of the most powerful examples of Flow State principles in action comes from my wife Michelle's creation of Hearts, Hands and Hope (HHH), and my subsequent involvement as Executive Director.

The journey began not with me but with Michelle. In 2016, six years after my television career ended and while I was working on my degree (this time for computer science), Michelle founded HHH. The organization emerged from two significant events: her deep appreciation for our neighbor Rhoda, who had helped our family during our darkest times, and her decision to transition from her role as PTA President after being recognized as "Dividend of the Year" for the entire county. With so many projects and responsibilities, she needed help to gain focus and have some direction for her considerable energy and talent for community service.

Initially, I supported from the sidelines while finishing my coursework. After graduating in 2018, I contributed my technical skills—building a website, designing flyers, creating payment systems, and establishing the digital infrastructure that would help the organization grow. What started as technical support would eventually evolve into a more comprehensive role.

Then came 2020 and the COVID-19 pandemic—a global challenge that transformed the scale and significance of HHH's work. During this unprecedented time, the organization became the primary distributor of food for government programs in our county, serving families for nearly two years, 91 consecutive weeks. This expanded role revealed both the immediate need for food distribution and the deeper systemic issue of food insecurity that affected so many in our community.

It was during this period of intense activity and responsibility that the Flow State principles we've been exploring throughout this book proved their practical power. As I stepped into the role of Executive Director, I found myself facing complex logistics, resource limitations, volunteer coordination, and the emotional weight of serving people in crisis—all challenges that could easily have overwhelmed me not that long before this. Living with a fragmented consciousness makes one vulnerable to overwhelm.

This is where the Attention Compass became invaluable. Rather than approaching these challenges from Level 4 consciousness (Fear—focused on all the things that could go wrong) or Level 5 (Desire—focused on achievement and recognition), I practiced bringing attention back to center whenever I noticed it being pulled in those directions.

During one crisis when needs far exceeded available supplies, I took time to focus and tune into stillness through the practices outlined in Chapter 6. In that centered state, something remarkable happened—not a magical voice or dramatic vision, but a clear knowing that emerged from three-brain alignment.

The insight was simple but transformative: HHH could be more than a food distribution site. We could actually work toward solving food insecurity through a comprehensive three-phase system. This wasn't just an incremental improvement to existing operations but a fundamental shift in vision that expanded our impact far beyond emergency response.

What makes this example so illustrative of Flow State principles isn't just the positive outcome but the qualitative difference in how it emerged. This was not the result of strained analysis or desperate problem-solving; the "ah-ha" came from aligned awareness that could perceive patterns and possibilities that are invisible to a more fragmented consciousness.

The implementation wasn't without challenges. Resources were limited, systems needed development, and the immediate needs of food distribution demanded constant attention. But approaching these challenges from Flow State awareness rather than fragmented reaction created a fundamentally different relationship with them—not as obstacles to overcome through force but as elements to work with through aligned intelligence.

This wasn't a mysterious manifestation where challenges simply disappeared. It was practical engagement from a consciousness that could hold multiple dimensions simultaneously—immediate needs and long-term vision, practical limitations and creative possibilities, individual contributions and systemic patterns.

The results spoke for themselves. What began as an emergency response evolved into a comprehensive approach to food insecurity that addressed not just immediate hunger but underlying causes and sustainable solutions. Partnerships formed that might have seemed unlikely from conventional perspectives. Resources appeared from unexpected sources.

Volunteers brought talents and connections that fit precisely with emerging needs.

These outcomes weren't coincidental or simply "lucky." They represented the natural reflection of a consciousness operating from higher frequencies—Level 7 (Acceptance) and occasionally Level 8 (Peace)—where perception isn't limited by fear-based filtering or desire-driven attachment to particular forms.

My experience with HHH not only transformed the organization's impact but also my understanding of how Flow State principles apply in high-stakes, real-world situations. It wasn't about escaping challenges through metaphysical bypassing or denying practical realities. It was about engaging those realities from a different quality of consciousness—one that could perceive patterns, possibilities, and connections which are invisible to a more fragmented awareness.

This phase of my journey also clarified a long-held aspiration: to return to public speaking, not as a weather forecaster but as someone sharing the Consciousness Levels and principles that had transformed my own life through the darkest times. The book you're reading represents fifteen years of research, experience, and insight—not just conceptual understanding but lived transformation through practices tested in the laboratory of real challenges.

What makes the HHH example particularly valuable is that it demonstrates how Flow State principles operate not just in controlled conditions or spiritual retreats but in the messy complexity of addressing urgent human needs during unprecedented circumstances. The same alignment of gut, heart, and mind that begins as personal practice eventually expresses as more effective service and contribution—not separate from practical action but as its foundation and guide.

This quote is from the first-hand account written by W.H. Murray, *The Scottish Himalayan Expedition* (1951).

"Until one is committed, there is hesitancy, the chance to draw back, always ineffectiveness. Concerning all acts of initiative (and creation), there is one elementary truth, the ignorance of which kills countless ideas and splendid plans: that the moment one definitely commits oneself, then Providence moves too. All sorts of things occur to help one that would never otherwise have occurred. A whole stream of events issues from the decision, raising in one's favour all manner of unforeseen incidents and meetings and material assistance, which no man could have dreamt would have come his way..."

Reprogramming Your Biology Through Flow

Our biological transformation happens through what scientists call "epigenetics"—the study of how our behaviors and environment can cause changes that affect the way our genes work. Dispenza's research shows that when we access coherent states of consciousness similar to the Flow State, we actually turn on different genes that promote healing, creativity, and resilience, while turning off genes associated with stress, inflammation, and disease.

One of Dispenza's most powerful examples comes from a week-long study where, through daily practice of entering "coherent brain states" (essentially Flow State by another name), participants showed significant decreases in stress hormones like cortisol and adrenaline, while increasing immune system markers and beneficial hormones like DHEA and oxytocin.

The most striking finding was that these changes weren't minor—in some cases, participants showed changes that would typically take months or years through conventional means. Some experienced healing from chronic conditions that had persisted for decades. Others manifested profound life changes in relationships, career, and creative expression that had previously seemed impossible.

What's happening here at the biological level? When we enter the Flow State, we shift from the sympathetic (fight-or-flight) nervous system to the parasympathetic (rest-and-restore) system, which activates the body's natural healing capacities. But it goes even deeper. The coherent electromagnetic field generated by the heart in Flow State actually communicates directly with our DNA, signaling it to express differently.

Dispenza notes that "when we combine a clear intention with an elevated emotion, we change our energy and broadcast a new electromagnetic signature to the quantum field." This signature affects not just our own biology but the field of possibility around us, which explains why synchronistic events and "coincidences" increase dramatically when operating from Flow State.

I experienced this biological reprogramming personally after incorporating Flow State practices daily. Chronic inflammation that had plagued me for years began to subside. My sleep quality improved dramatically. Energy levels that had been consistently low during my period of collapse rebounded to levels I hadn't experienced in decades. These weren't just subjective improvements but measurable physical changes that conventional medical approaches had failed to address.

The revolutionary implication is that your body is not a fixed, unchangeable entity but a dynamic system that responds moment by moment to your consciousness. As Dispenza puts it, "Your body is your unconscious mind." In other words, your physical condition is largely a manifestation of your habitual thought patterns, emotional states, and perceptions—all of which transform when you access the Flow State.

Beyond Survival: Flow State in Daily Life

While the creation of Hearts, Hands and Hope represents a beautiful example of Flow State manifestation, there are many, many everyday examples that are easy to see, once you understand what to look for.

As you read these stories I've gathered here for you, think about similar occurrences in and around your own life. They are there.

Creative Problem-Solving: During a particularly challenging period in developing a program for Hearts, Hands and Hope, we faced a seemingly insurmountable obstacle—needing an actual location that was far beyond our budget at the time. We found out we couldn't keep working from a rented storage place. In order to provide food, you must pass state agriculture regulations, etc plus we really needed a larger building.

Rather than forcing solutions through conventional approaches (aggressive fundraising, scaling back the program, etc.), I took time to access the Flow State through stillness practice. From that aligned state, an approach emerged that hadn't been visible from fragmented problem-solving: we found a location which was zoned as industrial and we were the second tenants. They learned about our mission and provided the building.

The next task was to get approval from the city, pass food guidelines from the state and so on. We didn't know if this was going to work. Eventually they all approved us, and it was amazing! The building had an office, a meeting room and a huge warehouse. Others donated needed desks, tables and industrial shelving. We became sponsored by competing hospitals through their Corporate Social Responsibility programs. By sharing resources, and from generous donations and partnerships that immediately followed, the impossible became possible and we were able to scale up our operation to help even more food insecure families. A win for all concerned, and beyond my imagination. "…A whole stream of events…raising in one's favour all manner of unforeseen incidents and meetings and material assistance, which no man could have dreamt would have come his way…"

This solution wasn't available to conventional thinking because it required seeing beyond traditional organizational boundaries and competitive mindsets. The Flow State produces synchronicities, every time.

Interpersonal Harmony: A couple I knew had been caught in escalating conflict for months, with communication deteriorating despite both partners' genuine desire for resolution. Their attempts at reconciliation consistently failed because they approached conversations from Level 4-5 consciousness (Fear and Desire), where defensive positioning and need for validation dominated.

I guided them through practices to access stillness individually before attempting communication. When they eventually spoke from this more aligned state, the conversation had an entirely different quality. Rather than repeating familiar patterns of accusation and defense, they found themselves genuinely curious about each other's experience and naturally oriented toward mutual understanding rather than individual vindication.

The situation they were dealing with stayed the same, but the way they looked at it completely changed. Their awareness grew clearer and more whole, and that allowed new answers to appear—answers they couldn't see before. They didn't fix the problem by giving in or pretending it didn't exist, but by moving to a higher level of understanding, a higher frequency. From that place, what once felt like a clash turned into a partnership. Each person saw their own and the other person's needs and naturally moved toward giving to and receiving from each other.

Health Integration: A woman in one of my workshops had struggled with chronic digestive issues for years, cycling through countless treatments, diets, and approaches with limited improvement. Her consciousness around health had become dominated by anxious research, frustration with her body, and desperate seeking for the "right" solution.

Through stillness practice and guided work with the three-brain alignment approach, she accessed a different quality of awareness regarding her body—not the fragmented consciousness that positioned health as something to achieve through striving, but an integrated perception that could listen to the body's wisdom directly.

From this Flow State awareness, she received clear guidance about specific dietary adjustments and lifestyle changes that differed from what experts had recommended but resonated deeply with her intuitive knowing. Following this guidance, her symptoms improved dramatically within weeks, not because she had found the universally "right" approach for everyone else but because she had accessed her own body's individual intelligence through aligned, rather than fragmented, awareness.

This example aligns perfectly with Dr. Dispenza's research on spontaneous remissions and healing. He documents how people who recover from "incurable" conditions often describe accessing a state of consciousness where they no longer feel separate from a healed state—they embody it completely, just as Aidan embodied the reality of having already won the Marvel figures. This embodiment creates what Dispenza calls "the placebo effect without the placebo"—healing that comes from consciousness shift rather than external intervention.

Career Transition: A man in his mid-fifties had spent decades in a career that provided financial security but left him feeling empty and disconnected from his authentic gifts. His attempts to find more fulfilling work consistently faltered because they emerged from fragmented consciousness—analytical planning disconnected from heart wisdom, emotional yearning without practical grounding, fearful clinging to security vs. his desire for meaning.

Through regular Flow State practice, he gradually accessed a more integrated awareness where these seemingly opposing needs no longer appeared contradictory. From this alignment, he didn't abandon his existing career but transformed his relationship with it, bringing more of his authentic gifts to current responsibilities while gradually developing a side business in an area of genuine passion.

The transformation wasn't what he had initially imagined (a complete career change), but what naturally emerged from aligned awareness—integration rather than replacement, evolution rather than revolution. The outcome was even better than he first imagined because it solved the deeper pattern behind the problem, not just the surface issue.

Relationship Transformation: A couple I worked with had reached a breaking point after years of increasingly hostile communication patterns. Rather than focusing on specific techniques or communication rules, I guided them through Flow State practices to access Level 7 consciousness before attempting difficult conversations.

The husband, who typically retreated into analytical problem-solving when emotions ran high, learned to integrate his gut awareness with his thinking mind. His wife, who had been operating primarily from emotional reactivity, discovered how to incorporate thoughtful perspective without abandoning her heart wisdom. The shift wasn't in what they discussed but in the Consciousness Level from which they engaged.

Within weeks, they reported a fundamental change in their relationship quality. 'The issues we argue about haven't completely disappeared,' the wife explained, 'but they no longer define our relationship. It's like we're standing on different ground together.' Their conflicts became opportunities for deeper understanding rather than battles to be won.

Creative Breakthrough: An artist friend had been struggling with creative block for months, attempting to force inspiration through discipline and technique alone. His frustration was palpable as deadline pressure mounted and his usual approaches yielded only derivative work he didn't feel connected to. If you are an artist, I'm sure you can relate.

I introduced him to the three-brain alignment practice combined with the "feeling it in" approach. Rather than trying to visualize completed artwork, he learned to access the feeling state of creative flow itself, independent of specific outcomes. This subtle shift created space for his natural creativity to emerge without the constriction of fear-based forcing.

The resulting work not only met his deadline but represented a significant evolution in his artistic expression. 'It's not that I didn't have to work hard,' he told me later, 'but the work came from a completely different place—more like discovery than manufacturing.'

This creative breakthrough illustrates what Dr. Dispenza describes as the shift from beta brain waves (the analytical, problem-solving state) to alpha and theta waves (the receptive, intuitive states where new connections and insights naturally emerge). When we access the Flow State, we temporarily suspend the analytical mind's dominance, allowing what Dispenza calls "the subconscious mind" to offer solutions beyond our conscious reasoning.

Health Transformation: The more desperately she tried to sleep, the more elusive it became. A woman in my workshop had struggled with chronic insomnia for over a decade, cycling through medications, strict sleep hygiene protocols, and various therapeutic approaches with limited success.

Through the Attention Compass practice, she began recognizing how her consciousness fragmented each night—part of her demanding sleep, another part anxiously monitoring her sleeplessness, yet another catastrophizing about the next day's consequences. From Level 4 (Fear) consciousness, sleep was an enemy to be conquered rather than a natural process to be allowed.

Using the body anchor practice from Chapter 6, she learned to bring attention back to center whenever she noticed it fragmenting at bedtime. Without directly 'trying' to sleep, she created conditions where sleep could naturally emerge. Within three weeks, her sleep had improved dramatically. "I'm not sleeping perfectly every night," she reported, "but the difference is I no longer fight with sleep. When I do have difficult nights, they don't create the same suffering they once did."

What unites these diverse examples is a consistent principle: When consciousness shifts from fragmented to aligned, reality responds not through magical manifestation but through resonant reflection. The Flow State doesn't override natural laws or eliminate practical considerations; it accesses a different order of intelligence that can work with these factors more effectively than fragmented awareness ever could.

This is why Flow State manifestation often produces results that differ from initial concepts but more precisely address underlying patterns. The universe doesn't deliver what we think we want; it reflects the frequency we embody. When that frequency emerges from three-brain alignment rather than fragmented striving, the reflection naturally exhibits greater harmony, effectiveness, and alignment with deeper purpose.

The Code Connection: Level 9 in Action

The examples above represent Level 9 consciousness (Enlightenment) in action—not as permanent transcendence of normal human experience, but as glimpses of non-dual awareness expressing through practical engagement with life's full spectrum.

Remember that each Consciousness Level in The Code represents not just a psychological state but a distinct energy frequency that shapes how we perceive and interact with reality. Level 9 represents the highest frequency currently accessible to human consciousness that I am aware of—a state where the artificial boundaries between self and other, internal and external, personal and universal temporarily dissolve. Then and there we find the underlying unity from which all apparent separation emerges.

This doesn't mean Level 9 eliminates individuality or practical distinction. You don't lose your unique perspective or functional boundaries. Rather, these elements are recognized as temporary expressions of a unified field rather than fundamentally separate realities. Again, think of waves on the ocean—distinct in form and movement while remaining always a part of the whole, the sea. The wave appears to be separate while in fact it is part of the entire ocean with no separation, just energy.

When functioning from Level 9, even momentarily, several distinctive qualities become apparent in how reality manifests:

Effortless Effectiveness: Action from Level 9 exhibits a quality of ease that defies conventional understanding of effort and result. Things happen, not through straining or forced effort, but through aligned participation with the natural flow of energy and information. This isn't bypassing necessary steps, but accessing pathways that remain invisible from more fragmented perspectives.

The creation of Hearts, Hands and Hope demonstrated this quality. The necessary components—space, funding, expertise, community— emerged through aligned action that naturally attracted resonant elements. This wasn't luck or coincidence, but the natural consequence of operating from a consciousness frequency that could perceive and engage with patterns beyond conventional awareness.

Synchronistic Timing: From Level 9, timing exhibits an uncanny precision that can't be engineered through analytical planning. The right connections, opportunities, or insights appear at exactly the moment they're needed, not because the universe is magically catering to personal desire but because perception has expanded to include dimensions typically filtered out by fragmented awareness.

This aligns with Dr. Dispenza's findings about synchronicity. He notes that participants in his advanced workshops consistently report dramatic increases in meaningful coincidences after practicing coherent states. These aren't random events, but the natural outcome of broadcasting a more coherent signal to the quantum field. As he puts it, "When you change your energy, you change your life."

Harmonious Integration: Think about how water flows around obstacles in a river. Instead of trying to push straight through a boulder (which would be impossible), it naturally finds the path of least resistance, creating beautiful patterns that work with the landscape rather than against it.

Flow State solutions work in a similar way. When we're stuck in fragmented thinking, we often see only two options: push through the obstacle with force or give up entirely. It's like trying to navigate that river by either ramming into the boulder or turning back completely. This either/or approach limits our options and often creates new problems while trying to solve the original one.

But when we operate from the integrated awareness of the Flow State, we perceive the situation differently. Like water finding its natural path around obstacles, our solutions emerge with an unexpected elegance that honors the reality of what's there while still moving forward. We see how seemingly opposing needs can actually complement each other, like how the pressure of water against rock eventually shapes both into something beautiful.

Evolutionary Alignment: Level 9 manifestation consistently serves not just personal preference but evolutionary purpose—the larger patterns of development and integration that transcend individual desires while including them within more comprehensive movements. This isn't about sacrificing personal fulfillment for some abstract greater good, but accessing a level of awareness where these dimensions are recognized as inseparable rather than competing.

Hearts, Hands and Hope didn't just meet my need for meaningful work and financial contribution to the family; it addressed a genuine need in the community that aligned with larger movements toward greater inclusion, support for vulnerable populations, and community resilience. This alignment wasn't engineered through moral calculation but emerged naturally from the frequency of Level 9 consciousness.

Understanding these qualities helps clarify why Flow State manifestation doesn't always match our initial concepts or timelines. It's not that our desires aren't being heard or that manifestation principles don't work; it's that Level 9 consciousness responds to patterns beyond what the individual ego can perceive from its limited perspective.

The Flow State connects us with Level 9 consciousness not as permanent transcendence but as increasingly available perception that can inform practical action even amid normal human experience. We don't need to abandon individuality or practical distinction to access this frequency; we simply need to recognize these elements as functional aspects of experience rather than ultimate reality.

How Reality Mirrors Our Consciousness Level

One of the most powerful principles revealed through Flow State experiences is how consistently reality mirrors the consciousness level from which we engage with it. This isn't supernatural manifestation but natural resonance—the immutable tendency of similar frequencies to attract and amplify each other.

We've all heard of the "tuning fork phenomenon," and I think it fits here: If you strike a tuning fork, creating a specific tone, a second identical, un-struck tuning fork nearby will begin to vibrate in harmony. Energy is transferred invisibly to the second, causing it to resonate without ever being touched.

Let me share a revealing example from my own journey:

During the early stages of career collapse, I attended a networking event specifically designed for professionals in career transition. Externally, everyone there faced similar circumstances—job loss, financial uncertainty, need for new opportunities. But the consciousness frequencies people embodied seemed to vary, creating strikingly different experiences of the same event.

Sometime after, I reflected on what I'd seen, heard, and felt in that room. Some attendees appeared to operate primarily from Level 4 (Fear), radiating anxiety about the future and desperately seeking security. Their interactions had a grasping quality, focused more on what they could get than what they could contribute. From what I overheard, they tended to attract similarly fearful connections, creating a reinforcing field of scarcity consciousness that generated few meaningful opportunities despite considerable effort.

Others seemed to function mainly from Level 5 (Desire), projecting confidence and ambition while internally craving validation and achievement. Their networking had a performative quality—impressive on the surface, but lacking authentic connection. They typically attracted flashy opportunities, ones that seemed promising yet lacked what I would call stability.

I observed that a small number seemed to operate from Levels 7-8 (Acceptance/Peace), approaching the situation not from desperate need or ambitious striving but from authentic presence and genuine interest in contribution. Their interactions had a quality of ease and authenticity that naturally attracted meaningful connections. They may have left pocketing fewer business cards, but with more substantial relationships that could lead to unexpected opportunities aligned with deeper purpose.

I began that event operating from Levels 4-5, feeling the familiar mix of anxiety and ambition that had characterized much of my career. But halfway through, something shifted. Through a brief moment of stillness practice in the venue's restroom (not the most glamorous meditation setting!), I accessed a quality of Level 7-8 consciousness that transformed my experience completely.

Returning to the same room with the same people, everything appeared different. Instead of seeing a competitive field of limited opportunities, I perceived a community of individuals with unique gifts and challenges. Instead of focusing on what I needed, I became genuinely curious about how I might contribute. Instead of anxiously evaluating each interaction for potential benefit, I engaged with authentic presence regardless of apparent utility.

The external responses to this shift were immediate and unmistakable. Conversations that had felt strained or awkward became flowing and generative. People who had seemed closed or distant suddenly appeared open and engaged. Connections formed not through strategic positioning but through authentic resonance.

The transformational outcome that still makes me smile today? One of these connections led to a consulting opportunity that provided bridge income during the early development of Hearts, Hands and Hope. This wasn't because I had suddenly become more qualified or impressive, but because the consciousness frequency I was broadcasting had shifted from fear/desire to acceptance/peace, naturally attracting corresponding reflections.

This mirroring principle doesn't just apply to interpersonal connections, but to all dimensions of experience:

Environmental Reflection: The places we live and spend time in often reflect the level of awareness we're operating from. When our mindset is at a lower level, life around us seems full of problems, dangers, and limits. It's not that the world itself is against us—it's that our minds notice and focus on what matches the way we're feeling inside.

During periods when I was caught in Level 3-4 consciousness, even beautiful natural settings appeared threatening or depressing. The same lake that later became a source of profound peace initially seemed to mock my failure with its serenity or threaten me with its vastness. The environment hadn't changed; the consciousness perceiving it had.

When consciousness shifts to higher levels (6-9), the same environments reveal resources, opportunities, and beauty previously filtered out. During moments of Level 7-8 consciousness, ordinary settings consistently displayed extraordinary qualities—geometric perfection in everyday objects, vibrant energy in seemingly mundane interactions, elegant solutions in apparent obstacles.

Temporal Reflection: Our consciousness level directly affects our experience of time, which in turn shapes the nature and pace of manifestation. Lower levels (1-5) create a contracted relationship with time—either fixated on past regrets/traumas or anxiously anticipating future threats/rewards. This means delay, poor timing, and missed opportunities. At this level, we often suffer with a sense of "time starvation."

During periods caught in Level 4 consciousness, I experienced constant timing misalignment—arriving at opportunities just after they closed, discovering resources just after the need had passed, connecting with people just after relevant projects had been assigned. This wasn't bad luck but the natural reflection of consciousness that wasn't present enough to perceive and engage with the actual unfolding of events.

At higher levels of awareness, our sense of time starts to feel bigger than just one moment following another. Things seem to happen at the right time, as if by coincidence—but it's really not luck. It's a natural flow where events line up perfectly because they're following the true rhythm of growth, not a schedule we try to force.

During the creation of Hearts, Hands and Hope, timing repeatedly displayed an uncanny precision that couldn't be engineered—resources appearing exactly when needed, connections forming at precisely the right moment for maximum synergy, insights emerging just when they could be most effectively applied. This wasn't mysterious intervention but natural alignment with temporal patterns that remain invisible to more contracted levels of awareness.

Dr. Dispenza has documented similar timing phenomena in his research. He notes that participants who maintain coherent brain states (AKA Flow State) begin to experience what he calls "synchronistic opportunities"—events that seem impossibly well-timed from a conventional perspective. One participant in his workshop had been struggling to find funding for an innovative health project for years. After four days of practicing coherent states, she received a call from a previously uninterested investor who had suddenly decided to fully fund her initiative—with no external prompting. As Dispenza explains, when we shift our energy, we broadcast a different electromagnetic signature that attracts different possibilities.

Informational Reflection: The information we encounter—whether through conversations, media, or seemingly random exposure—consistently mirrors our consciousness frequency. This explains why some people seem to easily discover exactly the knowledge they need while others remain caught in cycles of confusion despite access to the same external sources.

When operating from lower frequencies (1-5), information tends to appear contradictory, overwhelming, or insufficient. During my early career collapse, research into new opportunities consistently generated confusion rather than clarity—experts contradicted each other, data seemed incomplete, and new information often invalidated previous understanding rather than building upon it.

From higher frequencies (6-9), the same information landscape reveals patterns, connections, and relevant specificity that naturally supports coherent action. During Flow State periods in developing Hearts, Hands and Hope, needed information seemed to appear precisely when required—articles addressing exact challenges we faced, conversations that revealed specific resources we needed, or insights that connected previously separate understandings into comprehensive patterns.

This informational resonance aligns with Dispenza's concept of "tuning the brain" to different frequencies. He explains that our brains are literally receivers that can be tuned to different "stations" of information. When we operate from coherent states, we tune into information frequencies that were always broadcasting but were previously inaccessible to our fragmented awareness. As he writes, "When you change your energy, you change what you're capable of perceiving."

That reminds me of the quote, "If you change the way you look at things, the things you look at change," most famously attributed to Dr. Wayne Dyer. It's also associated with physicist Max Planck and suggests that changing your perspective can fundamentally alter your experience of reality. Changing your perspective is accomplished through changing your frequency, your Level of Consciousness.

Understanding this mirroring principle transforms how we approach manifestation. Instead of trying to force specific outcomes through increasingly detailed techniques, the focus shifts to embodying the consciousness frequency that naturally attracts and sustains desired experiences. The primary question becomes not "How do I get what I want?" but "What frequency am I broadcasting, and does it match what I claim to desire?" This is where using your feelings as a guide can be the best approach to discover where you are at any time.

This understanding doesn't eliminate the role of action but transforms its quality and foundation. Action still matters enormously, but its effectiveness depends far more on the consciousness from which it emerges than on its external form or intensity. Action from aligned consciousness naturally manifests results that transcend what could be achieved through even the most determined effort from fragmented awareness.

Becoming Your Own Placebo: The Biology of Belief

Dr. Dispenza's groundbreaking work in *You Are the Placebo* provides a scientific framework for understanding how the Flow State creates tangible change in our biology and, by extension, our external reality. The placebo effect—where patients experience real healing after receiving an inert substance they believe is medicine—demonstrates the remarkable power of belief to create physiological change.

What Dispenza discovered through his research is that we don't need the external "sugar pill" to activate this healing response. We can become our own placebos by creating the same internal states that produce the placebo effect—primarily belief and elevated emotion.

This connects directly to our exploration of the Flow State. When we align the three brains (gut, heart, and mind) in the Flow State, we create precisely the conditions that Dispenza identifies as necessary for becoming our own placebo:

1. A coherent belief that isn't contradicted by competing thoughts

2. An elevated emotional state that reinforces rather than undermines the belief

3. Surrender to a higher intelligence beyond the analytical mind

I experienced this principle most powerfully during the period when we were facing foreclosure on our home. Every external circumstance pointed to the inevitable loss of our house. Family members warned, "The sheriff is going to put your stuff out on the lawn if you don't move." Everyone I spoke with delivered the same verdict—we would be living in our car by the end of the year.

But something within me refused to accept this seemingly inevitable (and disastrous) outcome. Despite overwhelming external evidence, I maintained an unshakable inner knowing: "This is my house." This wasn't blind denial but a deep, resonant feeling state that transcended current circumstances. I would visualize coming home from a vacation to this house, fully embodying the feeling of returning to my permanent home, not a temporary residence about to be taken away.

I didn't just think about how much I wanted and needed to keep my house; I lived from the feeling state of already having secured it. I felt the relief, the stability, the sanctuary that this home represented—not as a future hope but as a present reality. This emotional stance wasn't based on any external evidence. By all rational measures, foreclosure was inevitable. But I maintained this inner state regardless of what everyone else believed.

And then a remarkable thing happened. About a month before we would have been homeless, a realtor reached out unexpectedly, telling me I could keep my house if I met with a particular lawyer. If the lawyer determined we had a case—which was often not the situation in similar circumstances—he would represent us. This opportunity appeared seemingly out of nowhere, aligning perfectly with the inner state I had been maintaining.

For two and a half years, we lived without paying a mortgage, trusting that the lawyer would find a resolution. Eventually, we received notification that the house was indeed ours, with an adjusted mortgage that we could afford—at a time when finding "two nickels to rub together" was challenging. Random luck or coincidence? No, it was the natural manifestation of maintaining a coherent emotional frequency despite contradictory external circumstances. The belief wasn't just mental assent to a possibility; it was a complete embodiment of the feeling state associated with the desired outcome. This is exactly what Dispenza means when he explains that the body must "emotionally understand" the future reality before it can manifest in our experience.

What makes this understanding so revolutionary is that it gives us practical access to what mystics have described for centuries—the power of consciousness to transform physical reality. As Dispenza writes, "Thoughts are the language of the brain, and feelings are the language of the body." When these align in the Flow State, we create what he calls "whole-brain thinking" which allows us to become our own placebo.

This principle applies far beyond saving a house from foreclosure. Every aspect of our lives—from relationships to creative expression to professional opportunities—responds to the same mechanisms. When we operate from fragmented consciousness, our biology reflects that fragmentation with stress hormones, inflammatory responses, and limited neural connectivity. When we operate from the Flow State, our biology shifts toward coherence, creating conditions where new possibilities can literally emerge at the level of our cells.

Overcoming Common Obstacles to Maintaining Flow

While the principles of Flow State manifestation are natural and consistent, maintaining alignment amid life's complexities presents real challenges. Even after experiencing the transformative power of three-brain alignment, most people encounter obstacles that temporarily interrupt flow and return consciousness to more fragmented frequencies.

These obstacles aren't failures or indications that the process isn't working; they're natural aspects of the evolutionary journey from fragmented to integrated awareness. Understanding and working skillfully with these challenges is essential for developing stable access to the Flow State rather than experiencing it as an occasional accident or fleeting grace.

Let's explore the most common obstacles and practical approaches for working with them:

Emotional Gravity: Each of us has a "set point" in consciousness—a frequency range we naturally return to without specific practice or intention. This set point is established through a combination of biological predisposition, early conditioning, cumulative experience, and habitual patterns of thought and emotion.

When we access higher frequencies through Flow State practice, emotional gravity naturally pulls consciousness back toward this set point, creating what feels like regression or loss of connection. This pull isn't something going wrong; it's the natural tendency of established neural patterns to reassert themselves until new pathways become equally established.

Working with Emotional Gravity: Rather than fighting against this pull or becoming discouraged by it, recognize emotional gravity as a natural aspect of consciousness evolution. Instead of expecting continuous maintenance of peak states, focus on:

- Gradually raising your set point through consistent practice rather than attempting to permanently escape it

- Shortening recovery time when gravity pulls you to lower frequencies

- Developing the capacity to recognize the pull before complete identification with lower states

- Creating environmental supports that counter gravity rather than reinforce it

During my early experiences with the Flow State, I would often access Level 7-8 consciousness during stillness practice, only to find myself pulled back to Levels 4-5 within hours or even minutes of returning to normal activities. Initially discouraging, this pattern became informative when I recognized it as natural gravity rather than personal failure.

By focusing on shortening recovery time and recognizing the pull earlier in the process, I gradually shifted from spending days caught in lower frequencies after a "fall" to recognizing the gravitational pull within minutes and implementing practices that could interrupt complete identification with it.

Environmental Triggers: Our physical and social environments are designed to maintain specific consciousness frequencies, often centered around Levels 4-5 (Fear and Desire). Media broadcasts primarily fear-based content. Advertising targets desire and insufficiency. Social structures reward conformity to established patterns rather than authentic alignment. Don't even get me started on "Social" media; what a waste of time, emotions, and attention (energy).

Even with strong internal practice, these environmental triggers can rapidly pull consciousness out of flow and back into fragmented patterns. A single news headline, challenging interaction, or environmental stressor can activate neural pathways associated with lower frequencies, creating an automatic shift difficult to counteract once fully triggered.

Working with Environmental Triggers: Instead of attempting to eliminate all triggering elements (rarely possible) or pretending they don't affect you (rarely honest), develop a strategic relationship with your environment:

- Consciously design your immediate physical space to support higher frequencies rather than trigger lower ones

- Develop awareness of specific environmental elements that consistently trigger fragmentation for you personally

- Create buffer practices that prepare consciousness before entering potentially triggering environments

- Establish pattern interrupts that catch triggering reactions before they fully activate lower frequencies

For me, certain social environments consistently triggered Level 4-5 consciousness; particularly professional gatherings where comparative achievement and status were emphasized. Rather than avoiding these environments entirely (impractical given my responsibilities) or pretending they didn't affect me (ineffective given the reality of triggers), I developed specific practices.

Before entering such settings, I would take five minutes of stillness practice in my car, establishing three-brain alignment that created a buffer against immediate triggering. During events, I established pattern interrupts like briefly stepping outside or practicing conscious breathing whenever I noticed comparative thinking or status anxiety arising. After exposure, I implemented "consciousness decontamination" practices to release absorbed frequencies that didn't serve higher alignment.

Integration Challenges: Perhaps the most subtle obstacle to maintaining flow comes from integration challenges—the difficulties that arise when attempting to embody higher consciousness within systems and relationships designed for lower frequencies. Family systems, work environments, and social groups often unconsciously resist changes in established patterns, creating pressure to return to familiar frequencies even when they don't serve genuine well-being. Family gatherings come to mind especially as they are entrenched as the oldest neural networks; but they can be overcome.

This pressure rarely appears as direct opposition to growth but as subtle invalidation, redirection, or concern that can be more challenging to navigate than outright resistance. Well-meaning friends express worry about changes in behavior. Family members respond to new patterns with confusion or withdrawal. Work systems interpret aligned action as non-compliance with established norms.

Working with Integration Challenges: These social dynamics require particularly skillful navigation:

- Recognize that resistance from systems and relationships isn't necessarily opposition to growth but natural homeostatic response to pattern disruption

- Implement changes in behavior gradually rather than abruptly when possible, allowing systems to adapt incrementally

- Communicate about shifts in consciousness through practical outcomes rather than conceptual language that may trigger resistance

- Find or create relationships and environments that support higher frequencies to balance those that unconsciously resist them

During my early experiences with higher consciousness, I made the mistake of attempting to directly communicate these shifts to people operating primarily from Levels 4-5, using language and concepts that made perfect sense from aligned (higher) awareness but appeared threatening or nonsensical from more fragmented (lower) perspectives. I needed a technique.

Learning from these missteps, I shifted to embodying changes with less explanation and more demonstration—letting altered behavior and its practical outcomes speak for themselves rather than trying to convince others of conceptual frameworks they weren't yet prepared to recognize. This approach reduced resistance while allowing genuine integration to proceed at a pace that systems could absorb. Simply, meet your audience where they are.

Success Loops: Paradoxically, one of the most challenging obstacles to maintaining flow can be initial success itself. When Flow State practice produces desired outcomes, the calculating mind often attempts to formalize and systematize what was essentially an organic, aligned process. "It worked when I did X, so I'll repeat X exactly to guarantee continued results." Nope. That's the old pattern we've all been taught and failed at.

This attempt to mechanize flow ironically interrupts it, replacing authentic alignment with formulaic repetition. The consciousness shifts from open participation to controlled replication, moving from Level 7-8 frequencies back to the Level 4-5 desire for guaranteed outcomes and fear of losing what's been gained.

Working with Success Loops: This subtle trap requires particular awareness:

- Recognize success as confirmation of principles rather than validation of specific techniques

- Maintain curiosity and openness even (especially) when particular approaches have produced positive results

- Focus on the quality of consciousness rather than replication of external forms or behaviors

- Allow each engagement with flow to be fresh rather than attempting to clone previous experiences

After the initial success of Hearts, Hands and Hope, I began attempting to formalize exactly what had "worked" so I could reliably repeat it in other contexts. This mechanistic approach ironically blocked the very flow that had generated the original success. The breakthrough came when I recognized that what mattered wasn't the specific sequence of actions, but the consciousness quality from which they had emerged.

By returning focus to three-brain alignment rather than technique replication, I restored access to flow that could respond freshly to new situations rather than mechanically applying formulas derived from previous ones. The principles remained consistent, but their expression remained organic rather than mechanical. This process is revolutionary, yet so natural to us all.

Spiritual Bypassing: A final obstacle worth mentioning involves what contemporary psychology calls "spiritual bypassing"—using higher states of consciousness to avoid rather than transform challenging emotions, situations, or developmental tasks. This pattern uses flow experiences as escape from complexity rather than capacity for engaging with it more effectively.

Signs of bypassing include using flow language to deny genuine difficulties, prematurely claiming transcendence of normal human needs and vulnerabilities, or employing consciousness practices to avoid necessary confrontations with internal and external challenges that require engaged resolution rather than transcendent avoidance.

Working with Spiritual Bypassing: This subtle distortion requires honest self-assessment:

- Recognize that authentic flow enhances rather than eliminates engagement with life's full spectrum

- Check whether consciousness practices are being used to avoid necessary developmental work or challenging emotions

- Notice whether language about higher awareness is being employed to create spiritual identity rather than genuine integration

- Maintain grounded authenticity about both transcendent experiences and human limitations

Imagine you're hiking along a beautiful mountain trail when you come across a deep ravine in your path. There are two ways you might respond: try to leap over it entirely (pretending it's not there) or find a way to climb down, cross, and climb back up the other side.

I fell into this exact trap in my own journey with the Flow State. For a while, I used my newfound access to higher states of consciousness like a personal helicopter, trying to fly over the ravines of my past—the childhood wounds, the unprocessed grief, the patterns formed in my relationships with my parents. I'd use beautiful spiritual language about transcendence and higher awareness whenever these painful areas surfaced, essentially saying, "I don't need to deal with that old stuff anymore because I'm operating at a higher level now."

It was my therapist who gently called me on this avoidance pattern during a particularly challenging session. "Eric," he said, "you're using transcendence as a bypass. What you are calling your 'Flow State' isn't meant to help you avoid your humanity—it's meant to help you embrace it more fully."

This insight hit me like a thunderclap. True growth wasn't about leaping over the ravines but finding a wiser, more compassionate way to navigate through them. The Flow State wasn't an escape hatch from my developmental work—it was a more spacious container for doing that work effectively.

When I finally brought my Flow State awareness into direct contact with my early childhood experiences of abandonment, something remarkable happened. Instead of those painful memories contaminating my higher awareness, my higher awareness created room for those experiences to be felt, understood, and integrated in ways that years of traditional therapy hadn't accomplished. It was like the difference between examining a wound with a dim flashlight versus in clear daylight—the light didn't heal the wound by itself, but it made healing work much more effective.

Understanding and working skillfully with these obstacles transforms them from disappointing setbacks to informative aspects of consciousness evolution. The path toward stable flow isn't continuous upward progression, but spiral development that includes apparent regressions, resistances, and challenges as essential elements of genuine integration rather than failures to be avoided.

When we learn to understand and handle our challenges wisely, they stop feeling like failures and start showing us how our awareness is growing. The journey toward steady flow isn't a straight climb upward— it's more like a spiral that includes steps backward, moments of resistance, and hard times. These aren't mistakes; they're part of real growth.

The goal isn't to be perfect, but to build strength and awareness. It's not about never feeling low, but about noticing it sooner, handling it better, and finding your balance again more quickly when life's difficulties knock you off track.

Dr. Dispenza acknowledges these challenges in his research, noting that lasting transformation requires consistent practice rather than one-time events. As he explains, "Change is an inside job that takes time. If you keep reproducing the state on a daily basis over time, the change in your energy and your life becomes permanent." This is why he emphasizes daily meditation practice to strengthen the neural pathways that support coherent brain states, making them more resilient against the challenges we've explored.

The Dream Deepens: The Collaborative Dance

As Hearts, Hands and Hope began to take form, my recurring dream evolved yet again. One night, the dream began with me standing on a stage.

◆

I can't make out individual faces in the darkened theater. Music begins playing—something classical, but with contemporary elements woven through it, a composition that seems to bridge different worlds. I sense that is exactly what my life is doing.

I begin to dance. My movements feel both spontaneous and inevitable, as if I'm discovering the choreography in the moment of performing it. This is a new dancing experience, neither controlled nor chaotic, but flowing from a deeper intelligence that knows exactly what I want to express through this body.

From the wing of the stage, the disheveled man appears. Rather than the rejection or hesitation I might once have felt, I find myself extending a hand toward him, inviting him to join the dance without a moment's uncertainty about whether he belongs here.

As he steps into the light, I see that he has changed. The grime and desperation that had once defined him are barely noticeable. He is not polished like the weatherman, but he carries a natural dignity, an unaffected presence that needs no external validation. His movements as he walks are not precisely graceful, but they possess something more compelling—an authenticity that no amount of training could produce.

We begin to dance together—not in synchronized movements but in complementary ones, creating patterns that neither of us could have created alone.

Where I am structured, he is fluid. Where I am calculated, he is intuitive. Where I am trained, he is raw. Yet somehow, these differences create a harmony rather than a conflict, a conversation rather than a competition.

The audience, initially silent, began to respond—first with murmurs of appreciation, then with applause that built to a standing ovation. They weren't applauding performance or skill, but the authentic expression of integration unfolding before them. They were witnessing a cohesive self in a beautiful dance of collaboration.

"This is flow," the once-disheveled man said as we moved together, his voice now indistinguishable from my own internal knowing. "Not perfection, but wholeness in motion."

◆

I woke with the sensation of movement still flowing through my body, as if the dance continued even in waking life. As I walked into a meeting at HHH that day, I noticed how different aspects of myself naturally took the lead in different situations—sometimes the structured analyst, sometimes the intuitive feeler—without internal conflict or the need to maintain a singular identity. I was no longer the weatherman pretending the disheveled man didn't exist, nor was I defined by what I had lost. I was the dancer, constantly discovering the next movement by being fully present to what wanted to emerge through me.

Exercise: Moving from Theory to Application

This integrative exercise helps translate Flow State principles from conceptual understanding to lived experience in specific areas of your life. Rather than a generic practice, it focuses on applying these principles to actual situations you're currently navigating.

You'll need:

- 45-60 minutes of uninterrupted time

- A journal or writing device

- A specific life situation you'd like to engage from flow rather than fragmentation

Part 1: Situation Assessment (10-15 minutes)

Begin by clearly defining a current life situation where you'd like to apply Flow State principles:

1. Briefly describe the situation in factual terms without interpretation or judgment

2. Identify what makes this situation challenging or significant for you

3. Notice what outcomes or experiences you desire in this situation

4. Observe what emotions typically arise when engaging with this situation

5. Recognize what consciousness levels (1-9) you typically operate from when dealing with this situation

Be honest about your current patterns without judgment. This isn't about criticizing yourself but creating clear awareness of the starting point. If we never start, we never move.

Part 2: Three-Brain Alignment (10-15 minutes)

Now create the foundational state from which effective application becomes possible:

1. Find a comfortable position that allows both relaxation and alertness

2. Begin with several conscious breaths, allowing attention to ride the natural rhythm of breathing

3. Bring attention to your gut center (lower abdomen), noticing sensations and allowing tension to release

4. Move attention to your heart center (middle chest), feeling any emotions present without trying to change them

5. Bring attention to your head center (space between and slightly behind eyes), noticing thought patterns without getting caught in content

6. Gradually expand awareness to include all three centers simultaneously, feeling them as an integrated field rather than separate locations

7. Notice the quality of awareness that emerges when these centers operate in harmony rather than isolation or hierarchy

Don't force a particular state or judge your experience. Simply allow the natural alignment that occurs when awareness includes all three centers without fragmentation.

Part 3: Situation Reimagining (10-15 minutes)

From this aligned state, revisit the situation you identified in Part 1:

1. Without forcing change in external details, notice how the situation appears when perceived from three-brain alignment rather than fragmented awareness

2. Observe what aspects become more prominent or recede when viewed from this integrated perspective

3. Feel what emotional tone naturally arises toward the situation from alignment rather than fragmentation

4. Notice what possibilities or responses become visible that weren't apparent from more divided awareness

5. Recognize what wisdom or guidance emerges about engaging with this situation from flow rather than fragmentation

This isn't about denying challenges or imagining magical solutions but accessing a different order of intelligence that can engage more effectively with the situation's actual complexity.

Part 4: Aligned Action Planning (10-15 minutes)

Now translate insights into practical application:

1. Identify 2-3 specific actions that emerge from aligned awareness rather than from fragmented reaction

2. Notice the qualitative difference between these actions and what you might have done (or did do) from the more common divided consciousness

3. For each action, define what makes it aligned rather than merely strategic or reactive

4. Recognize potential challenges to maintaining flow while implementing these actions

5. Develop specific supports that will help sustain alignment during practical engagement

The goal isn't elaborate planning but clarity about how aligned awareness translates into different qualities of action in this specific situation.

Daily Integration Practice:

To support ongoing application beyond this exercise:

1. Situation Check-ins: Before engaging with the identified situation in daily life, take 30-60 seconds to reset attention through conscious breathing and brief three-brain alignment.

2. Alignment Anchors: Create physical, visual, or auditory anchors that remind you of the aligned perspective when actively engaged in the situation. This might be a small object you carry, an image on your phone, or a specific phrase that reconnects you with the aligned state.

3. Course Corrections: When you notice yourself being pulled into fragmented awareness while dealing with the situation, implement brief pattern interrupts that create space for realignment rather than continued fragmentation.

4. Reflection Journaling: After significant engagements with the situation, take a few minutes to journal about what consciousness you operated from, what results emerged from that consciousness, and what you're learning about the relationship between awareness quality and external manifestation.

5. Appreciation Practice: Regularly appreciate any evidence that aligned awareness is creating different results, regardless of whether those results match your initial concepts of a successful outcome.

This exercise isn't a one-time solution but a template for ongoing practice that gradually shifts the consciousness from which you engage with important life situations. The goal isn't perfection but increasing capacity to choose alignment rather than defaulting to fragmentation when challenges arise.

Beyond Achievement: The Deeper Purpose of Flow

As we conclude this chapter on Flow State manifestation, it's important to recognize that the deeper purpose of flow goes beyond achieving specific outcomes or improving life circumstances. While these benefits naturally occur when consciousness shifts from fragmented to aligned awareness, they're secondary effects rather than the primary purpose of Flow State development.

The deeper value of flow lies in what it reveals about the nature of consciousness itself and our relationship with reality. When we experience the qualitative difference between fragmented and aligned awareness—not just conceptually but directly—we discover something profound: consciousness isn't just registering reality; it's participating in its emergence, producing something new for you to see and feel.

This realization changes the way we see life. Instead of thinking we're separate people moving through a world that runs on its own, we start to see that we're part of a shared process where our inner world and the outer world constantly influence each other. This isn't just an idea or theory—it's something you can actually experience more and more through regular Flow State practice.

During my own journey, this shift in understanding proved more valuable than any specific manifestations that accompanied it. While the creation of Hearts, Hands and Hope resolved practical challenges and provided meaningful purpose, the deeper transformation came from recognizing that consciousness itself is the ground of experience rather than just its witness.

Dr. Dispenza captures this profound recognition when he writes that "your personality creates your personal reality." This seemingly simple statement contains a revolutionary understanding—that who you are being (your personality or state of consciousness) quite literally creates what you experience as your personal reality. Not just subjectively, but through measurable changes in your biology and electromagnetic field that influence how you perceive and interact with the world around you.

This recognition doesn't eliminate challenges or guarantee particular outcomes. The challenges of human existence continue—health fluctuates, relationships evolve, practical needs persist.

But our relationship with these challenges transforms fundamentally when we experience them not just as problems to solve but as aspects of a reality that consciousness itself is helping to generate.

The invitation isn't to escape normal human experience through perpetual peak states or to deny life's genuine difficulties. It's to engage with the full spectrum of existence from a different quality of presence— one that participates rather than merely reacts, creates rather than merely responds, and recognizes patterns rather than merely navigates circumstance.

This transformed relationship with reality isn't an achievement to complete but an evolution to continue. It doesn't reach a final destination but spirals through ever-deepening levels of awareness and integration. The Flow State isn't the end of the journey but its authentic beginning— not an escape from engagement but its most genuine expression.

As you continue exploring and applying these principles in your own life, remember that the most significant manifestation isn't what appears externally, but what emerges internally—not just what you create but who you become through the process of creation. The Flow State manifests not just better circumstances but more authentic presence—not just improved conditions but expanded awareness of the consciousness that generates all conditions.

This is the Flow State manifested in its fullest sense—not just as occasional peak experience or manifestation technique but as a fundamental shift in how consciousness relates to the reality it simultaneously perceives and creates. This shift doesn't eliminate the human journey but transforms its quality from fragmented struggle to aligned participation—from separated striving to connected co-creation. Living from this state and working with Universal Mind is a heaven on Earth.

"A good traveler has no fixed plans and is not intent upon arriving." This quote from Lao Tzu reflects his philosophy of living in the moment, enjoying the journey, and remaining adaptable.

This ancient wisdom beautifully aligns with the message about the Flow State. Just as the good traveler finds value in the journey itself rather than fixating on the destination, the Flow State is about the quality of presence we bring to each moment rather than some final achievement we're striving toward.

In the Taoist tradition, this idea of process over destination is fundamental. Another Lao Tzu quote reinforces this concept: "Stop leaving and you will arrive. Stop searching and you will see. Stop running away and you will be found." This paradoxical wisdom suggests that our constant striving toward a goal often prevents us from experiencing what we already have.

The Flow State is "not just what we do but who we are in the doing of it" echoes this ancient understanding that the path itself is where transformation occurs. The vehicle (the Flow State) and how we travel in it matters more than any destination we might reach.

In the next chapter, we'll explore how this transformed relationship with reality is expressed in daily life through the integrated practices that sustain access to flow amid normal human experience.

CHAPTER 9
The Integrated Life

Take a moment and recall a time, no matter how distant or brief the moment, when everything in your life *felt right*, like everything was simply in perfect harmony. Bring to mind as vivid a picture as possible of that scene.

Like when you're standing at the ocean's edge, and you feel completely in sync with the rhythm of the waves, the song of the wind, and the vast expanse of the sky. Or perhaps the experience you remember is not an alone time, but with a loved one, and you're dancing and laughing. That sensation—that extraordinary alignment where boundaries dissolve and everything flows with effortless grace—does not have to occur as only a rare moment of bliss; it's a glimpse of what's possible when you live from the Flow State. You can not only find those moments more and more frequently, you can expand them, you can have them become *your life*.

The invitation of this chapter isn't just theoretical—it's a call to action based on my lived experience. This book stands as a testament to a profound truth: the Flow State isn't some mystical concept but a tangible, achievable reality that transforms everything it touches. I've walked this path from complete collapse to extraordinary rebirth, and what I've discovered isn't just personally meaningful—it's universally accessible. I know this because I have lived it. I have seen firsthand the transformative power within stillness and appreciating the moment I am in.

The feeling is hard to put into words, though many have both in the past as well as currently. The best thing I can offer is my peace of mind, which without the flow state would not have been possible. I also have seen this with many of those I have worked with. Lives changed, peace gained.

The ancient Taoist sage Chuang Tzu captured this experience perfectly when he wrote: "The perfect man employs his mind as a mirror. It grasps nothing; it refuses nothing. It receives, but does not keep." This mirror-like quality of consciousness—clear, receptive, and undisturbed—is the essence of what I've come to understand as the integrated life.

I remember standing in my kitchen one ordinary Tuesday morning, surrounded by the chaos of everyday life. My son was running late for school, emails were piling up on my phone, and the morning news was broadcasting another global crisis. In the past, my attention would have scattered like light through a broken prism—part of me rushing Aidan out the door, another part mentally composing email responses, yet another absorbing the troubling headlines and spinning anxiety about the future.

But something different happened that morning. Instead of my attention shattering into disconnected fragments, I felt myself settle into a state of coherence—a unified awareness where all these dimensions existed within a single clear field of perception. Not by escaping the situation or pushing anything away, but by fully inhabiting it from a different place within myself.

Time didn't slow down, but my relationship to it shifted. I moved through the morning with a strange paradox of complete presence and expanded awareness, responding to each need without becoming captured by it.

This coherent state is what the ancient traditions have pointed to across millennia. The Buddhist concept of "samadhi" describes it as *unification of mind*. The Taoist idea of "wu-wei" captures it as effortless action. The Hindu tradition speaks of "yoga" (literally, union), where consciousness operates as an integrated whole rather than divided parts.

Nothing external had changed in my kitchen that morning. But everything was different because of where I was operating from. This is what integrated life looks like—not some mountaintop existence separate from normal challenges, but everyday life experienced from an extraordinary place of wholeness.

Living from the Inside Out

Most of us have been taught to live from the outside in—allowing external circumstances, others' expectations, and cultural programming to determine our internal state. The 13th-century Sufi poet Rumi described this common condition perfectly: "I have lived on the lip of insanity, wanting to know reasons, knocking on a door. It opens. I've been knocking from the inside!"

This powerful metaphor reveals our fundamental misunderstanding. We keep looking outside ourselves for the key to peace, clarity, and purpose, never realizing we're already on the inside of what we seek. We've been taught to believe that our inner state is at the mercy of outer conditions—that we can only feel centered, whole, and alive when circumstances align with our preferences. We become stuck in "when this happens, THEN ____________."

The integrated life flips this pattern completely, operating from the inside out. Instead of letting external reality determine your internal state, you establish inner coherence first—then engage with external reality from that unified foundation. As Wayne Dyer said, "When you change the way you look at things, the things you look at change." That's a game-changer.

As I shared previously, I discovered the power of this inside-out approach during one of the most challenging periods of my life. Walking through our neighborhood with numerous problems weighing heavily on my mind, I stopped at a small pond near our home. For once, instead of mentally rehearsing everything that could go wrong or frantically searching for solutions, I simply watched the water. As my attention settled, something shifted—not in the external situation, but in my relationship to it.

The surface of the pond was disturbed by ripples and moved by the wind, but beneath that surface activity, the deeper water remained still. In that moment, I understood what the ancient wisdom traditions have been teaching for centuries: that beneath the constantly changing surface of thoughts, emotions, and circumstances lies an unchanging depth of awareness.

As the Bhagavad Gita expresses it: "For one who has conquered the mind, the mind is the best of friends; but for one who has failed to do so, the mind will remain the greatest enemy." I had been allowing my mind to scatter my attention in a dozen different directions, creating an experience of life as fragmented, overwhelming, and unmanageable. But in that moment of coherence by the pond, I experienced the mind as friend rather than enemy—a unified field of awareness that could hold complexity without breaking into pieces. With one's mind as "friend," power is withdrawn from urges to drown it out or numb it (such as with workaholism or substance abuse).

This shift from scattered to coherent attention transforms everything. The Zen tradition captures this transformation with elegant simplicity: "Before enlightenment, chop wood, carry water. After enlightenment, chop wood, carry water." The external activities don't change, but the consciousness behind them is utterly transformed.

A spiritual bypass or a denial of reality's challenges? No. It's precisely the opposite—a way of engaging those challenges from a consciousness that can actually address them effectively rather than adding to their complexity through divided attention and fragmented awareness.

Imagine trying to help someone who's drowning while you're panicking and thrashing around yourself. Not only are you ineffective, but you might actually pull them under in your own distress. But if you remain centered and whole, you can reach out from a place of strength and stability and offer genuine assistance. The drowning person's situation hasn't changed, but your capacity to respond effectively has transformed completely.

The *Talmudic* wisdom expresses this perfectly: "We do not see things as they are. We see things as we are." When our attention is scattered and divided, we perceive a world of disconnection, conflict, and insurmountable problems. When our attention becomes coherent and unified, we perceive a world of connection, harmony, and solvable challenges—not because the world has magically changed, but because the consciousness perceiving it has fundamentally shifted.

The Dance of Balance: Maintaining Coherence Amid Life's Currents

One of my favorite ways to understand the integrated life is through the metaphor of surfing. A skilled surfer doesn't stand rigid and unmovable on the board—that's a recipe for wiping out. Nor do they simply surrender control and let the wave throw them wherever it wants. Instead, they maintain a dynamic balance that constantly adjusts to changing conditions while maintaining overall direction and purpose.

This dance of balance perfectly captures what it means to maintain coherence amid life's constantly changing currents. The 6th-century BCE Chinese philosopher Lao Tzu described this dynamic perfectly when he wrote: "Nothing in the world is as soft and yielding as water. Yet for dissolving the hard and inflexible, nothing can surpass it." Like water, coherent consciousness combines perfect softness with irresistible power—flowing around obstacles rather than fighting against them while gradually reshaping even the most rigid resistance.

I discovered this mysterious water-like quality during a business negotiation that initially seemed impossibly deadlocked. Everyone involved had taken rigid positions with seemingly no room for movement. In the past, I would have either pushed harder against the opposition (creating more resistance) or surrendered my position entirely (creating resentment and poor outcomes).

Instead, I took a moment to center myself through the Attention Compass practice, feeling the coherence of all three brains—gut, heart, and mind—working in harmony rather than pulling in different directions. From this unified state, I suddenly saw the situation from an entirely new perspective. Like water finding the path of least resistance, my attention flowed naturally to openings and possibilities invisible to divided awareness.

What emerged wasn't a compromise where everyone loses something, but a creative solution where everyone gained what truly mattered to them. Not by magic or manipulation, but through the capacity to perceive connections and patterns that remained invisible to scattered attention.

The 13th-century Zen Master Dogen captured this seemingly magical quality when he wrote: "To study the Buddha Way is to study the self. To study the self is to forget the self. To forget the self is to be actualized by myriad things." When we release the fragmented attention that creates our usual sense of separate self, we discover connection with everything—and from that connection emerges wisdom beyond our limited personal perspective.

This capacity to maintain coherence amid life's constant changes isn't about rigid control or passive surrender. It's about what the martial arts tradition of Aikido calls "centered movement"—action that emerges from stability rather than reaction triggered by external forces. The founder of Aikido, Morihei Ueshiba, described it as "standing at the center of the world," a place where you can respond to any attack without being destabilized by it.

I've found this centered movement invaluable during challenging interactions with others, particularly those who arrive in states of high emotional intensity. Rather than either absorbing their scattered energy (and losing my own center) or defensively pushing against it (creating more conflict), I've learned to maintain inner coherence while still remaining fully engaged and responsive.

During one particularly volatile community meeting, emotions ran high as people voiced legitimate concerns and fears about changes affecting their neighborhood. The usual pattern in such settings is either escalating conflict or suppressed tension—both products of scattered, divided attention. But by maintaining inner coherence through the Attention Compass, I discovered a third possibility: holding space for intense emotion without either fueling it or shutting it down.

This centered holding created something remarkable—a shift in the field of the entire meeting. People who arrived in an agitated state gradually settled into more coherent expressions.

Perspectives that initially seemed irreconcilably opposed revealed unexpected points of connection. Solutions emerged that transcended the usual polarized positions.

The ancient Upanishads describe this field effect with the simple phrase "Tat Tvam Asi"—"Thou Art That." When we recognize that consciousness is not contained within a separate individual's skull, but flows between and through us all, we understand how one person's coherent attention can create ripples that affect an entire system.

This doesn't mean we can control others, impose our will, or force particular outcomes. It means we can contribute coherence to any field we enter—whether family, workplace, community, or beyond—creating conditions where wisdom beyond individual limitation becomes increasingly available to all. The practice of maintaining this dynamic balance involves several specific approaches that anyone can develop, regardless of circumstances:

The Anchor Practice: Develop a physical anchor that instantly reconnects you with coherent attention when you notice yourself becoming scattered. This might be feeling your feet on the ground, bringing awareness to your breath, or placing your hand on your heart center. These simple physical anchors create a bridge between mind and body, reuniting dimensions of experience that scattered attention artificially separates.

The Buddha taught a similar practice 2,500 years ago, instructing: "If your mind is scattered, bring it back to the breath." This simple instruction recognizes that embodied awareness naturally unifies what conceptual thinking divides. The breath isn't just air moving in and out of lungs—it's the constant reminder that we exist as unified beings rather than disjointed collections of parts.

The Witness Perspective: When you notice your attention becoming scattered amid challenging circumstances, practice shifting to the perspective of the witness—the awareness that can observe thoughts, emotions, and reactions without becoming completely identified with them. This isn't disconnection from experience but expansion beyond being captured by any single dimension of it.

The *Bhagavad Gita* describes this witness consciousness as "seated in the body, yet beyond the body; not affected by the qualities of nature, yet observing them." This witness isn't separate from experience but also isn't limited to any particular aspect of it—creating space to hold multiple dimensions simultaneously without fragmentation.

The Both/And Perception: When facing situations that present apparent either/or choices, practice shifting to both/and perception that can hold seeming opposites simultaneously. This isn't a compromise that waters down both sides but integration that honors the truth in different perspectives while transcending their limitations. My friend uses this example as a reminder:

Jana says rainy days at the beach are wonderful. Luke says sunny days at the beach are wonderful. So…*Both* rainy days *and* sunny days at the beach are wonderful.

The Taoist symbol of yin and yang perfectly captures this both/and awareness—not as opposing forces fighting for dominance but as complementary aspects of a single unified reality, each containing the seed of the other within it. This perception reveals the artificial nature of many apparent conflicts, dissolving problems created by divided thinking rather than solving them within its limited framework.

The Field Awareness: Develop sensitivity to the larger "field" or context in which individual experiences arise, recognizing that everything exists in relationship rather than isolation. This expanded awareness naturally shifts attention from fragmented parts to meaningful wholes, revealing connections that before were invisible with a more limited perception of self.

Indigenous wisdom traditions worldwide share this field awareness, expressed in the Lakota phrase *Mitakuye Oyasin*—"All Are Related." This isn't a poetic metaphor but direct recognition that everything exists within a web of interconnection, where each part affects and is affected by the whole. From this field awareness, solutions emerge that serve the entire system rather than privileging isolated parts at others' expense.

These practices don't eliminate life's complexity or the need for difficult choices. What they offer is a different relationship with complexity itself—one that engages from coherent wholeness rather than scattered division, seeing connections and patterns invisible to consciousness that perceives life's dimensions as inherently opposed.

The ancient Chinese text, the *I Ching* (Book of Changes), describes this integrated awareness as "the creative force that emerges when heaven and earth unite." When the different dimensions of our experience—intuitive and analytical, emotional and practical, material and spiritual—unite in coherent wholeness rather than pulling apart in scattered fragments, we access creative capacities beyond what divided consciousness can imagine.

Reprogramming Identity: From Scattered Self to Coherent Being

As our practice of maintaining coherence amid life's currents deepens, we begin to recognize that the most fundamental obstacle to sustained flow isn't external circumstance but internalized identity—the deep-seated patterns that define how we experience ourselves and our relationship with the world.

Most people operate from identities constructed of scattered, often contradictory elements—the achiever who believes worth comes from accomplishment, the people-pleaser who needs others' approval, the controller who must manage outcomes, the victim who feels perpetually at life's mercy. These fragmented aspects create a self-concept that resembles a house built from mismatched parts.

The medieval mystic Meister Eckhart captured this predicament perfectly when he wrote: "The seed of God is in us. If it received a wise and industrious cultivator, it would thrive and grow up into God, whose seed it is, and its fruits would be God-nature." Our essential nature is coherent wholeness, but it requires conscious cultivation to flourish amid the scattered conditioning that typically shapes identity.

As I continued practicing the Attention Compass amid my own dark days of my financial and identity crisis, something unexpected emerged.

I discovered that beneath the scattered fragments of who I thought I was existed a presence that hadn't changed at all despite external circumstances. The Buddhist tradition calls this "original face before you were born"—the fundamental consciousness that precedes all acquired identities and remains unchanged by life's constant fluctuations.

This discovery marked the beginning of what I now understand as *identity reprogramming*—not creating a new improved self-concept, but allowing the coherent wholeness that already exists at your core to gradually replace the scattered fragments that previously dominated experience. This reprogramming doesn't happen through force or control, but through the consistent cultivation of conditions that allow natural coherence to express itself.

The ancient Greek philosopher Plotinus described this process with remarkable clarity: "Cut away all that is excessive, straighten all that is crooked, bring light to all that is overcast, labor to make all one radiance of beauty. Never cease to sculpt your own statue, until there shines out upon you from it the divine glory of virtue."

This sculptural metaphor captures the nature of identity reprogramming. It's not about adding more elements to who you think you are but removing the excess that obscures the coherent wholeness already present. It's not constructing something new but revealing what was always there beneath the scattered accumulations of conditioned identity.

How does this reprogramming actually work in practice? Through several key approaches that gradually shift the center of gravity from scattered to coherent identity:

The Identity Witness Practice: Begin noticing the scattered identity patterns that automatically activate in different situations—the achiever in professional contexts, the people-pleaser in social settings, the controller amid uncertainty, the victim when facing obstacles. Simply witnessing these patterns without judgment creates space between awareness itself and the particular patterns it observes.

The Sufi tradition expresses this witnessing capacity through the practice of "muraqaba"—watchfulness or observation that neither indulges nor suppresses what arises. As the great Sufi master Ibn Arabi taught: "The eye through which I see God is the same eye through which God sees me." This reciprocal seeing creates a relationship with identity patterns rather than fusion with them, allowing conscious choice rather than automatic reaction.

The Source Connection: Regularly connect with the "original" consciousness that remains unchanged despite life's fluctuations. This connection might occur through meditation, time in nature, creative flow, or any experience where the scattered thoughts that maintain fragmented identity temporarily subside.

As stated before, the Upanishads describe this connection as recognizing "Tat Tvam Asi"—"That Thou Art." The coherent source of being is the very essence of who you are beneath the scattered accumulations of conditioned identity. Regular contact with this source gradually shifts the center of gravity from fragmented self-concept to a coherent presence.

The Integration Dialogue: When scattered identity patterns activate, engage them in conscious dialogue rather than either identifying completely with them or trying to eliminate them. This dialogue acknowledges their presence and typically protective intention while gently introducing the perspective of more coherent awareness.

The psychological approach of Internal Family Systems recognizes this dialogue as engagement with "parts" of ourselves that developed to protect against perceived threats. By approaching these parts with curiosity and compassion rather than identification or rejection, we facilitate their gradual integration into more coherent wholeness.

The Embodied Coherence: Your body is there to help you. Pay particular attention to how scattered identity expresses through the body—specific tensions, postures, breathing patterns, and energy signatures. As you notice these physical manifestations, allow them to gradually release—not through force but through bringing coherent awareness to bodily experience.

Ancient wisdom traditions worldwide recognize the centrality of embodiment in identity transformation. The Taoist practice of *qigong*, the Indian tradition of *yoga*, the Japanese art of *aikido*—all work directly with the body as the ground where scattered identity patterns can be recognized and transformed through coherent attention.

The Field Reinforcement: Consciously engage with people, environments, activities, and teachings that reinforce coherent identity rather than triggering scattered patterns. This isn't avoidance of challenge but strategic cultivation of conditions that support the emerging shift from fragmentation to wholeness.

Indigenous traditions worldwide recognize this principle through ceremonial practices that temporarily create fields of coherent awareness where participants can experience themselves beyond the limitations of scattered identity. While we may not have access to traditional ceremonies, we can consciously create environments and relationships that serve similar functions in contemporary contexts. Actually, it's critical to make the effort to connect with and spend time around others with the same intention of living a grounded life of wholeness, not one of identity-based striving and drama.

Through consistent application of these approaches, identity gradually reprograms from scattered fragments to coherent wholeness—not as perfect achievement but as ongoing evolution where the center of gravity steadily shifts toward greater integration. This shift manifests in several recognizable ways:

Reduced Identity Defense: As coherent identity becomes more established, the automatic defensive reactions triggered by perceived threats to self-concept gradually diminish. Criticism, setbacks, and challenges that previously provoked intense reactivity become opportunities for learning and growth rather than existential threats requiring immediate defense.

Expanded Perspective: The artificial boundaries that scattered identity creates between "self" and "other" become increasingly permeable, allowing perception that includes rather than excludes. This expanded perspective naturally recognizes connection and mutual influence, where fragmented awareness sees only separation and conflict.

Authentic Expression: The energy previously consumed by maintaining scattered identity becomes available for authentic creative expression that emerges from coherent wholeness rather than fragmented parts. This expression has a quality of naturalness and flow that contrasts sharply with the effortful performance characteristic of scattered identity.

Flexible Response: Rather than rigid reactions determined by fixed identity patterns, coherent selfhood allows a flexible response appropriate to actual circumstances rather than habitual defense. This adaptability combines stability and responsiveness in ways that scattered identity cannot sustain.

Synchronistic Experience: As identity becomes more coherent, synchronistic connections—meaningful "coincidences"—become increasingly common. These aren't supernatural interventions but natural expressions of consciousness operating from wholeness rather than fragmentation.

The 20th-century Swiss psychiatrist Carl Jung, who coined the term "synchronicity," described this phenomenon as "a meaningful coincidence of two or more events where something other than the probability of chance is involved." From coherent identity, such meaningful connections appear not as rare anomalies but as the natural expression of consciousness operating beyond the artificial separations created by our scattered attention.

I experienced this synchronistic dimension dramatically during a period when I was working on a creative project that had stalled due to seemingly insurmountable obstacles. After several days of practicing coherent identity amid this frustration, I "randomly" met someone at a community event who possessed exactly the expertise and connections needed to move the project forward.

This wasn't magic or a stroke of luck. It was the natural expression of consciousness operating from coherence rather than fragmentation—perceiving connections invisible to our scattered attention and engaging in possibilities beyond what our fragmented awareness can imagine.

The integrated life doesn't require belief in supernatural intervention or abandonment of practical reality. It simply recognizes that consciousness itself operates differently when it is coherent rather than when it is scattered—accessing dimensions of experience that have always been present but remained invisible to divided attention.

The ancient Hermetic axiom, "As above, so below; as within, so without…" describes this principle perfectly. The coherence or fragmentation we experience internally directly corresponds to what we perceive and create externally—not through magical thinking but through the actual mechanics of how consciousness shapes reality through perception, attention, and action.

I came to realize the reality that "What we see is in direct proportion to how we feel. If you want to change what you see 'out there' then change how you feel inside."

Creating Ripples of Coherence

As we develop increasing capacity for living from coherent wholeness rather than scattered fragments, something remarkable becomes apparent: the effects of our personal integration

extend far beyond individual experience, creating ripples that influence every field in which we participate.

The influential physicist David Bohm described this ripple effect through his theory of "implicate order"—the understanding that everything exists within a unified field, where each part contains and affects the whole. From this perspective, one person's shift from scattered to coherent consciousness doesn't just change their own experience, but contributes to the transformation of the entire field in which they participate.

I witnessed this ripple effect most dramatically during a conflict that had become increasingly polarized and hostile. People had taken rigid positions, communication had deteriorated into accusation and defense, and the possibility of mutual understanding seemed impossible.

Rather than adding my voice to either camp or attempting to force reconciliation through external intervention, I focused on maintaining my own coherent presence amid the scattered energy. This wasn't detachment or passivity but my conscious contribution to the field— offering a different quality of attention that could potentially catalyze a shift beyond what force or persuasion could accomplish.

I practiced the Attention Compass while simply listening to the various perspectives being expressed. Instead of mentally sorting them into "agree" or "disagree," I allowed each voice to be received by coherent attention that could hold apparent contradictions without fragmenting into opposition. Did I say any magic words or try to validate each different viewpoint? No. Did I move to a neutral place in the room to show I wasn't taking sides? No. Did I ask insightful questions that could give each side pause to think? No. As I'll explain more a little later, *the most profound contribution you can make to any situation isn't necessarily what you do but the quality of consciousness you bring to whatever you do.*

Then, something remarkable happened. Without any explicit intervention on my part, the quality of communication began to shift. People who had been speaking in absolute certainties began acknowledging complexity and nuance. Those who had been attacking others' positions began recognizing legitimate concerns beneath opposing viewpoints. The rigid boundaries between "sides" gradually softened into more permeable membranes, allowing genuine exchange.

This shift wasn't magic or manipulation. It was the natural expression of how coherent consciousness affects the fields it enters. The 20th-century philosopher Pierre Teilhard de Chardin captured this understanding when he wrote: "The day will come when, after harnessing space, the winds, the tides, gravitation, we shall harness for God the energies of love. And, on that day, for the second time in the history of the world, man will have discovered fire."

The fire de Chardin describes is the actual transformative power of coherent consciousness—the energy that naturally emerges when scattered attention unifies into coherent wholeness. This energy affects everything it contacts, not through force or control, but through resonance that allows similar coherence to emerge in whatever it touches.

The ripple effect of coherent consciousness operates through several specific mechanisms worth understanding if we want to consciously participate in collective transformation:

Resonant Field Dynamics: Consciousness itself generates measurable energy fields. When one person maintains coherent consciousness amid scattered energy, they offer a baseline frequency that others can naturally attune to through resonance rather than being repeatedly pulled into fragmentation.

The HeartMath Institute has documented this resonance effect through research showing that one person's coherent heart rhythm can measurably affect others' physiological states without any explicit intervention.

Pattern Disruption: Coherent consciousness naturally disrupts the habitual patterns that maintain scattered collective fields. Most human systems—families, organizations, communities—develop recurring cycles of reactivity and fragmentation that become self-reinforcing over time. One person consistently maintaining coherence creates a pattern interruption, allowing new possibilities to emerge without forcing particular outcomes.

Systems theorists recognize this principle as "perturbation"—small inputs at leverage points that can shift entire system dynamics without proportional force. Coherent consciousness functions as precisely this kind of leverage perturbation, interrupting established patterns enough to create space for greater coherence.

Mirror Neuron Engagement: The human brain contains specialized cells called *mirror neurons* that automatically simulate and reproduce states observed in others. When one person maintains coherent presence amid scattered energy, their integrated state engages others' mirror neuron systems, creating an internal simulation of coherence that can potentially become an actual embodied state.

This mirror neuron effect explains why being around someone in coherent presence feels so different from interaction with scattered consciousness. The brain literally "catches" the patterns it observes, particularly when those patterns represent integration rather than fragmentation. Think of a time when you experienced someone's joy being "contagious," just as another's negative emotions can cast a shadow on everyone around them.

Expanded Solution Space: Coherent consciousness naturally perceives connections and possibilities invisible to scattered attention, introducing these expanded perspectives into collective fields where they become available to others regardless of their individual state. This creates what complexity theorists call "expanded solution space," where a wider range of potential resolutions form.

Indigenous wisdom traditions worldwide recognize this principle through practices of council, where diverse perspectives are held within coherent collective attention that allows solutions to emerge beyond what any individual viewpoint could generate. One person maintaining coherent consciousness amid scattered collective energy contributes to this expanded solution space regardless of formal role or explicit contribution.

Understanding these ripple effects transforms how we approach both personal practice and collective change. The question shifts from "How can I fix this broken system?" to "How can I embody coherence that naturally affects the fields I enter?" The focus moves from controlling outcomes to cultivating consciousness quality. This, we find, is far more powerful. There is still a need for practical action or structural change. And, the effectiveness of any action depends fundamentally on the consciousness from which it emerges. The same external behavior arising from coherent presence versus scattered fragmentation creates entirely different effects in the systems it engages.

The most profound contribution you can make to any situation isn't necessarily what you do but the quality of consciousness you bring to whatever you do. As Mahatma Gandhi expressed in his famous invitation to "be the change you wish to see in the world," the most powerful transformation begins with embodying (becoming) the coherence you hope to create rather than fighting against the fragmentation you hope to eliminate.

The Dream Deepens: The New Host

The dream returns with increasing frequency. Each time, the Great Hall transforms further.

◆

No walls. As I look around, I see that the Great Hall walls have been replaced by columns with views of mountains, forests, the ocean, and the city in each direction. The separation between inside and outside has dissolved, allowing fresh air and birdsong to mingle with conversation and laughter.

The ceremony continues, but I observe from a different perspective. Rather than being at the center of attention or lurking, rejected at the door, I move through the gathering as host—equally at ease with dignitaries in formal attire and unexpected guests in work clothes, children running between tables, and elders sharing quiet conversations in corners.

I notice the disheveled man across the room, but he, too, has transformed. He is not polished, but he carries himself with natural dignity. His face, once contorted by rejection and anger, now holds a peaceful presence. His clothes are simple but clean, his manner direct but kind. He catches my eye and smiles with recognition—not as a separate entity seeking acknowledgment but as an aspect of myself fully welcomed home.

I move toward him, and as I pass a mirror, I catch a glimpse of myself. I am neither the weatherman nor the disheveled man, but someone who contains elements of both, while being defined by neither. The weatherman's ability to communicate clearly is there, but without the desperate need for approval. The disheveled man's authenticity is present, but without the wounded rage of rejection. I seem, perhaps for the first time, simply myself—not a role or a reaction, just the human being I had always been beneath all the layers of construction and collapse.

As I reach him, words are not necessary. We stand side by side, surveying the gathering—not as separate entities but as integrated aspects of a whole self.

"Remember when you couldn't bear to look at me?" he asks, his voice holding no resentment, only gentle acknowledgment of how far we had come.

"I was afraid you were all that remained after I lost everything," I admit, the words emerging from a place of complete honesty that required no defense.

His laugh is warm, genuine. "Instead, you discovered I was everything that remained after you lost nothing of value."

<hr>

When I woke up, I was filled with a profound sense of belonging, of homecoming. I wiped away my tears and sat straight up, feeling more refreshed than I usually do upon waking. Throughout the day, I noticed how much more energy I now had. Before, so much energy was spent maintaining the division between who I presented myself to be and who I feared I actually was. That energy, no longer tied up in internal conflict, flowed naturally into creation, connection, and presence with everyone I encountered. I also felt more connected with myself, and had frequent bursts of creativity and optimism.

Exercise: Integration Practices for Sustained Flow

This exercise integrates the principles we've explored throughout this chapter into practical approaches for sustaining coherent consciousness amid everyday life. Rather than treating flow as separate from normal experience, these practices support its integration into the full spectrum of human activity.

Part 1: The Coherence Reset

This foundational practice helps you quickly return to coherent consciousness whenever you notice yourself becoming scattered:

1. **Pause and Breathe:** When you notice scattered attention—mind pulled in multiple directions, thoughts racing, emotions intensifying—pause and take three conscious breaths, feeling the physical sensation of breathing throughout your body.

2. **Engage the Three Brains:** Place one hand on your lower abdomen (gut center) while continuing conscious breathing. Feel this center activate and relax. Move your hand to your heart center, continuing conscious breathing and feeling emotional energy without trying to change it. Finally, rest your attention in the space between and slightly behind your eyes, noticing mental activity without engaging with specific content.

3. **Feel Coherent Wholeness:** Expand awareness to include all three centers simultaneously. Feel them not as separate systems but as aspects of a single integrated field of consciousness. Notice the quality of coherent wholeness when these dimensions operate in harmony rather than pulling in different directions.

4. **Engage from Coherence:** From this reset foundation, engage with whatever situation triggered scattered attention, bringing coherent presence to circumstances that previously fragmented awareness. Notice how the same external conditions look and feel different when perceived from wholeness rather than fragments.

This reset practice takes only 30-60 seconds and creates a crucial pattern interruption whenever you notice attention becoming scattered. With consistent application, the return to coherence becomes increasingly natural and immediate, requiring less deliberate effort and happening before fragmentation fully captures awareness.

Part 2: The Coherence Expansion

This practice helps expand coherent consciousness beyond brief moments into more sustained capacity:

1. **Map Your Coherence Landscape:** Notice when, where, and with whom you most naturally experience coherent consciousness. What activities, environments, relationships, and circumstances support your natural coherence? What consistently triggers scattered attention? Write about each of these. This mapping creates strategic awareness of conditions that either support or challenge your integrated presence.

2. **Design Coherence Bridges:** Create intentional transitions between activities that typically pull attention in different directions. Before ending one engagement and beginning another, take 30 seconds for the Coherence Reset, consciously completing the previous activity before turning attention to the next. These brief bridges prevent the accumulation of scattered momentum that typically builds throughout busy days. It can be helpful to say out loud, "Stop. Change. Start." This lets your attention know and follow your intention.

3. **Establish Coherence Anchors:** Develop physical anchors that instantly reconnect you with coherent awareness amid challenging circumstances—feeling your feet on the ground, placing your hand on your heart center, touching thumb to forefinger, or any gesture that creates embodied connection with integrated presence. An example my friend uses is to take off her shoes and feel/notice her feet touching the ground. These anchors become increasingly powerful through consistent association with coherent consciousness.

4. **Create Coherence Reminders:** Place visual cues in environments where scattered attention most commonly occurs—a small stone on your desk, a symbolic image on your phone, a meaningful object where you'll regularly notice it. These reminders (some

like to call them "totems") create brief pattern interruptions that allow a return to coherence before fragmentation fully captures attention.

With consistent practice, these approaches gradually extend coherent consciousness from occasional moments to more sustained capacity. The emphasis isn't perfectionist achievement but ongoing development through practical engagement with actual life circumstances rather than idealized conditions.

Part 3: The Coherence Engagement

This practice helps maintain coherent consciousness during challenging interactions that typically trigger scattered attention:

1. **Prepare with Coherence:** Before entering potentially challenging engagements—difficult conversations, complex decisions, stressful environments—take 2-3 minutes for conscious coherence preparation. This isn't trying to control what will happen, but establishing the foundation from which you'll engage whatever actually occurs. Imagine an actor taking a deep breath and standing tall before stepping out onto the stage. You can "gather yourself" any time you choose.

2. **Maintain the Witness:** During any interaction, practice maintaining witness awareness that can observe thoughts, emotions, and reactions without becoming completely identified with them. This witness isn't disconnected from the experience, but rests beyond the reach of being captured by any single dimension of it.

3. **Track Body Signals:** Pay close attention to physical sensations that indicate scattered attention—tension in specific areas, shallow or held breath, constricted energy, postural collapse or rigidity. These bodily signals often precede conscious awareness of fragmentation, allowing earlier return to coherence before scattered patterns fully activate.

4. **Create Coherence Pauses:** When noticing yourself becoming scattered during extended engagements, create brief pauses—a moment of silence, a conscious breath, a simple question that

interrupts momentum long enough for coherence to reestablish. These pauses aren't avoidance of difficulty but strategic pattern interruptions that allow more effective engagement. "The pause that refreshes."

With practice, this coherence engagement becomes increasingly natural amid challenging circumstances that previously triggered automatic fragmentation. The capacity to maintain integrated presence doesn't eliminate difficulty but transforms your relationship with it— from scattered reactivity to coherent response.

Part 4: The Coherence Reflection

This practice supports ongoing integration through conscious reflection on your coherence journey:

1. **End-of-Day Reflection:** Take 3-5 minutes each evening to reflect on your coherence practice throughout the day. When were you most naturally coherent? What triggered scattered attention? How quickly did you notice fragmentation and return to center? What patterns are becoming more clear through consistent observation?

2. **Appreciation Practice:** Specifically appreciate moments of coherence rather than judging moments of fragmentation. This appreciation reinforces neural and energetic pathways associated with integrated presence, gradually shifting from effortful practice to natural expression.

3. **Integration Journaling:** Keep brief notes about your coherence journey, recording insights, challenges, and patterns that emerge through consistent practice. This journaling isn't elaborate analysis but simple documentation that reveals developmental patterns invisible to day-by-day perception.

4. **Weekly Review:** Take 10-15 minutes each week for a more reflective review. What patterns have emerged over seven days that might not be visible in daily reflection? What adjustments to your practice would support continued development based on actual experience rather than abstract ideals?

Notice your progress in your Level of Consciousness, while also noting how you can improve your environment to better support coherence.

◆

Remember that this journey isn't about achieving perfect coherence but developing increasing capacity to return to center when temporarily pulled away. Each recognition of scattered attention and subsequent return to coherence strengthens the neural and energetic pathways that support integrated presence. Progress isn't measured by elimination of challenge but by changing relationships with it—quicker recognition, reduced identification, and faster return to wholeness.

The integrated life doesn't require belief in supernatural intervention nor abandonment of practical reality. It simply recognizes that consciousness itself operates differently when coherent than when scattered—accessing dimensions of experience that have always been present but remained invisible to divided attention.

As the ancient Hermetic text *The Emerald Tablet* expresses: "That which is below is like that which is above, and that which is above is like that which is below, to perform the miracles of one thing." The miracle of coherent consciousness is completely natural. It's the restoration of what was always true beneath the scattered fragmentation we've come to accept as normal.

When you apply the principles and practices shared in these pages, you will fundamentally transform how you experience reality itself. The coherent wholeness awaiting your discovery isn't just a philosophical idea—it's a powerful force that will reshape your relationships, your work, your health, and your understanding of what's possible in this lifetime.

My journey proves that even from the darkest depths of financial ruin, identity collapse, and shattered certainty, the Flow State can emerge as an extraordinary new foundation. This isn't about returning to some imagined natural state—it's about evolving into a higher expression of human potential that most people never discover because they're trapped in scattered attention without realizing there's another way to live.

With each day you practice my suggested exercises, you're building momentum toward a quantum shift that will make your previous life seem like you were living in black and white before discovering color.

EPILOGUE
The Continuous Awakening

Searching for enlightenment, a young monk travels around for years, the Zen story goes. He makes his way to distant temples, studies with renowned masters, and practices rigorous meditation. After a decade of seeking, discouraged and exhausted, he returns to his home village. While drawing water from the well he has used since childhood, he sees the moon's reflection on the water's surface. It is a breathtaking moment, and he experiences a complete awakening. What he had traveled the world to find had been available all along in his own village well.

I smile whenever I recall this story, because it mirrors my own journey so perfectly. The "This is it!" moments that I spent decades seeking through achievement, status, and external validation had always been present, waiting quietly at the center of my attention compass—the Flow State. This treasure wasn't hidden in some distant, exotic location; it did not lie just over the next hill and then the next…but in the stillness I had been too busy to notice within myself.

This paradox—that precisely what we seek with such desperate effort is already here—marks the beginning of our journey, not the end game. The Flow State isn't a final goal you reach. It's more like a path on a map that keeps unfolding, helping you wake up to deeper levels of experience as you go. It's an open invitation to keep learning, growing, and deepening your awareness over time.

The Journey That Never Ends

When I began writing this book, I imagined sharing a journey with a clear beginning, middle, and triumphant conclusion—the story of how I found the Flow State and permanently solved the challenges that had defined my life. But the deeper truth I've discovered is both more humble and more magnificent: There is no final destination, no ultimate achievement, no permanent resolution. There is only the continuous awakening to what has always been true beneath the surface of our scattered attention.

Is my life now challenge-free? Of course not. I sometimes get pulled into old patterns of fear, desire, and separation. My attention becomes fragmented, my presence less powerful. The difference isn't the elimination of these human experiences, but my relationship with them—quicker recognition when they arise, reduced identification with their narrow perspective, and faster return to the coherent wholeness that remains my true home.

Picture a spiral—the beautiful, mathematical design found in nature. For me, you, and everyone, this ongoing, natural journey reveals itself not as a linear progression toward a fixed destination, but as a spiral evolution that continuously revisits familiar territory from expanding awareness. Each turn of the spiral doesn't just add new information, but transforms the foundation from which we perceive and engage with all experience.

Recently, I faced a challenge that would have completely overwhelmed me in the past—a complex situation involving financial pressure, relationship dynamics, and professional uncertainty all converging at once. The old pattern would have fragmented my attention into panic-driven reactions, creating chaos both internally and externally as I tried to solve separate problems that were actually interconnected facets of a unified field.

But through consistent practice with the Attention Compass, I was able to maintain a coherent presence amid these swirling complexities. This didn't magically eliminate the challenges, but it transformed how I perceived and engaged with them—not as threats to resist or problems to solve, but as aspects of a unified field. Through my intention to bring a coherent presence to the moment and to maintain non-fragmented attention, the entire challenging situation was resolved, wholly and effectively.

The ancient Zen tradition captures this process perfectly in the saying: "Before enlightenment, chop wood, carry water. After enlightenment, chop wood, carry water." The external activities don't change, but the consciousness behind them is utterly transformed. The tasks remain the same, but the one performing them experiences reality from an entirely different dimension of awareness.

This continuous awakening isn't reserved for monks, special individuals, or particular life circumstances. It's the natural birthright of every human being—the inherent capacity to experience reality not through scattered fragments of divided attention but through the coherent wholeness that is our essential nature beneath accumulated conditioning.

The Magic That Was Always Within

Perhaps the most profound discovery of my journey has been recognizing that what appears magical from the perspective of scattered attention is actually the natural expression of consciousness operating from its essential coherence. I hesitate to use the word "magical" because it might suggest something outside the natural order, accessible only through special powers or esoteric techniques. But I've come to recognize that what feels magical is simply the experience of consciousness operating as it was designed. Before becoming fragmented through conditioning and cultural programming, life is magic.

When the three brains—gut, heart, and head—align in coherent harmony, our perception transforms through natural integration, revealing dimensions of reality that were always present but remained invisible to scattered attention.

We've all had experiences that are difficult to describe or explain. Understanding the Flow State is perhaps the closest we'll ever get to seeing the magic with no veil. In the Flow State, the way life "occurs" for us is transformed. What does that look like?

Synchronicities that defy conventional causality become increasingly common—meaningful connections and "coincidental" encounters that provide exactly what's needed precisely when it's needed. Not through cosmic orchestration but through perception freed from the artificial separations created by scattered attention.

Creative solutions emerge for challenges that previously seemed insurmountable—not through denial of practical reality but through access to possibilities invisible to fragmented awareness. These solutions often transcend conventional either/or thinking, revealing both/and approaches that honor apparent opposites as complementary aspects of unified reality.

Manifestation occurs not through magical thinking but through the resonant field created by coherent consciousness—a field that naturally attracts experiences matching its frequency, not through supernatural manipulation but through the physics of energetic resonance that governs both quantum and psychological reality.

Healing accelerates across physical, emotional, and relational dimensions through coherent attention that allows natural integration of aspects previously held separate by fragmented awareness. This integration creates conditions in which wholeness can express itself across all dimensions of experience.

Magic isn't something you need to find, create, or import from somewhere else. It's what naturally emerges when the obstacles to your essential coherence temporarily dissolve. What emerges is the wholeness that has always been your true nature beneath the scattered attention you've been taught to accept as normal.

The Invitation to Your Own Discovery

As our journey together through these pages comes to completion, I offer an invitation—an opening rather than closure, a beginning rather than an ending. The Flow State is something you must discover through your own direct experience, available whenever your attention returns from scattered fragments to coherent wholeness.

I invite you to *recognize what you already know* at levels deeper than conceptual understanding—the coherent wholeness that remains your essential nature, regardless of how scattered your attention might temporarily become.

You've experienced this coherence in moments you might have considered exceptional—occasions of creative flow, athletic performance, intimate connection, or natural immersion where the usual boundaries between self and other temporarily dissolved. What if those weren't exceptional moments but glimpses of your natural state, available not just in special circumstances but in every dimension of ordinary life?

The Attention Compass isn't something I "invented." It occurred to me as a representation of the natural capacity within human consciousness to recognize when attention has been pulled away from the center, and to gently return it to the coherent wholeness that is its home. This capacity doesn't require special talent, spiritual advancement, or particular life circumstances. It's the inherent faculty of every human being.

I invite you to experiment with the practices shared throughout this book, not as techniques to achieve something you lack, but as pointers to recognize what has always been present beneath the scattered attention you've been conditioned to accept as normal.

The **three-brain alignment**, the **"feeling it in"** approach, the **identity reprogramming**—all are simply different doorways to the same fundamental recognition of your essential coherence.

Wherever you are right now is actually the perfect place to start— with the circumstances that are present in your life rather than waiting for ideal conditions or special preparation. The challenges that seem to prevent coherence are often where its transformative potential can most powerfully express—not because difficulties magically disappear, but because the relationship with them fundamentally transforms.

Be patient with the process of continuous awakening, recognizing that it unfolds not through perfect achievement but through consistent engagement that gradually shifts the center of gravity from scattered to coherent attention. Each recognition of fragmentation and subsequent return to center strengthens the neural and energetic pathways that support natural integration. Your patience will pay off as this ability grows in you and becomes easier and more habitual.

Share your journey with others who recognize and support coherent attention rather than reinforcing fragmented patterns. This sharing isn't about convincing or converting but about creating fields of resonance where natural coherence can more easily express through mutual recognition and reinforcement.

Trust your direct experience more than any concept, teaching, or authority—including the words on these pages. The consciousness reading these words contains wisdom far deeper than language can capture or concepts can contain. The still center of your own awareness remains the most reliable guide through territories no map can fully represent.

Above all, remember that the Flow State isn't a special achievement reserved for exceptional circumstances or specially gifted individuals. It's the natural expression of consciousness when artificial divisions temporarily dissolve.

Consciousness as the Ultimate Creative Force

I offer one final reflection on the **nature of consciousness** itself—not as philosophical speculation but as practical recognition with profound implications for how we engage with every dimension of existence.

Consciousness isn't just perceiving reality; it's participating in its emergence. The quality of attention we bring to any experience directly affects not just our subjective response but the actual unfolding of what we call objective reality. This is the natural expression of consciousness as the fundamental creative force from which all experience emerges.

In every corner of our world, ancient traditions have recognized this participatory nature of consciousness. The Hermetic axiom, "As above, so below; as within, so without," captures the direct correspondence between inner state and outer experience. The Buddhist understanding that "Mind is the forerunner of all things" recognizes consciousness as the primary creative force rather than a secondary response. The quantum physics principle that observation affects the observed confirms scientifically what wisdom traditions have taught experientially for millennia.

My own journey has revealed this **creative nature of consciousness** not as abstract theory but as lived reality, expressing through everyday experience. When attention fragments into scattered pieces, reality appears as disconnected problems requiring separate solutions. When attention unifies in coherent wholeness, the same external circumstances reveal previously invisible connections, allowing an integrated response that transforms apparent problems into opportunities for creative evolution.

Consciousness and matter exist in continuous creative dialogue—each affecting and being affected by the other in ways that transcend conventional understanding of cause and effect.

The implications of this understanding transform how we approach both personal development and collective change. Instead of trying to manipulate external reality through force or control, we recognize that the most profound transformation begins with the consciousness we bring to whatever circumstances actually exist. As Mahatma Gandhi expressed in his now-famous invitation to "be the change you wish to see in the world," the most powerful creation starts with embodying the quality of consciousness we hope to manifest, rather than fighting against what we hope to change.

As you continue your own journey beyond these pages, I invite you to recognize the creative power of your consciousness in every dimension of experience. Not as a burden of responsibility or source of blame, but as recognition of your inherent capacity to participate consciously in the emergence of reality through the **quality of attention you bring** to each moment.

The ancient Tibetan Buddhist master Padmasambhava expressed this understanding with remarkable clarity: "If you want to know your past life, look at your present condition. If you want to know your future life, look at your present actions." The consciousness we embody now directly shapes the reality we experience, not through magical manifestation but through the creative nature of attention itself.

Again, the good news is that this creativity isn't something you need to work on, develop, or achieve. It's the inherent nature of consciousness itself, expressed continuously whether we recognize it or not. The question isn't whether your consciousness is creating but what quality of creation emerges from coherent versus scattered attention.

What is and has always been true: consciousness itself is the ultimate creative force, and the quality of attention you bring to each moment directly shapes the reality that emerges through your unique expression of universal awareness.

The journey continues beyond these pages through the silent dialogue between your awakening consciousness and the intelligence that permeates all existence. Listen closely to what emerges in the space between structured practice and spontaneous insight, between dedicated effort and grace beyond effort, between individual journey and collective unfoldment.

Listen closely. In the quiet space between these words and your understanding lies the most powerful discovery of your life.

I've shared my journey from weatherman to bankruptcy to awakening not just as a story, but as a map you can follow. The compass I've placed in your hands isn't theoretical—it's been tested in the crucible of real-world challenges and proven its worth beyond measure.

What awaits you isn't just improved focus or occasional moments of clarity. It's a complete revolution in how you experience reality. Imagine moving through your days with a sense of coherence so powerful that challenges which once overwhelmed you become opportunities for creative expansion. Picture relationships transforming not through techniques or strategies but through the quality of presence you bring to every interaction.

This transformation isn't gradual or incremental—it's a quantum leap into a dimension of experience most people never discover. The distance between your current reality and what's possible isn't measured in years of practice but in millimeters of attention. One conscious breath can bridge that gap when you understand the principles revealed in these pages.

My intention and greatest hope for you is to remember that the magic you seek isn't a distant achievement but a present possibility, available whenever attention returns from scattered fragments to the coherent wholeness that is your essential nature. The Flow State awaits not as a future goal but as a present reality, accessible now and always when the plumb bob returns to center—not just occasionally in special circumstances but increasingly in every dimension of ordinary life.

Take that first step. Center your attention. Feel the coherence that has always been your true nature. And watch as the world transforms not through magical intervention but through the extraordinary power of a unified consciousness seeing itself in everything it touches.

Your adventure with the power of attention awaits. And it will be magnificent.

Reunion Notes: The Expanding Circle

The dream visits me less frequently now, but when it does, it has transformed in ways I never expected. Last time, there was no Great Hall, no stage, no lake—just the boundless expanse of earth and sky stretching to infinity.

———◆———

The disheveled man stands beside me, but with each moment that passes, the distinction between us blurs. The boundaries of identity have become so permeable that "he" and "I" exist more as perspectives than as distinct beings.

From where we stand at this center point, I can see concentric circles rippling outward, like waves from a stone dropped in still water. (Later, I realize that the innermost circles represent the journey documented in this book—from division to recognition, from rejection to integration, from fragmentation to flow. And beyond them expand larger circles, suggesting journeys yet to unfold, questions still to be answered, depths still to be explored.)

"It never ends, does it?" I ask, not really expecting an answer.

"The awakening is continuous," comes the reply, the voice now indistinguishable as his or mine. "Each integration reveals new divisions to heal, each realization uncovers new depths to explore."

*Oh…*I feel a moment of exhaustion at the thought of this endless nature of the journey, but it quickly gives way to exhilaration. The work of integration is not a burden to deal with, but an adventure to embrace—

not a destination to reach but a landscape to explore with ever-expanding awareness.

"What happens now?" I ask.

The only answer is a gentle expansion of perspective, like a slowly turning lens that reveals thousands of others in the landscape. Each is standing at the center of their own concentric circles, each is engaged in their own journey of integration. Yet somehow, all these individual journeys form a single pattern when viewed from my new perspective—a vast, complex, lovely tapestry of awakening consciousness. I see a flower pattern, each petal unique yet part of the same unfolding. If natural beauty has a heart, I'm seeing it here.

◆

I woke with tears on my face, but they were neither sad nor happy tears—simply the natural response to glimpsing, however briefly, the immensity and beauty of the journey we're all sharing. With amazing clarity, I could see that my personal journey of integration is part of something far larger than myself. I am one wave in the ocean, as each of us is a unique wave—while also being a part of the one great ocean. In recognizing and embracing my own rejected aspects, I am playing my small but necessary part in the healing of a divided world.

We all play a vital part in this collective awakening. Your awakening matters. Your integration heals not just you, but the collective consciousness we all share. As I move through my days now, I carry this knowing: that every moment we choose coherence over fragmentation, every time we embrace rather than reject what arises within us, we contribute to the healing of a world that desperately needs our wholeness.

May we stay awake to this truth—that our individual healing ripples outward, touching lives we may never know, contributing to a transformation we may never fully witness, but one we help create simply by becoming whole.

The journey continues, wave by wave, breath by breath, awakening by awakening.

The center of your attention compass is waiting for you now.

It all starts with simply paying attention.

WORKS THAT INFLUENCED
MY JOURNEY

Arntz, William, Betsy Chasse, and Mark Vicente. *What the Bleep Do We Know!?: Discovering the Endless Possibilities for Altering Your Everyday Reality.* Health Communications, 2005.

Bandyopadhyay, Anirban. "Direct Experimental Evidence for Quantum States in Microtubules and Topological Invariance." *Toward a Science of Consciousness* conference, Tucson, Arizona, 2010.

Coelho, Paulo. *The Alchemist.* HarperOne, 1988.

Davidson, Richard J., and Antoine Lutz. "Buddha's Brain: Neuroplasticity and Meditation." *IEEE Signal Processing Magazine*, 25(1), 2008, pp. 176-174.

Desbordes, Gaëlle, Lobsang T. Negi, Thaddeus W. Pace, B. Alan Wallace, Charles L. Raison, and Eric L. Schwartz. "Effects of Mindful-attention and Compassion Meditation Training on Amygdala Response to Emotional Stimuli in an Ordinary, Non-meditative State." *Frontiers in Human Neuroscience*, 6, 2012, p. 292.

Dispenza, Joe. *You Are the Placebo: Making Your Mind Matter*. Hay House, 2014.

Dispenza, Joe. *Breaking the Habit of Being Yourself: How to Lose Your Mind and Create a New One*. Hay House, 2012.

Dispenza, Joe. *Becoming Supernatural: How Common People Are Doing the Uncommon*. Hay House, 2017.

Goddard, Neville. *Feeling Is the Secret*. DeVorss & Company, 1944.

Hameroff, Stuart. "How Quantum Brain Biology Can Rescue Conscious Free Will." *Frontiers in Integrative Neuroscience*, 6, 2012, p. 93.

Hameroff, Stuart. "The Brain Is Both Neurocomputer and Quantum Computer." *Cognitive Science*, 31(6), 2007, pp. 1035-1045.

Hameroff, Stuart, and Roger Penrose. "Consciousness in the Universe: A Review of the 'Orch OR' Theory." *Physics of Life Reviews*, 11(1), 2014, pp. 39-78.

Hancock, Graham. *Supernatural: Meetings with the Ancient Teachers of Mankind*. Century, 2005.

Hölzel, Britta K., James Carmody, Mark Vangel, Christina Congleton, Sita M. Yerramsetti, Tim Gard, and Sara W. Lazar. "Mindfulness Practice

Leads to Increases in Regional Brain Gray Matter Density." *Psychiatry Research: Neuroimaging*, 191(1), 2011, pp. 36-43.

Lazar, Sara W., Catherine E. Kerr, Rachel H. Wasserman, Jeremy R. Gray, Douglas N. Greve, Michael T. Treadway, Metta McGarvey, Brian T. Quinn, Jeffery A. Dusek, Herbert Benson, Scott

L. Rauch, Christopher I. Moore, and Bruce Fischl. "Meditation Experience Is Associated with Increased Cortical Thickness." *Neuroreport*, 16(17), 2005, pp. 1893-1897.

Lutz, Antoine, Heleen A. Slagter, John D. Dunne, and Richard J. Davidson. "Attention Regulation and Monitoring in Meditation." *Trends in Cognitive Sciences*, 12(4), 2008, pp. 163-169.

McCraty, Rollin. *Science of the Heart: Exploring the Role of the Heart in Human Performance*. HeartMath Institute, 2015.

McCraty, Rollin, and Doc Childre. "Coherence: Bridging Personal, Social, and Global Health." *Alternative Therapies in Health and Medicine*, 16(4), 2010, pp. 10-24.

McCraty, Rollin, and Maria A. Zayas. "Cardiac Coherence, Self-regulation, Autonomic Stability, and Psychosocial Well-being." *Frontiers in Psychology*, 5, 2014, p. 1090.

McCraty, Rollin, Mike Atkinson, and Dana Tomasino. "Impact of a Workplace Stress Reduction Program on Blood Pressure and Emotional Health in Hypertensive Employees." *The Journal of Alternative and Complementary Medicine*, 9(3), 2003, pp. 355-369.

McCraty, Rollin, Mike Atkinson, Dana Tomasino, and Raymond Trevor Bradley. "The Coherent Heart: Heart-brain Interactions,

Psychophysiological Coherence, and the Emergence of System-wide Order." *Integral Review*, 5(2), 2009, pp. 10-115.

Moss, Richard. *The Mandala of Being: Discovering the Power of Awareness.* New World Library, 2007.

Penrose, Roger, and Stuart Hameroff. "Consciousness in the Universe: Neuroscience, Quantum Space-time Geometry and Orch OR Theory." *Journal of Cosmology*, 14, 2011, pp. 1-17.

Tolle, Eckhart. *The Power of Now: A Guide to Spiritual Enlightenment.* New World Library, 1999.

ABOUT THE AUTHOR

Eric Edward Wilson spent twenty years as a broadcast meteorologist before a career collapse in 2010 catalyzed a profound personal transformation. What began as financial ruin and identity crisis became a 15-year journey of consciousness exploration that led him to develop the Attention Compass methodology.

In 2016, Eric co-founded Hearts, Hands and Hope with his wife Michelle, where he currently serves as Executive Director. The organization has served over 3 million meals to food-insecure families in Seminole County, Florida, and helps hundreds of families achieve employment stability through their comprehensive Three-Phase Program.

Eric's approach to consciousness and attention draws from personal experience rather than academic psychology—a journey that included career collapse, bankruptcy, and the profound lessons learned while raising his son Aidan, who is on the autism spectrum. These experiences, combined with 15 years of research into consciousness, neuroscience, and ancient wisdom traditions, form the foundation of his work.

Today, Eric speaks to groups about the transformative power of attention, sharing practical insights through engaging anecdotes drawn from his journey from broadcast meteorologist to consciousness guide. He offers one-on-one coaching to individuals seeking to navigate their own transformation from fragmentation to flow.

Eric lives in Lake Mary, Florida, with his wife Michelle and son Aidan, where he continues his work with Hearts, Hands and Hope while sharing the Attention Compass methodology with audiences seeking greater coherence in an increasingly fragmented world.

CONNECT WITH ERIC:

Website: www.theattentioncompass.com
Email: eric@theattentioncompass.com

www.ingramcontent.com/pod-product-compliance
Lightning Source LLC
Chambersburg PA
CBHW051552030726
47592CB00001B/247